Case Methods
in
Teacher Education

Case Methods
in
Teacher Education

Edited by
JUDITH H. SHULMAN

Teachers College, Columbia University
New York and London

This book is dedicated to my parents,
Ethel and Joe Horwitz

Published by Teachers College Press, 1234 Amsterdam Avenue
New York, NY 10027

Copyright © 1992 by Teachers College, Columbia University

Library of Congress Cataloging-in-Publication Data

Case methods in teacher education / edited by Judith H. Shulman.
    p.   cm.
  Includes bibliographical references and index.
  ISBN 0-8077-3130-7 (alk. paper).—ISBN 0-8077-3129-3 (pbk. :
  alk. paper)
  1. Teachers—Training of—United States. 2. Teaching—United
States—Case studies. I. Shulman, Judith.
LB1715.C34 1992
370′.71′0973—dc20   91-28441

ISBN 0-8077-3141-2
ISBN 0-8077-3129-3 (pbk.)

Printed on acid-free paper
Manufactured in the United States of America
98 97 96 95 94 93 92   8 7 6 5 4 3 2 1

Contents

Foreword

This volume makes a fine contribution to the literature on teacher education, demonstrating the wide ranging role that case-based teaching can play. Most of us hold a conventional image of the case method. We think of the orthodoxy enshrined in legal education—the magisterial law professor firing questions at a roomful of trembling students—or the presenting case in medicine. Teacher educators may yearn for their own set of codifying conventions to rationalize their work to a skeptical public, but this collection of cases about the case idea celebrates the diversity of practices that are emerging, testimony to the complexities of teaching.

The book has a practical aim in concretely conveying a range of uses for cases in teacher education, and many of the chapters include descriptions of case use together with actual cases and case commentaries. This combination provides a genuine advance over the case texts now appearing, for here we learn how instructors use various cases, how students respond to and construct cases, and how cases provoke multiple interpretations of teaching situations. The illustrative cases in the volume are situated in extended descriptions of development and use, a marked advance over the simple collection of cases coupled with sample questions and brief introduction. Readers interested in how cases may be used have a rich feast before them, for the chapters reveal both the versatility of cases and the inventiveness of the authors. Cases, we learn, are helpful in teaching about subject matter, classroom management, inquiry and reflection on teaching, and knowledge traditionally conveyed in foundations courses.

This is not a methods text in the usual sense of the term, but it does send a message about case methods in teacher education: to experiment, to be eclectic, to think broadly about the contexts and purposes of case use. In future, the field of teacher education may rely more extensively on case-based teaching, but not in any uniform way. There is much to be learned about how to employ cases effectively in teacher education, and this volume begins to suggest the possibilities.

The selections also reveal a great deal about teaching. The accounts rendered in these chapters, the stories that are told, portray a wide variety of situations, decisions, dilemmas, and difficulties that routinely confront teachers and teacher educators. Although one line of research today portrays teacher expertise in terms of efficient routines, stable patterns of practice, and typical, recurring events, these chapters convey the feel of teaching as frought with uncertainties, difficult decisions, and competing considerations. The speculative, contingent character of teaching is exposed to view, and this narrative perspective does not so much challenge the perspective from expertise as capture a different reality. Jerome Bruner describes narrative as fundamentally concerned with "the vicissitudes of human intentions," and this timeless, universal theme is surely central to the act of teaching and of learning to teach.

These cases also faithfully portray the inseparability of thought, feeling, and action in teaching. From an existential outlook, such old-fashioned terms as hope, fear, awe, disappointment, pride, joy, disgust, and satisfaction provide a window to teaching, for whatever else goes on in school and university classrooms, teachers and students experience a stream of emotions that affect all else. These accounts serve as reminders about this neglected dimension of teaching and learning, and this is no surprise, for the chapter authors are themselves teachers who cannot fail to notice their own feelings.

Such "insider" accounts increasingly supply ballast to the "outsider" renderings from social science, and this useful corrective is another great virtue of the turn to cases. For cases supply an accessible vehicle through which to sound the teacher's voice, to enter teachers' insights into our society's ongoing educational conversation. From Socrates onward, teachers have written about their work, but in the modern era, such accounts were suspect for their subjectivity and their particularity. In a scientific age, sagas of teaching might supply some color and some illustrative examples for more highly prized theoretical propositions, but their perceived utility was limited. A formative development in the postmodern era has been the widespread challenge to the domination of positivist science as a way of world-making. Today, knowledge represented in well-rendered cases enjoys increased status, and cases appear to be a most promising form for representing and conveying knowledge about teaching.

These chapters represent teaching and learning to teach in its felt complexity and constitute a cautionary reminder against ever-present simplifications. Teachers and teacher educators now pursue a daunting learning agenda that sets a high standard. We seek to promote conceptual understanding of school subjects together with advanced skills of critical thinking, problem-solving, and self-monitored learning. And, we set these aims for all children, not just for a "yuppie-techie" elite. I fervently believe that realizing this agenda requires substantial changes in teacher education. We cannot achieve higher standards for children's learning unless and until we provide and promote higher standards for teachers' learning. The case idea draws on a number of powerful intellectual currents in our time and appears as one promising resource for strengthening teacher education. For those interested in provocative early reports on this development, this volume serves as an excellent source.

Gary Sykes

Acknowledgments

The completion of this book was made possible by the support and encouragement of a number of individuals. First, I wish to thank the Office of Educational Research and Improvement and the Far West Laboratory where I work for consistently promoting and funding my work on a variety of case-related projects during the last 5 years. These include developing three teacher-authored casebooks and a monograph on case methods in teacher education and arranging a number of conferences on case-based teaching. In fact, the conception of this book originated in 1987 at one of these conferences. Here several teacher educators in the Laboratory's Western region gathered for the first time to discuss the role of cases in teacher education.

Several individuals at the Laboratory have been particularly significant in guiding my work. Linda Nelson, Don Barfield, Dean Nafziger, Jim Johnson, and Carolyn Cates offered unending encouragement and support; Carne Barnett gave wisdom during ongoing deliberations on issues of case development and pedagogy; Joan McRobbie provided feedback and editorial assistance on my chapter; and Rosemary De La Torre kept me organized during the many developmental stages of this book.

I also wish to thank Professor Yehuda Elkana, Director of the Van Leer Jerusalem Institute, for providing a serene setting for writing my chapter and Pam Grossman for her astute comments on its drafts. A special hug goes to my husband, Lee Shulman, who inspired all of us in our work on case-based teaching. He was the one who gave the opening remarks at our conferences, and he always added new insights and understandings on the role of cases in teacher education. Thanks, Lee!

Preparation for this volume by Teachers College Press was guided by an extraordinary editor, Ronald Galbraith. Ron worked closely with me from the time the manuscript was submitted to the press, offering thoughtful counsel and meticulous editing. Ronald Galbraith died in December 1990, victim of a tragic accident that took his life at the age of 32. I mourn his death and pray that this book will serve as one of the many memorials to his editorial talent.

Introduction

This is a book about teaching with cases. Its purpose is to show teacher educators and staff developers how to develop and use a variety of case materials in their preservice and inservice classes. Most chapters describe how and why the author uses cases, and present an illustrative case for examination. In short, each chapter can be conceived as a case of case-based education.

This volume also begins to lay out a set of connections between the use of case methods and the emerging knowledge base for teaching and teacher education. Selected chapters examine recent research on why case methods may be particularly effective and discuss theoretical principles that can guide case development and case-based instruction.

BRIDGING THE GAP BETWEEN THEORY AND PRACTICE

The book responds to a growing concern among both teacher educators and their critics about the limitations of traditional teacher preparation and inservice training programs. They point to the gap between the complex reality of classroom life and the theoretical principles taught as quasi-prescriptions in university and staff development curricula. Moreover, many new teachers maintain that their university preparation simply did not equip them to deal with the day-to-day ambiguities of the classroom.

Traditionally, teacher educators draw on theoretical research, such as classroom management and multicultural studies, and proceed to teach this information as formal principles to their students. They expect that novices will apply this knowledge when they are out in real classrooms. Unfortunately, it is rarely that simple. The ambiguity and complexity of teaching meaningful and relevant lessons to real children in today's classrooms make it almost impossible for neophytes (and often veterans) to apply the generic prescriptions they learned in their preservice and inservice programs. Besides, in the flurry of decisions teachers are forced to make each day, it is often difficult to remember specific principles, much less invoke them in practice.

Teaching is not alone in confronting this fundamental gap between theory and practice. It is the challenge facing all education for the professions. Indeed, our colleagues in the law, business, and medical schools have already developed traditions for teaching principles through reality-based cases. The case, in this sense, is a piece of controllable reality, more vivid and contextual than a textbook discussion, yet more disciplined and manageable than observing or doing work in the world itself.

In the past few years, the role of case-based teaching in the education of teachers has received increasing attention as a way to bridge the gap between theory and practice. Though not a new idea, the use of case methods in teacher education has been relatively ignored in the literature on teaching. This approach gained visibility with the 1986 publication of *A Nation Prepared: Teachers in the 21st Century*, the landmark report by the Carnegie Task Force on Teaching as a Profession. It recommended that "teaching 'cases' illustrating a great variety of teaching problems should be developed as a major focus of instruction" (p. 76). Cases could provide opportunities for prospective teachers to grapple with the ambiguities and dilemmas of schooling, such as grading, racism, plagiarism, diversity, appropriate instruction, and uncooperative students.

At about this time, other educational scholars also began to write about the importance of cases to the knowledge base of teaching (Doyle, 1986; L. Shulman, 1986). For example, Lee Shulman argues that case knowledge—a potentially codifiable body of knowledge conveying the wisdom of practice—is as essential to the knowledge base of teaching as is the knowledge of principles derived from educational research. Case-based teaching provides teachers with opportunities to analyze situations and make judgments in the messy world of practice, where principles often appear to conflict with one another and no simple solution is possible. Shulman maintains that a pedagogy for teacher education needs to incorporate the "careful confrontation of principles with cases, of general rules with concrete documented events—a dialectic of the general with the particular in which the limits of the former and the boundaries of the latter are explored" (p. 13). Unfortunately, the case literature on teaching is currently quite limited. Therefore traditional forms of teacher education for new and experienced teachers rarely provide opportunities for them to apply their theoretical knowledge to practice within school settings.

Although case-based approaches in other professions are not new, we are only beginning to develop a body of theory and research that explains why they are so unusually effective. Several cognitive psychologists write about the importance of situated knowledge to the knowledge base of teaching (e.g., Brown, Collins, & Duguid, 1989). They suggest that propositional knowledge learned in academic settings does not necessarily transfer to nonacademic settings. Moreover, the theoretical research of Rand Spiro and his colleagues (1988) suggests the need for case-based teaching in their papers on cognitive flexibility theory. Educational practitioners work in an "ill-structured domain" where there are few right or wrong answers. They argue that "criss-crossing the landscape with cases" is necessary in order to understand the complexities of teaching. Lee Shulman and Pamela Grossman elaborate on this body of research in the opening and closing chapters of this book.

Finally, the literature on educational improvement makes it clear that reflection and substantive conversation among teachers are important ingredients in the improvement of schools (e.g., Little, 1987). We are now strongly convinced that cases become catalysts for pedagogical conversations among members of school communities. They stimulate teachers' individual reflections on their own teaching as well as providing a basis for dialogue and interaction among teachers themselves. Such talk is not idle chatter. Lipsitz (1984) observed, like Little, that effective schools are places where teachers can actively talk about their teaching in the interests of improving it.

DESCRIPTION OF THIS BOOK

This book presents a wide variety of case samples and methodologies of case-based teaching. The opening chapter by Lee Shulman presents a framework for thinking about case-based teaching and what it means to learn from a case. Shulman discusses the pedagogical implications for the use of case methods in teacher education, suggests a definition for the term *case*, and sets parameters for the application of its definition. Parts I and II highlight the differences in how chapter authors use cases in their teacher education programs—as teaching tools and as learning tools. The last part synthesizes what we do and do not know about case-based teaching and raises some questions about its limitations.

In Part I, the authors describe how and why they use cases to teach a concept or disposition. Judith Kleinfeld (Chapter 2) uses extended cases (approximately 50 pages) written by veteran practitioners to help her students learn to "think like a teacher." She is particularly interested in preparing teachers emotionally and intellectually to teach in multicultural settings. Katherine Merseth (Chapter 3) uses cases that she constructs herself to teach students both the analytic and decision-making skills essential to thoughtful decisions and appropriate actions. The next three authors adapt their cases from longer research-based case studies. Suzanne Wilson (Chapter 4) examines how to use cases to teach students both theoretical and pedagogical understanding of what it means to know and to teach subject matter. Suzanne Wade (Chapter 5) shows us how to use a case to analyze the problems that reading specialists and regular education teachers may experience as they attempt to work together. Kathy Carter (Chapter 6) explores how to use cases to understand the variety of ways teachers interpret the task of managing their classrooms. In Chapter 7 I focus on the development of teacher-written cases and commentaries that can be used as teaching cases. I also examine what can be learned from writing a case.

In Part II the three authors explore the importance of case writing in promoting reflective inquiry with their students. All of the authors have incorporated case-writing assignments in their classes. Anna Richert (Chapter 8) focuses on the process of working with students to write meaningful narratives, often quite difficult for some teachers. Vicki LaBoskey (Chapter 9) describes her novel approach of introducing "case investigations" into her teacher preparation program. And Jean Easterly (Chapter 10) examines why and how she uses the format of a structured case report to link her students' theoretical understanding of models of classroom management with their student teaching experience in classrooms.

Part III explores the limitations and prospects for a case approach to teacher education. Grace Grant (Chapter 11) writes with a cautionary note on the use of case-based teaching as she examines one of her rather unsuccessful lessons on critical thinking. Pamela Grossman (Chapter 12) synthesizes the current status of case-based teaching and raises questions about the limitations of its use.

This book appears during a time when case-based teaching is gaining increasing attention from the educational community. We must be cautious in our enthusiasm, for it is not a panacea for all the ills of education. Yet our obligation as teacher educators is to achieve not perfection, but improvement. Unquestionably, case methods are the most exciting potential source of improvement for the contemporary pedagogy of teacher education.

REFERENCES

Brown, J. S., Collins, A., & Duguid, P. (1989). Situated cognition and the culture of learning. *Educational Researcher, 18*(1), 32–41.

Carnegie Task Force on Teaching as a Profession. (1986). *A Natïon Prepared: Teachers for the 21st Century.* New York: Carnegie Forum on Education and the Economy, Carnegie Corporation.

Doyle, W. (1986, April). *The world is everything that is the case: Developing case methods for teacher education.* Paper presented at the annual meeting of the American Educational Research Association, San Francisco.

Lipsitz, J. (1984). *Successful schools for young adolescents.* New Brunswick, NJ: Transaction Books.

Little, J. W. (1987). Teachers as colleagues. In V. Richardson-Koehler (Ed.), *Educator's handbook: A research perspective* (pp. 491–518). New York: Longman.

Shulman, L. S. (1986). Those who understand: Knowledge growth in teaching. *Educational Researcher, 15*(2), 4–14.

Spiro, R. J., Coulson, R. L., Feltovich, P. J., & Anderson, D. K. (1988). Cognitive flexibility theory: Advanced knowledge acquisition in ill-structured domains. In *Tenth annual conference of the cognitive science society* (pp. 375–383). Hillsdale, NJ: Erlbaum.

CHAPTER 1

Toward a Pedagogy of Cases

LEE S. SHULMAN

If philosophy begins in wonder, pedagogy typically begins in frustration. Educators rarely invent new modes of teaching simply out of a sense of mystery or longing. More often, they are fed up with the kind of teaching they have been doing in the past. They are looking for better ways to educate their students. Such has certainly been the case with case methods.

Educators have long been critical of academic programs dominated by the twin demons of lecture and textbook, each a method designed to predigest and deliver a body of key facts and principles through exposition to a rather passive audience of students. These educators were critical of methods of recitation used by teachers to check whether the students had "mastered" the expounded materials in the lecture or textbook. They argued that students had grown bored, dulled by uninspired pedagogy, mindlessly memorizing and rotely rehearsing. They were surely not learning to connect theory to action, nor were they coming to think analytically or critically. In Whitehead's (1929) preface to *The Aims of Education*, he protested "against dead knowledge, that is to say, against inert ideas" (p. 1). The proponents of case methods have felt that existing pedagogies were breeding "inert ideas" fated to clog and suffocate good minds. Case methods were seen as a solvent for such problems.

This is surely the case in teacher education today. We observe widespread (and well-deserved) criticism of the quality of instruction in teacher preparation programs, as well as of the quality of learning. Case methods are expected to be more engaging, more demanding, more intellectually exciting and stimulating, more likely to bridge the vast chasm between principle and practice, and more likely to help neophytes to learn to "think like a teacher."

1

The case method of teaching does not exist. The character of cases and case methods varies widely from field to field, and even at times within a single field. Even the juxtaposition of *case* with methods of *discussion* is not universal. And when discussion methods are advocated, it is not always in the same manner and toward the same ends. In areas such as business school education, we encounter a more *canonical* or orthodox conception of case methods, based heavily on the remarkably successful approaches of the Harvard Business School and the writings of Christensen (1987). Certainly in teacher education we are far from any received doctrine or orthodoxy regarding case methods.

I propose to discuss a number of questions in this chapter:

- What is the variety of purposes for which cases and case methods are employed?
- What variations do we encounter both in the organization of case materials and in the methods employed for using them?
- How might the growing interest in case methods relate to changes in how scholars view the substance of their fields and the acceptable methods of inquiry for their research?
- Why do cases work?
- What are both the virtues and the liabilities of case methods?

PURPOSES

It seems most appropriate to begin our discussion with a survey of the purposes for case methods. Cases and case methods are employed to teach:

1. Principles or concepts of a theoretical nature
2. Precedents for practice
3. Morals or ethics
4. Strategies, dispositions, and habits of mind
5. Visions or images of the possible

In addition, cases can be viewed as:

1. Creating or increasing motivation for learning
2. Providing unique benefits to practitioners who participate in writing as case authors or commentators

3. Providing specific antidotes to the dangers of overgeneralization from either the learning of principles or from prior cases
4. Serving as the instructional material around which participants can form communities for discussion or discourse

Theoretical Principles

I begin with principles because, in a very real sense, the use of cases to teach principles is counterintuitive. Nothing seems so obvious as the concrete, particular, here-and-now story that is a case. Yet Christopher Columbus Langdell, first dean of the Harvard Law School in 1875, proposed the case method in legal education precisely because he believed that cases could become the most powerful medium for teaching theory (Stevens, 1983). Although studying cases certainly can serve to enlighten students regarding specific precedents, the dialectic of legal case methods drives students to explore ever deeper reasons for applying principles in particular ways. Only through carefully analyzing the reasoning of judges as they decided important cases, argued Langdell, could the underlying principles of the law be discerned.

Consider the typical Socratic exchange between the teacher and student of law. The teacher may begin with either a general question or a specific case. "Imagine that a person is walking across the street while the light says 'walk' and he is hit by a car driven by Mr. Jones, who has driven against the red light. Who is responsible for the injuries?" "Mr. Jones, of course." What is the reason for assigning responsibility to Mr. Jones? A legal reason is now advanced. Now imagine another case, in which Mr. Jones's car is determined to have faulty brakes. Now who is responsible? What if it is a rented car? Why do you argue that position?

Cases are occasions for offering theories to explain why certain actions are appropriate. Once theoretical reasons are advanced, their utility is tested through new cases, accounts in which circumstances change and conditions alter. The previous theoretical explanation now changes to accommodate to the challenges. Often new principles are adduced to conform to the new cases. In either event, cases are used to teach the theory of the law, not primarily to present specific precedents. Cases thus come to exemplify or to test principles.[1]

When constructing a case-based curriculum, therefore, the first step is to identify the theoretical principles one wishes to teach. Once the desired set of principles has been identified, or the theories have been identified, then teaching cases can be selected or constructed that exemplify those principles. A good example can be found in the work of James B. Conant (1947) in the teaching of college science.

In 1946, the 53-year-old Harvard president confronted a new challenge: How to conceive of a science education for nonscientists that would overcome the ineffectiveness of traditional science teaching and lead to a well-grounded understanding of science. Conant turned to a strategy in which the use of historical cases of scientific work played the central role. He argued that the goal of teaching science to nonscientists ought properly to be the learning of principles that explain the tactics and strategies of science. These, he felt, could best be conveyed through vividly presented case histories of scientific discoveries and, even more effectively, through cases describing failures to make discoveries even when all the "facts" were ostensibly available. One of his primary goals was to provide contrary evidence for the prevailing oversimplified view of the scientific method too often promulgated by authors of science textbooks.

He was stimulated in this enterprise by his own deep interest in and understanding of the history of science, as well as by his impressions of the success with case methods of the Harvard Business School. Conant did not associate case methods of teaching with use of a discussion method, in spite of the fact that cases and discussion-based approaches are inseparable in the business school model. Indeed, he seems to assume that instruction would continue to use lectures much as it always did. The centrality of the case histories would provide the lecturer with much more interesting material, intrinsically motivating stories that could be presented with some dramatic flair. The case histories themselves would convey an understanding of the processes of science. His purposes were novel, his case histories were beautifully wrought, but for reasons known only to Conant, no new conception of pedagogy accompanied their development.

Conant believed that the major purpose for teaching scientific understanding through original cases was to help students understand "principles of the tactics and strategy of science" (p. 102). He was not interested in the teaching of particular scientific concepts—for example, adaptation, tropism, evolution—through cases. Among the principles he valued, and which he identified with the understanding of science, was the understanding that "new concepts evolve from experiments or observations and are fruitful of new experiments or observations" (p. 104). But he wished students to grasp that the "evolution" of scientific concepts was not a simple linear process of aggregation. Good ideas did not expel poor ones from the scientific world in some inexorable fashion.

The principles valued by Conant come alive in the context of case histories of scientific discovery. Stripped of such narrative contexts, the principles of science can become quite meaningless cants, memorized and even explicated by students, but not deeply understood. Hence the value of the case for the learning of theory lies in the ways cases instantiate and contextualize principles through embedding them in vividly told stories.

Precedents for Practice

When a case presents the portrayal of a problem situation confronted by a teacher, a variety of possible approaches that could have been taken, and some account of how the problem was resolved, readers may treat that teacher's actions as a model for practice, a kind of precedent for future action. Thus, in the law, when a formal judgment has been rendered regarding a particular case, that judgment stands officially as a precedent and demands the attention of other lawyers and jurists when they face analogous situations.

Although we typically associate the idea of precedents with the law, nowhere is the notion of precedents more clearly expressed than in approaches to learning chess. Chess writers often contrast approaches to learning chess that stress principles and maxims with those that emphasize reviewing and replaying games of champions, games that comprise the precedents for chess.

Reuben Fine (1943), grandmaster and former world champion, expressed this view beautifully in his *The Ideas Behind the Chess Openings*:

> Nobody has found a method of determining values which is superior to that of good master practice. That is, by sticking to well-established rules and principles we get to a position where there are pros and cons for both sides. In that event a game between two experts is the most important clue that we can possibly have. This is one of the chief reasons for quoting games. . . . (p. 2)
>
> The argument is simple enough. Two experts examined this game and came to the following conclusion. Their opinions have been checked by another expert who finds that both played reasonably well [if not, a comment to that effect will be entered]. Unless there is some excellent evidence to support the contrary, it is therefore to be assumed that the judgment of the book is to be accepted as substantially correct. (pp. 5–6)

Researchers who study chess players have concluded that expertise in chess consists mainly of organized memory for many thousands of chess games, the problem situations they presented, and the strategic solutions they exhibited. When a chess player finds herself in a difficult position, she retrieves from her chess memory all instances reminiscent of the spot she is in, and she thinks through ways in which to apply those precedents.

It is not unusual for a precedent to be generalized into a maxim, a more broad-gauged practical principle. This often happens in the education of teachers. Thus a well-crafted case of a young teacher who paid the price for attempting to be too informal and friendly with her high school students (see White 1988) can be summed up in the maxim "Don't smile until Christmas." In conjunction with the case, however, the cognitive economy of the maxim is likely to have far more impact.

Similarly, Jere Brophy tells the story of a teacher who repeatedly confronted the problem of her pupils' arriving at class without pens or pencils. Does she punish them by making them spend the day without writing instruments? Or should she provide them with pencils and thereby reinforce their irresponsibility? The teacher resolved this dilemma by accumulating a collection of the shortest stubs of pencil she could find. When confronted by students who had come unprepared, she generously required that they do the day's work with one of these stubs. The discomfort that followed her generosity rapidly taught most students that coming without pencils did not pay.

Brophy's story can be considered as a precedent for a type of problem often confronted by teachers. Beyond the specifics of pencil stubs, however, may well be lurking the basis for more general maxims and rules of thumb, even some pieces of practical theory. This example begins to illustrate how the question "What is this a case of?" is probably unanswerable in any absolute sense. Cases may be crafted and organized as exemplars of particular principles, maxims, or moral visions. But once apprehended and interpreted by their readers, cases can and will come to exemplify other ideas, attitudes, and practices as well. They are thus no different from any other literary creation. The author's intentions and the reader's constructions are rarely identical.

When cases serve as precedents for future practice, we confront both a potentially useful educational tool and a potentially dangerous one. If particularly well-crafted cases are too compelling, they may lead to overly slavish "precedent following" by readers who accept their approach unquestioningly. Nevertheless, the very fact that cases portray real people actually doing something in classrooms in ways that yield real consequences makes them valuable for future (and present) teachers.

Moral or Ethical Principles

There is probably no older tradition than the use of stories to convey moral or ethical principles. Whether in the form of timeless fables or traditional parables, preachers, prophets, and teachers of all kinds have used the power of stories to instruct their flocks in the rules of the good life. Cases can serve as parables when the teacher in the case provides a clear model of attitude or behavior worthy of emulation by another practitioner. Alternatively, the story of a learner—perhaps unexpectedly overcoming the vicissitudes of poor preparation or economic disadvantage—can send a moral or ethical message to teachers regarding the inappropriateness of prematurely labeling youngsters and limiting their growth through low expectations.

Cases have been employed for thousands of years as the vehicles for inquiry and debate regarding proper ethical or moral behavior. We will see in a subsequent section of this chapter how the intellectual traditions of ethics and moral philosophy can influence the ways in which we think about case methods and the underlying types of knowledge with which they connect.

Strategies, Dispositions, Reflection, and Habits of Mind

In all forms of professional education, there lurks an overarching goal: to teach the neophyte "to think like" a member of the profession. Learning to think like a lawyer, a teacher, a physician, or an anthropologist involves many aspects of practice. These features of professional performance go beyond the usual skills and knowledge that constitute the professional curriculum. They pertain to more general strategies, personal orientations, and habits of mind. They are more stylistic than rule-governed, more metacognitive than cognitive.

By presenting realistic problems to students, and asking them to respond as if they were more mature members of the profession, the discipline, or the policy community, case methods are seen as providing opportunities to practice "thinking like" a professional. Cases show little respect for disciplinary boundaries. They are messy and recalcitrant. They rarely admit of a single right answer. They are therefore ideal for inducting the neophyte into those worlds of thought and work that are themselves characterized by unpredictability, uncertainty, and judgment. They fit well with the goals of education in the professions, especially teaching. Moreover, most other fields of human accomplishment, including the sciences, are inherently messy beneath their patinas of order and regularity. Thus case methods model modes of thinking in many fields far more accurately than do the simplifications of didactic pedagogies.

In the teacher education literature, we often read arguments for case methods predicated on the goal of teaching teachers to be more reflective. The immense popularity of Donald Schön's (1983, 1987) work bears witness to the growing feeling among teacher educators that while the average teacher could hardly be characterized as reflective, the image of reflective practice corresponds to the most desirable vision of proper pedagogy. Because of their inherent complexity and multiple layers, cases lend themselves to programs that value such a view of the purposes of teacher education.

Visions or Images of the Possible

In most forms of professional preparation, there exists a continuing tension between the realities of current practice and the ideals of desired reforms. This tension becomes particularly acute when students are sent out as observers, interns, student teachers, or apprentices to learn the work under real conditions. By definition, most real work settings are mundane, prosaic, conservative, unimaginative. Students who accept the status quo's definition of how the work should be done will merely reproduce last generation's solutions to this generation's problems. Yet how can newcomers learn to perform without supervised observations and practice in the real world? Moreover, many of the reform ideals endorsed by educators may be utterly unrealistic and utopian, properly objects of disdain by those veterans of practice who serve as mentors for the neophytes.

Case studies of unusually visionary yet well-grounded exemplars of good practice may present the ideal middle ground between the unfettered fantasies of the dreamers and the unimaginative practices of the uninspired. These cases can play the same role for teachers as do myths in other fields. They portray concrete human images of activities and values worthy of emulation. They thus can serve to stimulate those learning to teach to consider alternative forms of practice that are rooted in real teaching, not only in the passions of idealists.

I have been particularly impressed in this regard by the case studies of her own teaching written by Magdalene Lampert. These case studies have been conducted for research purposes rather than as teaching cases, but I will discuss their implications for the preparation of teachers. In a recent paper, Lampert (1990) presents a vivid account of her teaching, complete with extensive classroom dialogues. Her portrayal begins, however, with an examination of three aspects of the nature of mathematics: as a field of study, as a way of thinking, and as a community of scholars. She grounds her creation of a classroom context for mathematics teaching on those features of the discipline. Students study what is important in the discipline, they are encouraged to think in ways that are mathematically interesting, and they interact with one another as do mathematicians conducting exchanges about mathematical work.

In her case we observe how the children are confronted with mathematical questions and address them by generating conjectures. These conjectures are shared with their classmates, whose job is to examine, refute, confirm, and amend them. The mathematical work of the class becomes the doing of the mathematics largely invented by classmates. The case presentation is so beautifully rendered that the reader is both instructed and inspired. I learn theoretical principles about mathematics and its pedagogy; I learn practical maxims for the organization and management of a mathematics classroom; and I come to believe with enthusiasm that this sort of classroom represents how math should be taught and that it is possible to do so in imaginable settings.

Additional Purposes

Cases motivate. They stimulate interest in the problems they represent. This is not a controversial claim. Were it the only value of case methods, they still would merit our interest. They certainly merit the interests of the learners.

Case *writing* may well bring special benefits to those who write them, prompting them to reflect on their practice and to become more analytic about their work. Moreover, authoring cases may well instill deserved pride in practitioners, especially teachers, whose own professional insights are rarely afforded the respect they deserve. Judith Shulman has written about the impact of case authoring in several publications (e.g., J. Shulman & Colbert, 1989; J. Shulman, Colbert, Kemper, & Dmytriw, 1990) and adds to that account in Chapter 7 of this volume.

The contextualized detail and verisimilitude of a good case serves as a powerful antidote to simplistic overgeneralizations of principles or maxims. Collections of cases or analogies can temper the impact on cognition of any single entry. As I mentioned before, one danger of teaching either powerful principles or compelling individual cases is the likelihood that their message will become overgeneralized well beyond the proper limits of application. Well-placed cases can reduce the likelihood of unbridled extrapolation of simple rules of thumb.

Cases provide occasions for professionals to gather together for retelling, reflection, and analysis. Case conferences in medicine provide one prototype. In teaching, we have begun to observe how teachers can interact with one another around the examination of compelling cases.

I have reviewed a number of purposes for which cases and case methods can be used. But cases alone are not enough. How are they to be used instructionally? What formats of casebook design and case methods of teaching are appropriate for achieving some of these purposes?

THE PEDAGOGY OF CASES

Beware of references to *the* case method. Those who use cases in teaching become strong advocates of their own approach, zealous in defense of a particular way of building a lesson or unit of instruction around a case. Yet there are several ways to think about cases as occasions for teaching.

A central question revolves around one's conception of the role (if any) for the teacher. In the Harvard Business School tradition, the teacher is central as the manager of discussion. The teacher controls the pace and direction of the exchanges, ensuring that all participants have an opportunity to contribute, coaxing and leading the group to elicit a range of points of view. Although student participation is the key to successful business school instruction, the method demands a well-prepared teacher who is trained in group discussion methods and well-versed in the details of this particular teaching case. There is no case method of teaching in the business school without group discussion conducted by a skilled teacher.

The business school model also dictates the form of case material for discussion. Cases are almost always prepared in two (or even three) versions. The *A* case presents the basic circumstances and background of the case and portrays a set of alternate courses of action that might be taken by the protagonist. The *B* case, which is not introduced until after the teacher has conducted a thorough discussion of the *A* case, adds more information, usually including an account of what the actors did after the earlier time period and what consequences followed. The incompleteness of the initiating *A* case is essential to the approach; to foreclose the class's opportunity to engage in analysis and deliberation by presenting the completed account would be anathema.

One contrast to this model is the approach taken by Conant, in which the cases are designed to present a narrative of the discovery process, a tantalizing tale of conception and search, of blind alleys and epiphanies. Not only is the case presented for individual reading in its entirety—beginning, middle, and end; no *A* and *B* cases here— but the mode of instruction is likely to be a large-group lecture rather than any kind of discussion. Yet the case as narrative, as contextualized in space and time, as organized around processes of discovery, invention, disappointment, and triumph, remains at the center.

Traditions for publishing accounts of chess games present several alternate approaches for organizing cases. Chess provides three models to consider. Records of games (with associated commentaries) can be collected according to *topics*, for example, openings, defensive strategies, participants. These are normally full games that are meant to be vicariously replayed by the reader from beginning to end. A second genre is the incomplete game qua puzzle. Here we find sets of incomplete games edited to provide the reader with opportunities to practice strategy with particular problems, for example, responding to unusual openings or frequently encountered endgame positions. A third genre is the casebook of an entire match, a series of games played over a continuous period of time by two antagonists, such as Fisher versus Spassky. These become interesting because of the contingencies among games, since the consequences of strategies employed in an earlier game demand consideration when the player confronts problems in a subsequent game.

Another contrast is the cases-and-commentaries model presented in the J. Shulman and Colbert (1987, 1988) casebooks. Here the cases are presented in their entireties, and the commentaries follow directly after each case. Cases provide accounts of how a particular teacher/author experienced a problem, the analysis and strategies she employed, and the eventual resolution or stalemate that resulted. Lest the case be read as a precedent for action ("This is the best thing to do whenever you encounter a situation like this one"), the commentaries that follow add complexity to the case and offer other readings and additional views. These cases can be taught in a classroom, but they are also designed to be read by individuals who can mull over them in private.

The Role of Commentaries

There is growing controversy in the community of case methods scholars regarding the usefulness of commentaries as adjuncts to written cases. Proponents, such as myself, argue that commentaries "layer" cases by providing additional perspectives or lenses through which to view the events of the case. Skeptics fear that commentaries will function as verdicts that proclaim the one best way to interpret a case, thus foreclosing the deliberation and debate that makes case-based teaching educative. No empirical research exists that can support either position.

The claim that there is something intrinsically simplifying about a case commentary fundamentally misconstrues the potential role of multiple interpretations in the examination of a text. Perhaps the skeptics confuse commentaries with answer keys or with the discussion notes that follow some cases, which appear to provide a concise "resolution" to the complexities of the puzzle. I view commentary as an opportunity to take a particular case—whether apparently straightforward or undeniably perplexing—and to provide alternative lenses for viewing it.

I spent a number of years studying commentaries in the context of Biblical exegesis and Talmudic texts. These experiences have shaped my conception of commentaries as adding complexity and richness to the texts they gloss rather than simplifying or trivializing the text. Commentaries in the Jewish tradition build up over the centuries as additional, and typically conflicting, perspectives on canonical texts. As the years go by, later commentators offer their views of both the focal text and the earlier commentaries. New centuries demand new perspectives as new contexts with novel problems arise that earlier exegetes could never have imagined. The interplay among the commentaries creates a spirit of conversation, of dialogue and debate, all anchored around the original text, but enriching and extending its implications. Such is the vision I hold of the role of commentaries in a literature of teaching cases.

In order to encourage independent thought, should the commentaries be read only after the original case has been discussed (or individually analyzed) thoroughly by readers? Should commentaries be printed in conjunction with cases or in separate sections or even volumes of a text? (In the Talmud, the commentaries share the same page with the original cases. The older texts are literally in the center of the page, both vertically and horizontally, and the commentaries are printed above, below, and on either side of the central text.) I believe that with rich commentaries the danger of forestalling discussion and creativity is minimized.

On the other hand, there is a danger of cognitive overload if too much information must be processed by the reader at one time. For that reason alone, it may be pedagogically useful to segment the reading of a case into shorter chunks, including the possibility of *A* and *B* segments analogous to the business model. For the same reason, it may be wise to print commentaries in a separate section of a casebook, or at least on pages that separate them from the original case.

If the physical appearance of published cases is an important issue, it pales in comparison with the importance of group discussion as the vehicle for instruction. In the business school traditions, the use of discussion methods and the idea of a case method are essentially synonymous. A particularly lovely account of the role of discussion in teaching, which also illustrates why there is no *necessary* relationship between cases and discussion, is seen in the work of Joseph Schwab.

Joseph Schwab and the College Curriculum at Chicago

At about the same time that Conant was struggling with the reform of undergraduate science teaching at Harvard, a younger scientist was reconstructing the undergraduate science curriculum in the college of the University of Chicago. Joseph Schwab was trained in mathematical genetics, having completed his doctorate under Sewell Wright in 1938. Unlike Conant's Harvard model, the Chicago tradition to which Schwab contributed viewed an understanding of how knowledge grows and develops as essential for *all* students, even (perhaps especially) those destined to pursue science as their life's work.

Schwab, like Conant, wanted students to understand how scientific ideas developed, rather than simply have a grasp of contemporary scientific thought. He made an important distinction between understanding science as a "rhetoric of conclusions" and as a "narrative of enquiry" (Schwab, 1964). The latter, which had the stories of scientific discovery as their heart, rested on a curriculum combining original source materials with case histories of scientific work.

For Schwab, the materials of instruction were important. They could not be simplistic and doctrinaire if the goal was to engage students in active learning and critical reasoning. The materials had to be sufficiently complex and compelling to foster a proper atmosphere for discussion and debate. When overly simplistic or predigested readings were employed, these became "assignments" for students, read only because they were required for course credit. Actual cases, especially medical or legal cases, were highly useful in this regard; so were original source documents, never written as textbook material, whose complexity would permit alternative readings and multiple interpretations.

Schwab was far more interested in the conduct of class discussions than with the structure of instructional materials. He illustrates the approach to teaching he advocated, and which can certainly be considered part of the family of case methods of teaching, when he describes a class session that began with the reading of a medical case of a woman who was brought to the physician in a "cretinoid state," which I have adapted from his book *College Curriculum and Student Protest* (1969).

Schwab opens the discussion with a broad question: "What is the problem dealt with by the paper?" (p. 56).

After some hesitations, misconstruals of the question, and false starts, one student offers an answer to the question. The teacher probes for clarification, qualification, and purpose. The student revises and refines his proposal.

The teacher then calls for an alternative view. A second student now proposes another reading. After necessary clarification of the second proposal, the teacher turns back to the first student and asks him to consider and comment upon the second reading. He then asks the second student to reconsider and criticize the first reading.

At that time, other students begin to participate. What began as a debate between two views is steered into conjoint inquiry regarding several alternative readings. Under the teacher's direction, the number and extent of different readings is reduced and simplified. The discussants begin to consider the course of their own discussion, with members reflecting on the path taken by their deliberation.

The class concludes with several alternative proposals remaining on the floor, but after considerable refinement and analysis.

Schwab comments that in a properly conducted discussion of such a case, there are two distinct layers of discourse. In the first, the text or case itself is the object of inquiry as the group moves toward the collection and elaboration of multiple alternative readings. In the second layer, the dialogue becomes reflexive. The students begin to work reflectively on their own dialogue and analyses, treating them as a form of second-order text. They thus alternate between cognition and metacognition, between addressing the case and analyzing their own processes of analysis and review.

In the sciences, unlike law, cases and case methods are apparently methods of pedagogical transformation; no one would confuse case knowledge with real scientific understandings. In other fields, however, there exists substantial controversy over the best ways to represent the knowledge base of the domain itself; that is, there can be strong claims that knowledge of cases is precisely what defines the knowledge base of some fields. An instructive example comes from the study of ethics.

Stephen Toulmin and the Reemergence of Casuistry

Stephen Toulmin (1949/1986) argues that the study of ethics has gone through some interesting changes over the centuries. In its earliest phases, initiated by Talmudic treatments of moral issues, the field was dominated by a form of *casuistry*, an approach to ethics in which the ethicist reasons about quite specific cases and categories of cases. The case is clearly the unit of discourse, rather than the broad general principle. Indeed, Aristotle was skeptical about the possibility that ethics could be devised as a theoretical system. His general treatment of *phronesis*, practical (as contrasted with theoretical) reasoning, takes place in the *Ethics*, so convinced is Aristotle that ethical reasoning is the paradigmatic domain of the practical.

In the mid-nineteenth century, ethicists began to grow intolerant of the messy character of casuistry, with its cacophony of categories seeming to tumble over one another. They sought a more parsimonious system, in which more scientific formulations of ethical principles could be posited from which ethical decisions could be deduced as from first principles. William Whewell, perhaps better known to us for his debates with John Stuart Mill on the nature of induction, held the chair of ethics at Cambridge during that period. He had written a standard text on ethics, *The Elements of Morality*, which continued the casuistic tradition of focusing on specific concrete problems of different kinds rather than on general principles. But even Whewell was clearly somewhat uncomfortable with that approach. As Toulmin describes, during Whewell's tenure his professorship underwent a name change: from the Knightsbridge Professor of Casuistical Divinity to Knightsbridge Professor of Moral Philosophy. Whewell's successor, Henry Sidgewick, devised a method of argument in ethics that derived more elegantly and simply from the principles of Mill's utilitarianism. Finally, ethics was to rest on the more solid ground of theoretical principles and deductive logic, rather than on a shaky foundation of cases and analogical reasoning (Toulmin, 1949/1986).

By the time Toulmin wrote *The Place of Reason in Ethics* in 1949, the theoretical perspective was well entrenched at Cambridge. Toulmin's skeptical argument "placed limits on the universalizability of moral concepts and arguments, and so opened up the possibility of reviving older traditions of practical moral reasoning; especially, the much despised tradition of 'casusistry' or case morality" (p. *xiv*). In his book, Toulmin goes on to argue that "in either law or morality, the philosopher's task is not to find an underlying principle that binds all obligations and claims together: rather it is *to develop a sufficiently varied taxonomy of cases, circumstances and considerations*, allowing for (and doing justice to) the differences between them" (p. *xv*; emphasis added).

In *The Abuse of Casuistry* (Jonsen & Toulmin, 1988), Toulmin and his collaborator extend and deepen the argument. The import of their assertions for us goes beyond the domain of ethics, central though ethical concepts might be to the field of education. I suspect that all forms of professional activity rest on the capacity for practical judgment, however bound up they may be in elements of theory. Practical decisions are not deducible from general principles. Theoretical principles play a key role in practical arguments, but they share that role with the distinctive features and broad categories of past cases and the particular contextual details of present circumstances. The capacity to engage in legal, medical, or pedagogical judgment and action, therefore, rests as much on a combination of case knowledge and case-based reasoning as does the capacity to reason ethically.

To this day instruction in ethics is typically organized around the study of *paradigmatic cases.* A case is deemed paradigmatic because its particularities reflect the distinctive features of other cases belonging to a specific class. Members of the class bear a family resemblance to one another; through analogical reasoning regarding similarities and differences, as well as through invoking working principles as they become useful, the decision maker moves toward a moral judgment for a particular case.

I hold that teaching is a form of transformation, in which teachers create representations of complex ideas that connect with the constructions of their students (L. Shulman, 1987). Case methods are a particular strategy of pedagogical transformation—a strategy for transforming more propositional forms of knowledge into narratives that motivate and educate. If, however, the knowledge base and reasoning processes of teaching (or law, medicine, or other practical domain) are themselves case-based, then the use of case methods does not require a very elaborate transformation. We are not taking a field of study that is basically a propositional system and writing cases solely for pedagogical purposes. The field is itself a body of cases linked loosely by working principles, and case methods are the most valid way of representing that structure in teaching.

WHAT IS A CASE?

To call something a case is to make a theoretical claim. It argues that the story, event, or text is an instance of a larger class, an example of a broader category. In a word, it is a "case-of-something" and therefore merits more serious consideration than a simple anecdote or vignette. It implies an underlying taxonomy or typology, however intuitive or informal, to which a given case belongs. There can be cases of alienation—a thoroughly theoretical classification— and cases of students using foul language in class. To call something a case, therefore, is to treat it as a member of a class of events and to call our attention to its value in helping us appreciate more than the particularities of the case narrative itself. As observed earlier, however, the beauty of cases is their potential for reinterpretation and multiple representation. A case collected for one purpose may well turn out to be even more useful as a case-of-something-else. The very same case can be found to admit of several simultaneous classifications, just as my dog can be concurrently companion and nuisance.

There is a more powerful sense of the case as instance of larger theoretical class. As observed in the earlier discussion of ethics, we can speak of *paradigmatic cases.* These cases "point to" broader principles or situations that they exemplify in particularly evocative ways. What is more effective than the "overcrowded lifeboat" case to capture the complexities of a certain genre of moral reasoning? The case becomes paradigmatic when newly encountered ethical problems can be analyzed and explicated by reference to the paradigms. ("Is this new situation more like an overcrowded lifeboat case or like the case of a parent whose child is dying of starvation? Is it more like *Brown* v. *Board of Education* or *Roe* v. *Wade?*") Here again, even a paradigmatic case can change its function under new circumstances. The very same case that served as a precedent for one kind of judgment this year can become a precedent in an utterly different decision next year.

In those traditions, such as business, that use incomplete cases as triggers for analysis and discussion, cases are usually tales of crisis and unresolved tension. The *A* case ends with a moment of decision and the question: "What would you do now?" They are oriented toward crisis management, problem solving, and decision making. Nonetheless, much of what must be learned by professionals is the management of routines, coping with the predictable. For teachers, beginning the school year, establishing class rules, setting up a biology laboratory, or selecting culturally relevant literature are hardly the stuff that crisis-oriented *A* cases are made of. They are problematic because there are competing approaches to their accomplishment, based on different premises and aimed at contrasting purposes. They too might be better addressed using cases, but they would rarely be very dramatic in their plot. Premature commitment to crisis-oriented cases might well exclude this entire genre of important goals from a case-based curriculum.

Yet the presentation of routine cases can be either dull or dangerously prescriptive. A solution would be to insist on presenting teaching cases of managing routine or predictable pedagogy in contrasting pairs: two distinctive approaches to opening the school year, a couple of different ways to teach *Moby Dick* or the concept of natural selection. Although the case portrays the problematic ("How shall I teach this idea or arrange this classroom?"), it is not dealing with a crisis.

In addition to defining what a case is, we should also define a set of terms for discussing the types of cases and their uses. Few matters are as intrinsically dull as discourses on terminology. But the rapidly developing literature on cases and case methods is creating a cacophony of terms relating to cases. In the interests of clarification, I offer the following suggestions:

Case materials are the raw data from which cases are constructed, whether by the original author or by a third party. They are diaries, personal letters, student work samples, videotapes, observer's notes, and so on.

Case reports are first-person accounts, reports written by someone who is reporting her own experiences, activities, and interpretations. When the author is the protagonist of the narrative, we are reading a case report.

Case studies are third-person accounts—the anthropologist's write-up of a native ritual, the psychologist's portrayal of a classroom episode, the teacher's presentation of the story of a child. Even when the writer has a prominent role in the account, if another person is clearly the focus of the story, we are working with a case study.[2]

Teaching cases are original accounts, case reports or case studies that have been written or edited for teaching purposes. Cases used for teaching in business schools are always in this category, usually written on the basis of extensively gathered case materials, sometimes supplemented by case reports written by participants or elicited through interviews. Teaching cases can vary enormously in length, from the quite brief vignettes (a paragraph or two) used in teaching medical problem solving through the lengthier narratives (2 or 3 pages) employed in ethics courses, to the extended and often multichapter accounts used in business schools (as much as 50 pages or more). They are usually based on fact but in some fields, such as ethics, can be fictitious vignettes constructed to illustrate a vexing ethical dilemma.

Case methods of teaching are nearly independent of the types of cases used. They are the methods of pedagogy employed in conjunction with teaching cases. In business schools and in programs strongly influenced by the business models, they are prototypically quasi-Socratic interactions with high levels of student participation, and they demand skilled leadership from instructors. But not always. They can be autodidactic, self-instruction conducted by reading cases with commentaries and reflecting upon them. They can be interactive computer programs built around teaching cases. They can be lectures that use cases as their subject matter. They can be non-Socratic group discussions in groups that vary in size from 20 to an entire law school class of 150.

Casebooks are collections of case reports, case studies, or teaching cases selected, sequenced, organized, and glossed for particular educational purposes. There are a number of different ways these collections can be organized.

Casebooks for teacher education could be organized in a variety of ways. We could have casebooks that focus on predictably hard-to-teach topics or objectives in school subjects. These might include contrasting cases for teaching evolution or photosynthesis in biology, inequalities in mathematics, thematic analysis in literature, or the imperfect tense in Romance languages. Here the lesson or the unit would be the unit around which cases were organized.

Cases could focus on types of students and the challenges they present. They could describe policy conflicts in schools with which teachers must cope, or tensions arising out of relationships with parents, administrators, or peers.

The editing of casebooks has become a central scholarly activity for professors of law, who collect, annotate, and organize paradigmatic cases into topical casebooks that are used instructionally in law schools all over the country.

Case-based curriculum describes courses or whole programs built around the use of cases and/or casebooks. Conant's course in the understanding of science for nonmajors, certain medical school curricula such as those at Michigan State, McMaster University in Ontario, or Southern Illinois, and many business school courses are all examples of case-based curriculum. These usually include both particular genres of teaching cases along with prescribed methods of teaching.

WHAT IS IN A CASE?

Schwab, in discussing the kinds of teaching materials that can be successfully used in discussion, argued that the materials we have students read must be of sufficient complexity, must admit enough alternative readings and perspectives, must invite enough enthusiastic disagreements and contrary views to be worth the energetic investments in dialogue of a learning community. For Schwab, such material was very often a case, though it could also be an original piece of scientific writing (e.g., an essay by Newton, Galileo's *Two Dialogues*). For our purposes in this chapter, I would prefer to limit our discussion of cases to the variety of *narratives* that can be used in case reports, case studies, or teaching cases.

What, then, is in a case? I would stipulate that a case has a narrative, a story, a set of events that unfolds over time in a particular place. It probably includes human protagonists, though it need not. (For example, there can probably be biological, geological, or astronomical cases in which the central figures are species, planets, black holes, tectonic plates, or volcanoes that change or evolve over time). I will further stipulate that, in general, these teaching narratives have certain shared characteristics.

- Narratives have a plot—a beginning, middle, and end. They may well include a dramatic tension that must be relieved in some fashion.
- Narratives are particular and specific. They are not statements of what generally or for the most part is or has been.
- Narratives place events in a frame of time and place. They are, quite literally, local—that is, located or situated.
- Narratives of action or inquiry reveal the working of human hands, minds, motives, conceptions, needs, misconceptions, frustrations, jealousies, faults. Human agency and intention are central to those accounts.
- Narratives reflect the social and cultural contexts within which the events occur.

Cases therefore possess at least two features that may render them useful in learning: their status as narratives and their contextualization in time and place. A central question remains. Why might we find such narratives so powerful and relevant in teacher education?

There are a number of reasons why cases may teach more effectively than traditional expository texts and teaching techniques. From an epistemological perspective, cases may be more congruent with the forms of practical knowledge that undergird the varieties of practice, in teaching and other fields. From a professional perspective, cases may have more immediate credibility and relevance. In the next section I will attempt to answer this question of the efficacy of cases from the perspective I understand best, contemporary psychological theory and research.

WHY SHOULD CASE-BASED APPROACHES WORK?

We do not really have evidence that case-based approaches work any better than lecture or discussion approaches. It seems ironic that after so many years of applications in business, law, and medicine, no comparative evaluation studies exist that confirm the widely held belief that cases are more motivating, promote better transfer from theory to practice, and produce better problem solvers and critical thinkers. Therefore this section will present a variety of theoretical and empirical perspectives on why case-based approaches are likely to work and discuss the kinds of psychological mechanisms that would account for the potency of cases and case methods.

We are only beginning to develop the kind of psychology adequate for dealing with the complexities of learning from cases. Bruner (1986, 1990) proposes that there are primarily two ways of knowing, the *paradigmatic* and the *narrative*. Paradigmatic forms are the kinds usually associated with scientific knowing. (He uses the term quite differently from my use of it in our earlier discussions of paradigmatic cases in ethics.) They are analytic, general, abstract, impersonal, and decontextualized. To know paradigmatically is to know in general, to know quite independent of individual knowers and particular contexts. Boyle's law, reinforcement theory, and the principles of supply and demand are all paradigmatic forms of knowledge.

Narrative modes, in contrast, are specific, local, personal, and contextualized. We do not speak of the validity of a narrative, but of its verisimilitude. Does it ring true? Is it a compelling and persuasive story? A good piece of physics demonstrates its validity through meeting standards of prediction and control. A good work of tragedy demonstrates its verisimilitude by evoking in its audience feelings of pity and fear.

During most of its brief history, the psychology of learning and cognition has focused its attention on how individuals engage or fail to engage in paradigmatic learning. How are lists memorized, paragraphs comprehended, theories understood, and skills transferred? Why are rules so hard to remember and even harder to apply in new situations? In contrast, why do stories appear to lodge in memory more easily? Why do we so readily organize many performances via scripts and story grammars?

Although our paradigmatic sciences may have taught us that we are only entitled to place faith in the world of scientific generalizations and quantitative laws, both scientists and policy makers will often base their personal choices or explanations on the power of narratives. Should it be any surprise, then, that the narrative forms of cases possess such clear instructional impact? Cases engage our attention, lodge in our memory, and capture our commitment. We remember and believe the narratives of cases, and they effectively influence our subsequent dispositions and actions.

Situated Cognition

In addition to the quality of narrative itself, cases are also situated; they are embedded in contexts of application and emotion, of place and time. Concurrently with development of the kinds of psychology that help us understand the role of narratives in fostering human understanding, we have witnessed the development of a psychology of situated learning, in which the contextualization of performance occupies center stage.

During the 1980s psychology and anthropology met, courted, and consorted. The liaison left an indelible mark on psychology. Narrative modes of knowing had been employed by anthropologists for years. In spite of attempts to render anthropology into a nomothetic discipline that studied *culture* in general, the field remained rooted in thick descriptions, theory-laden narratives describing local, particular, and highly contextualized events in which the personal role and voice of the narrator were clearly visible. For anthropologists, stories were legitimate empirical data.

Anthropology had another disturbing challenge to throw at psychology, a challenge that moved well beyond method. Psychology is constructed around the experimental *task*, whether administered in the laboratory or as an item on a test or inventory. To call something a task or test item requires that any elements of context or person be removed so that it is "fair" to everyone. Psychologists then observe how individuals perform on these tasks and make inferences regarding their abilities, achievements, and other personal attributes. By removing the context, one presumably arrives at the essential qualities of the individual. Similarly, by removing the personal in experimental research, one presumably can discern the essential influences of contexts.

As anthropologists (and anthropologically infected psychologists) began studying human performances in other cultures, however, they began to make some disturbing discoveries. When individuals were working in their own local cultures, they were frequently capable of performances that could not have been predicted from their performances on tests. People who looked dumb on tests or in the laboratory frequently looked quite smart *on comparable tasks* when observed in situations with which they were familiar. Even within our own society, truck drivers and supermarket shoppers could intuitively perform fairly complex arithmetic calculations in familiar contexts that they could not solve when presented with them on tests. An ostensibly learning-disabled child could assume a leadership role in a complex group cake-baking activity by taking advantage of the complementary talents of his peers (Cole & Traupmann, 1981).

Cognition was situated. Many tasks individuals could not perform in general, they could perform readily in particular settings. Many things they could not perform alone, they could perform in collaboration with others. Apparently, learning is much more situation-specific than heretofore imagined, as is its transfer to new settings (e.g., Brown, Collins, & Duguid, 1989; Lave, 1988; Resnick, 1987).

Thus the specificity and localism of cases as instructional materials may not be problematic for learning; indeed, they may be far more appropriate media for learning than the more abstract and decontextualized lists of propositions or expositions of facts, concepts, and principles. The character of the narrative form may be particularly well suited to the situatedness of the learning process. While principles may be powerful in their efficiency and economy of representation, learners may find it far easier to remember and use ideas that are located in the narrative form of cases. Moreover, cases may reduce the problems of transfer because they simulate the way in which the most effective forms of learning are situated in specific contexts and circumstances.

Cognitive Flexibility in Ill-Structured Domains

If the kind of psychology we have traditionally pursued has focused on the paradigmatic rather than the narrative (in both its topics and its methods), it has also taught us much more about learning in well-structured domains, such as mathematics and physics or reading comprehension for fairly explicit expository prose, than in ill-structured domains such as those characteristic of most professions. Medicine, history, and law are ill-structured domains; teaching is a profoundly ill-structured domain. Another new line of work in contemporary psychology is helping us to understand how the instructional use of cases may help learners cope with the judgmental complexities of ill-structured domains of knowledge and performance. Rand Spiro argues:

> The best way to learn and instruct in order to attain the goal of cognitive flexibility in knowledge representation for future application is by a method of case-based presentations which treats a content domain as a landscape that is explored by "criss-crossing" it in many directions, by reexamining each case "site" in the varying contexts of different neighboring cases, and by using a variety of abstract dimensions for comparing cases. (Spiro, Vispoel, Schmitz, Samarapungavan, & Boerger, 1987, p. 178)

Spiro came to these conclusions after several years of studying a problem of teaching and learning in a complex setting of medical school courses in physiology.

Spiro and his colleagues observed that excellent medical students frequently emerged from courses in physiology holding misconceptions with which they had apparently not entered the courses. The study of misconceptions has become a central focus of research on cognition, as we have recognized the pervasive influence of prior knowledge on learning and thinking of all kinds. Whether one chooses to use the language of Herbart, Piaget, Bartlett, Ausubel, Bruner, Richard Anderson, or any of the contemporary schema theorists such as Spiro himself, the manner in which prior understandings serve to frame, organize, and scaffold future learning is undeniable. The message of a constructivist social science is consistent and clear.

The medical students studied by Spiro, however, did not appear to be afflicted with crippling preconceptions. Indeed, their maladies seemed *pedagogic*; that is, they were created by the instruction rather than antedating it. More specifically, the misconceptions appeared traceable to the power of initial analogies, metaphors, examples, or cases used by the teachers to introduce and frame the new topics in the course. Since all analogies, like all cases, breed distortion when overgeneralized, these organizing analogies had apparently overwhelmed the expositions and fine-tunings that succeeded them. If the instructor, in introducing the topic of the circulatory system, had asked the students to think of it as like the plumbing system of a large apartment building, then that organizing image would continue to frame their thinking well after its usefulness had ceased.

Spiro came to recognize that the problem lay not in the distortive power of analogies and cases, but in a pedagogy that permitted single representations to reign unchallenged. He therefore proposed methods of multiple representations and multiple cases, carefully designed and coordinated so that new cases would be introduced to compensate for the potential misunderstandings bred by powerful predecessors (Spiro, Feltovich, & Coulson, 1988).

There are several other features associated with Spiro's work. He argues that the dictates of traditional schema theory work particularly well in well-structured domains because these domains are hierarchical and relatively fixed. In ill-structured domains, however, "the meaning of a concept is intimately connected to its patterns of use" (Spiro et al., 1988, p. 380). This allusion to the situatedness of the cognitions in such domains leads to the need for knowledge to be organized flexibly into networks of concepts and cases rather than more rigidly into schemata and hierarchies.

We thus can see the variety of ways in which the new forms of cognitive psychology developed over the past decade or so have made possible a deeper understanding of the potential value and proper pedagogy for case methods. Our growing understanding of narrative ways of knowing, of the local and situated character of cognition, and of the conditions needed for the development of cognitive flexibility to cope with unpredictable and fluid domains lend credence to the claims of those who advocate case methods. Nevertheless, it would be folly to cast away all forms of exposition and didactic explanation and replace them with case-based approaches. The cognitive efficiency of propositional knowledge is undeniable. Its precision and structure are invaluable. Moreover, case methods also have some liabilities.

DISADVANTAGES OF CASES AND CASE METHODS

Amidst these paeans for case methods, some potential disadvantages of case methods should also be acknowledged.

- Cases are expensive and time-consuming to produce and demanding to field test.
- Cases are difficult to teach well. Especially when paired with Socratic teaching, they require well-trained, gifted teachers who are willing to invest longer periods of preparation than is typical for other methods.
- Cases are very inefficient; very little material is covered in rather long periods of time. Even though we may wish to

argue that content is far less important than process, we must attain a judicious blend of the two; case methods may make that difficult to accomplish.

- Cases are episodic, discontinuous, hard to structure and organize into larger wholes in the minds of students. In curricula (especially teacher education) already criticized because they are too fragmented and lack integration, case methods could exacerbate the problem. Learning through cases, therefore, could blind the learner to critical generalizations and principles because the particularities of the narrative overwhelm the general conceptions.
- Cases may be susceptible to overgeneralization. A single case may be so powerful that its apparent message is transformed into a rigid maxim by the learner.

Interesting paradoxes are associated with the use of cases and case methods. On the one hand, they certainly retard the pace of content coverage when compared to the swiftness of lectures or textbooks. Nevertheless, when compared to the logistical complexities and site limitations of student teaching and internships, they permit the student to experience vicariously a far larger number of different situations than would ever be possible through direct personal experience. Cases thus become simulated residencies, transporting students to settings and dilemmas they would be unlikely to experience directly. Given recent writings (e.g., Feiman-Nemser & Buchmann, 1985) on teacher education that warn against treating direct experience as a panacea, case methods may well be the ideal compromise between more field work and more controlled clinical experiences.

CASES AND CASE METHODS FOR TEACHER EDUCATION

I have reviewed the field of case methods in education with a rather broad brush. Case-based approaches are used rather widely in professional education, especially in business and law. They are rarely found in undergraduate general education. They have been almost nonexistent in teacher education.

I have examined the variety of purposes for which case methods have been used and the underlying theories of learning and teaching that support their value for education. Those who advocate case methods must do so without the support of research or evaluation studies. Those of us who wish to introduce such approaches to the education of teachers must not only commit ourselves to a generation of case writing, careful editing, and curriculum development; we must also plan to conduct serious investigations of learning and teaching with cases. Until now, there has been no unique pedagogy of teacher education. Law has had its Socratic case method, medicine its bedside teaching and patient rounds, and business its own form of case method. Since the demise of the normal school, the pedagogy of pedagogues has resembled the commonplace university classroom more than anything else, replete with its lectures and recitations, projects and field experiences.

I envision case methods as a strategy for overcoming many of the most serious deficiencies in the education of teachers. Because they are contextual, local, and situated—as are all narratives—cases integrate what otherwise remains separated. Content and process, thought and feeling, teaching and learning are not addressed theoretically as distinct constructs. They occur simultaneously as they do in real life, posing problems, issues, and challenges for new teachers that their knowledge and experiences can be used to discern.

I envision cases and case methods being employed in Foundations courses as well as Methods classes to bridge between theory and practice (L. Shulman, 1990). By using multiple cases and yeasty layers of commentary, teacher educators will resist the temptations of easy formulas, whether for five-step lesson plans or five-paragraph essays. Complex cases will communicate to both future teachers and laypersons that teaching is a complex domain demanding subtle judgments and agonizing decisions.

As Bruner once observed regarding discovery learning, it seems foolish to ask each generation to rediscover or reinvent all that its ancestors had learned. Our challenge as educators will be to devise that judicious blend of the economy of expository teaching with the complementary power of families of well-crafted, compensating cases. In the dialectic between principle and parable, we are likely to discover wisdom.

NOTES

Acknowledgments. The preparation of this chapter extended over a rather long period of time. I wish to thank Stanford University for support of a sabbatical leave, the Spencer Foundation and the Carnegie Corporation of New York for grants that contributed to the writing of this paper, and the Van Leer Jerusalem Institute for providing an ideal setting for its completion.

1. The contrast with the use of cases in business education is enlightening. Where legal case methods typically ask students to discern underlying principles, business cases are more likely to press students to examine the likely consequences of each action they propose. Legal cases focus student attention on judgments and reasons; business cases focus on actions and consequences.

2. A singular exception to this distinction between case report and case study is the relatively new genre of research in which the author is systematically studying his or her own practice in a disciplined manner, often with the assistance of other observers and frequently using videotape and other technologies. In these cases, such as Lampert (1990) and the papers by Ball (in press) and Wilson (in press), the discipline of case study is brought to bear on the first-person narrative to create a new form.

REFERENCES

Ball, D. L. (in press). With an eye on the mathematical horizon: Dilemmas of teaching elementary school mathematics. *Elementary School Journal.*

Brown, J. S., Collins, A., & Duguid, P. (1989). Situated cognition and the culture of learning. *Educational Researcher, 18*(1), 32–41.

Bruner, J. S. (1986). *Actual minds, possible worlds.* Cambridge, MA: Harvard University Press.

Bruner, J. S. (1990). *Acts of meaning.* Cambridge, MA: Harvard University Press.

Christensen, C. R., with Hansen, A. J. (1987). *Teaching and the case method.* Boston: Harvard Business School.

Cole, M., & Traupmann, K. (1981). Comparative cognitive research: Learning from a learning disabled child. In *Minnesota symposia on child psychology* (Vol. 14, pp. 125–154). Hillsdale, NJ: Erlbaum.

Conant, J. B. (1947). *On understanding science.* New Haven, CT: Yale University Press.

Feiman-Nemser, S., & Buchmann, M. (1985). Pitfalls of experience in teacher preparation. *Teachers College Record, 87*(1), 53–65.

Fine, R. (1943). *The ideas behind the chess openings.* New York: McKay.

Jonsen, A., & Toulmin, S. (1988). *The abuse of casuistry.* Berkeley: University of California Press.

Lampert, M. (1990). When the problem is not the question and the answer is not the solution. *American Educational Research Journal, 27,* 29–64.

Lave, J. (1988). *Cognition in practice.* New York: Cambridge University Press.

Resnick, L. (1987). Learning in school and out. *Educational Researcher, 16*, 13–20.

Schön D. A. (1983). *The reflective practitioner.* New York: Basic Books.

Schön, D. A. (1987). *Educating the reflective practitioner.* San Francisco: Jossey-Bass.

Schwab, J. J. (1964). *The teaching of science as enquiry.* Cambridge, MA: Harvard University Press.

Schwab, J. J. (1969). *College curriculum and student protest.* Chicago: University of Chicago Press.

Shulman, J. H., & Colbert, J. A. (Eds.). (1987). *The mentor teacher casebook: Cases and commentaries.* San Francisco: Far West Laboratory for Educational Research and Development.

Shulman, J. H., & Colbert, J. A. (Eds.) (1988). *The intern teacher casebook: Cases and commentaries.* San Francisco: Far West Laboratory for Educational Research and Development.

Shulman, J. H., & Colbert, J. A. (1989). Cases as catalysts for cases. *Action in Teacher Education, 11*(1), 44–52.

Shulman, J. H., Colbert, J. A., Kemper, D., & Dmytriw, L. (1990). Case writing as a site for collaboration. *Teacher Education Quarterly, 17*(1), 63–78.

Shulman, L. S. (1986). Those who understand: Knowledge growth in teaching. *Educational Researcher, 15*(2), 4–14.

Shulman, L. S. (1987). Knowledge and teaching: Foundations of the new reform. *Harvard Educational Review, 57*(1), 1–22.

Shulman, L. S. (1990). Reconnecting foundations to the substance of teacher education. *Teachers College Record, 91*(3), 300–310.

Spiro, R. J., Vispoel, W., Schmitz, J., Samarapungavan, A., & Boerger, A. (1987). Knowledge acquisition for application: Cognitive flexibility and transfer in complex content domains. In B. C. Britton & S. Glynn (Eds.), *Executive control processes* (pp. 177–200). Hillsdale, NJ: Erlbaum.

Spiro, R. J., Coulson, R. L., Feltovich, P. J., & Anderson, D. K. (1988). Cognitive flexibility theory: Advanced knowledge acquisition in ill-structured domains. In *Tenth Annual Conference of the Cognitive Science Society* (pp. 375–383). Hillsdale, NJ: Erlbaum.

Stevens, R. (1983). *Law school: Legal education in America from the 1850s to the 1980s.* Chapel Hill: University of North Carolina Press.

Toulmin, S. (1986). *The place of reason in ethics.* Chicago: University of Chicago Press. (Original work published 1949)

White, V. (1988). The breaking point. In J. H. Shulman & J. A. Colbert (Eds.), *The intern teacher casebook: Cases and commentaries* (pp. 33–35). San Francisco: Far West Laboratory for Educational Research and Development.

Whitehead, A. N. (1929). *The aims of education and other essays.* New York: Macmillan.

Wilson, S. (in press). Mastodons, maps, and Michigan: Exploring uncharted territory while teaching elementary school social studies. *Elementary School Journal.*

Part I

CASES AS
TEACHING TOOLS

CHAPTER 2

Learning to Think Like a Teacher
The Study of Cases

JUDITH KLEINFELD

Students entering Harvard Law School hear a story that has been passed down for at least 50 years. The story communicates to entering students a basic purpose of professional education in the law—teaching students the habits of skepticism, verbal aggressiveness, and readiness to challenge power of a "real lawyer." A powerful and brilliant professor (at least three have been the named figures, since this legend has outlasted retirements and successions) strides to the podium and surveys his domain—165 nervous first-year law students. He selects his victim.

"Sir," says the professor, "state the facts in this case."

The quaking student gives an answer that is inadequate. The professor demands a better one. The student stumbles.

The professor becomes silent. He reaches deep into his suit pocket, pulls out a dime, and puts it on the podium.

"Kid," he announces, "you'll never make a lawyer. Take this dime and call your mother. Tell her to come and get you. Tell her you're never going to be a lawyer."

The student freezes.

"What are you waiting for?" the professor roars. "Come here and get this dime. Call your mother."

The student gets up and staggers toward the door. He stops, draws himself up, and says, "Sir, you are a bastard!"

Go back to your seat," says the professor. "You're beginning to think like a lawyer."

This legend is not one of the official "cases" of the law school— these are appellate court decisions—but it is these kinds of stories that students remember years after they have forgotten most of their classwork. These stories and cases develop the frame of mind that characterizes a well-trained professional in this field of expertise.

Cases studied in law schools are decisions of appeals courts in actual, individual lawsuits. Such cases teach the law student how to "think like a lawyer," 'that is, how to spot the important issues in a complex, muddy situation and how to apply general principles of law to particular facts. The cases also give the student a great deal of vicarious experience of business administrative processes, criminal matters, and other domains of life previously unfamiliar. The application of general principles of law to particular cases is surprisingly complex and difficult and requires 3 years of law school and years of practice to master. The purpose of law school is to teach the student the principles used in the major fields of law, as well as the intellectual process of thinking like a lawyer.

Schools of education are less clear about their purposes than law or other professional schools. Indeed, the position that a fundamental aim of a school of education is to develop a particular professional way of thinking is only one of many competing paradigms of teacher education. In current discussions, this position is labeled the "reflective inquiry" model as opposed to "eclectic" or "technical-skills" models of teacher education (Tom, 1984; Zeichner, 1983). This chapter does not attempt to justify the position that teacher education programs should, above all, teach education students how to "think like a teacher," that is, learn how to formulate educational problems, design strategies that fit specific children, and reflect on the ethical and policy issues as well on the pedagogical issues embedded in everyday instructional decisions. I and others have made such arguments elsewhere (Feiman-Nemser, 1980; Kleinfeld & Noordhoff, 1988; Zeichner & Liston, 1987).

This chapter has a more specific purpose: I show how case methods can be used to develop the particular professional way of thinking characteristic of expert teachers. I use a particular case, "Malaise of the Spirit," to illustrate the way a case can give novices:

1. Vicarious experience with the kinds of problematic situations characteristic of teaching
2. A model of how an expert teacher goes about framing and constructing educational problems
3. A model of how a sophisticated teacher inquires about and reflects on such problems

4. A stock of educational strategies for use in analogous problem situations
5. A sense that teaching is an inherently ambiguous activity requiring continuous reflection

"Thinking like a teacher," case methods demonstrate to students, is a creative way of thinking, a process of problem framing and inquiry, a process of design.

In this chapter, I first describe the issues in our case example, "Malaise of the Spirit," written by an expert teacher who experienced the problems he is writing about (Finley, 1988). Second, I describe the context, the type of teacher education program I prepared this case for. Next, I describe how I go about getting expert teachers to write cases and how I conduct classes based on cases. Finally, I try to be clear and specific about my purposes in using cases—exactly what I want to help education students learn. I emphasize the importance of cases in preparing teachers emotionally, not only intellectually, for the kinds of problems they will face in the classroom. I show how case methods legitimize the discussion of crucial educational variables—such as the personality of the individual teacher—that the positivistic research tradition ignores.

FIGURING OUT THE ISSUES
IN ILL-STRUCTURED PROBLEMS

"Malaise of the Spirit" begins with a dilemma requiring fast professional judgment and immediate action: An Eskimo boy in Peter Wedman's English class has jumped a Caucasian boy and is pummeling him on the floor while the rest of the class circles the pair. The Caucasian boy is protecting himself, but he is not fighting back. Wedman does not know who or what started the fight. Nonetheless he has to act—immediately.

Wedman handles the fight in a way most education students find quite surprising. After pulling the Eskimo boy off the Caucasian boy, he orders the Caucasian boy to the principal's office and tells the rest of the class to go out into the hall. He leaves the Eskimo boy alone in the classroom. Why does Wedman do this? What problem does he see that he is trying to solve?

As the case unfolds, Wedman explains his thinking. What Wedman had spotted was the Eskimo boy's nonverbal reactions: the boy was on the verge of tears. Wedman considered the cultural context. For a traditional Eskimo male of high school age to cry in public is a humiliation beyond repair. The boy might respond by dropping out of school. Thus Wedman saw the critical, immediate problem as getting all the other students out—to give the Eskimo boy the opportunity to regain his composure.

Wedman had also sensed the emotions that had started the fight, although not until later was his intuitive judgment confirmed. When Wedman talked to the Caucasian boy in the principal's office, the boy admitted that he had looked at the Eskimo boy's folder and uttered the words, "D minus." When Wedman asked the Eskimo boy what had started the fight, the student said nothing. Wedman realized that an indirect means of communication was culturally more appropriate: he asked the Eskimo boy to write him a note. The Eskimo boy gave the note to another student to deliver (making the communication process even more indirect). It read: "I don't like it when he calls me a dumb Eskimo."

In sum, most teachers in Wedman's situation would define the central problem as how to stop the fight and get the class back on track. They would take what Dewey (1933) calls "routine action." They would ask who had started the fight, send that student to the office, and carry on with class routines.

A reflective professional like Peter Wedman defines the central problem quite differently. He sees the problem as how to figure out how to avoid humiliating a student in public, especially an Eskimo student who may drop out of school. He sees the secondary problem as learning what started the fight. The case thus shows students that educational problems are constructed; they are not inherent in a situation, even in such an obvious situation as a fight. The case shows that finding and framing a problem is a creative act, an act of professional imagination.

Wedman does not forget about the fight. He turns it over in his mind. The incident, Wedman realizes, symbolizes a more serious problem—the pervasive racial tensions disrupting his English class. This more fundamental problem requires not quick judgment and fast improvisation but long-term reflection and considered strategies for action. This is the second type of problematic teaching situation that the case brings to students' attention: the basic problems underlying a surface difficulty.

Wedman begins the business of thinking through the entire situation and constructing new problems that are amenable to action. The case displays for education students what Schön (1983) calls "reflection-in-action," the hallmark of professional thinking in many fields where the problems are inherently ill structured and precise, technical solutions are not available. "Malaise of the Spirit" shows how a teacher thinks through a complex situation, gathers evidence, applies theoretical insights to practical problems, and designs and tests a strategy. Wedman considers why his English classroom is tense with bad feeling between the Eskimo students and the Caucasian students. He thinks about why the Eskimo students do not talk much in class. He considers the reasons the Eskimo students see themselves as "dumb."

Like a quantitative researcher, he examines evidence. He looks at his gradebook and analyzes ethnic group differences in grades, tardiness, absenteeism, and standardized test scores. His analysis provides interesting clues, such as the pattern of absenteeism among Eskimo girls, who have baby-sitting responsibilities during the school day. Like a qualitative researcher, he seeks out key informants in the school and community who offer historical and cultural perspectives on the situation. He thinks about research articles he has read on identity formation and motivation that might illuminate the situation.

He worries about ethical questions. On the basis of what criteria does he actually assign grades, and are these criteria just or subtly racist? What does fair grading mean in an English classroom where some students have spoken standard English all their lives and other students speak "village" English, a dialect? Wedman self-consciously portrays himself as a "detective" doing investigative work. Indeed, he organizes the opening sections of the case into "incidents" and "clues"—drawing readers into his search for good problems, ones that suggest practical strategies for action.

The bases of his classroom problems, Wedman comes to understand, lie outside as well as inside his classroom. The town itself—inhabited by well-paid Caucasian government employees and Eskimos suspended between a subsistence hunting and wage-work culture—breeds a malaise of the spirit that is infecting him, the school staff, and the students. Many Eskimo parents view the teachers as invaders after high salaries and easily replaceable. ("You teachers are a dime a dozen," sniffs a school board member.) Some parents sanction children's absenteeism from school. The school itself is dilapidated due to district funding inequities. The school board is composed of people who are elected on an at-large basis from a region composed of many communities and schools. The board allocates more than twice the money per student to the small schools in village communities than to Wedman's school in the regional center. Teachers seethe with anger and resentment, but many are trapped in the community. They bought expensive houses, the economy collapsed, and they cannot sell and leave.

The depression and resentments that are infecting the teachers and the community, Wedman realizes, are infecting him as well. A seasoned veteran, known throughout the region for his innovative teaching, he had expected his transfer to Ruden, the regional center, to be uneventful. In Ruden he is shocked to see that he himself is deteriorating.

A second critical incident—a "lost weekend"—comes to symbolize Wedman's fear that he is losing his own identity and sense of self-worth. On most weekends Wedman grades papers and prepares for his classes. On this weekend, he sleeps and watches television. He comes to school on Monday without lesson plans.

Like an actual teaching situation, "Malaise of the Spirit" presents not one well-defined issue but many ill-defined ones, intertwined like the fibers of a thick rope. The first part of the case ends with a dramatic conflict. Will Wedman work his way out of this situation? Will he flee or will he, like Kurtz in *Heart of Darkness*, succumb?

IDENTIFYING STRATEGIES FOR TURNING AROUND A BAD SITUATION

An especially effective way to teach this case is to give students this first part and then ask them three fundamental questions: What do you see as the basic problems in this teaching situation? What, if anything, can Wedman do? What do you think will happen?

Even though the first part of the case is partially structured into definable problems, many students still find it difficult to identify the issues. Many students see very little Wedman can do; they are strategy-poor.

When students receive the second part of the case, they are shocked to discover how much one teacher can accomplish, even in a situation beset with long-term and complex institutional and cultural problems. Wedman spends a large part of his Christmas vacation thinking about the difficulties in Ruden and in his classroom. He comes back and takes action. Wedman begins with a small innovation of great symbolic import. He goes to a local publishing outfit and orders an engraved sign. The first day back at school, he removes the sign that reads "Teachers' Lounge" and replaces it with a sign reading "Faculty Room."

Next Wedman makes major changes in his classroom organization and grading system. He gives each student English assignments with a statement of objectives keyed to that student's achievement level. He assigns grades on the basis of student attainment of these specific objectives—an approach that equalizes opportunities for the Eskimo and Caucasian students. He asks a local teaching aide to call parents when students are not doing their homework. He organizes study sessions before and after school for students who cannot study at home. Soon homework starts coming in regularly. He initiates "roll call" procedures (going around the class so everyone gets a chance to talk) and "taking a speaking order" (writing down students' names when they raise their hands to talk) so that the more verbal Caucasian students do not jump in and dominate classroom discussions.

Wedman undertakes an enormous variety of other innovations to raise students' morale and change community attitudes toward the school. He takes photographs of students doing homework and sends their pictures to the local newspaper with tag lines such as, "Their parents should be proud. Working together on their homework are John Carl, Lisa Cook, and Pam Sheffield." He gives his English classes a section of the wall to decorate with the title "The Theme is Excellence." Before long, the board is filled with student awards, student writings, magazine photographs of fabulous cars and meals, and news articles about parent activities. A few parents "dropped by after school ostensibly to talk about their child, surreptitiously making sidelong looks for 'their article'" (Finley, 1988, pp. 44–45). Education students reading this case are taken aback by the success of Wedman's efforts and how much he accomplished.

THE CONTEXT: CASES IN THE
TEACHERS FOR ALASKA PROGRAM

"Malaise of the Spirit" is the first teaching case we use in an innovative teacher education program called Teachers for Alaska. This program is designed to prepare teachers for small village high schools in Eskimo and Indian communities and for large urban classrooms with culturally diverse students. It is a fifth-year program that offers two semesters of professional teacher preparation leading to secondary certification. Each year the program selects a small cohort of 15 to 20 students and prepares them for teaching through (1) seminars organized around cases presenting concrete problems of teaching and (2) field experience that offers other cases and examples of the best contemporary practice.

Teachers for Alaska is a problem-centered, case-based approach to teacher education modeled after the problem-based approach to professional education pioneered at McMaster University and New Pathways at the Harvard Medical School (Barrows & Tamblyn, 1980). This teacher preparation program has done away with the traditional sequence of Foundations courses followed by Methods courses. Students instead study problems and cases in small seminar groups. Educational research, theory, and methods are introduced as such material becomes useful in understanding and dealing with the classic problems of professional practice.

The Teachers for Alaska program is grounded firmly in a conception of good teaching as "reflective inquiry." We are trying to prepare teachers who can teach well in the type of complex and ambiguous world that Wedman inhabits. We can offer teachers no clear rules for navigating through the terrain. What we can do is to prepare teachers to think clearly about the complex empirical and normative questions they will face in such teaching situations. We can suggest to them what a few of the crucial issues and dilemmas may be. We can point to features of the situation they may want to attend to. We can offer them research knowledge and examples of successful teaching that may prove helpful. But, in the final analysis, they will be on their own.

The Teachers for Alaska curriculum is organized as a series of thematic blocks. Each block centers on the dilemmas of teaching particular subjects to culturally diverse student groups and includes teaching cases. "Malaise of the Spirit," for example, is taught in the literature and literacy block. It nests classroom questions about teaching English ("How do I organize English instruction in a class where some students are sophisticated English speakers and others speak a nonstandard dialect?") in the context of wider community issues ("How are community attitudes affecting students' motivation to learn?") and in the context of personal issues ("Why am I falling apart emotionally?").

Cases are the bricks and mortar of the Teachers for Alaska program. But we have also used cases in conventional Foundations and Methods courses. The case gives valuable concreteness to the philosophical, historical, and normative issues considered in Foundations courses. The case gives valuable context to the methodological choices discussed in Methods courses. Case methods work well in a single course and in an entire teacher education program.

USING EXPERT TEACHERS AS CASE WRITERS

Since an important purpose of a case such as "Malaise of the Spirit" is to model for students the clinical reasoning of an expert teacher, the logical person to write a case is an expert teacher. We therefore search for teachers/case writers who are both exemplary teachers in a multicultural context and accomplished writers.

Like a literary autobiography, the case reveals the teacher/case writer's personality and ways of thinking about experience. The length of a rich case becomes a way of handling a critical problem in case teaching: Is the teacher writing the case distorting the situation? The question of whether and how the teacher may be distorting the situation becomes not an invalidating concern but a critical issue for education students to discuss. How does this particular teacher see the situation? How might the situation appear to other participants—such as the members of the Ruden school board? A detailed case provides grist for such discussion; a mere anecdote does not. "We do not know if the world really is the way this teacher describes it," we say to our students. "Knowledge is constructed. Think about how this teacher went about constructing problems. When you try to make sense of your own situation, you too will be locked into your own skin."

The case offers evidence—literary detail—that enables us to discuss how the teacher's "person" shapes his or her interpretation of events, choices of action, and other people's responses. These subjects become an important part of a case discussion. The case thus opens for discussion critical issues that the positivistic research tradition gives us no way to talk about—the impact of teachers' manner and personality, the moral quality of their intentions, the passions that they communicate. The case method invites and legitimizes the discussion of such matters in ways that conventional approaches to teacher education do not.

CONDUCTING CLASSES WITH CASES

It is easy to use a case to have a stimulating and exciting class discussion. The question is whether such discussion leads to learning or whether it amounts to little more than loose talk.

To use cases productively, you must have a clear idea of what the case can teach and what you want the class discussion to accomplish. As Christensen and Hansen (1987) emphasize in their discussion of case method teaching at the Harvard Business School, preparation for teaching a case demands considerable work on the part of the teacher.

Since we use "Malaise of the Spirit" to model for students the process of framing and analyzing educational problems, our questions emphasize Wedman's clinical reasoning processes. We begin the case discussion by asking students, "What issues does this case present?" Usually we "poll the group"—asking each student to name issues and writing their answers on the board. (Indeed, we use and model the same polling technique Wedman uses to encourage class participation in culturally mixed classes.) We start discussion with whatever issue has aroused the most student interest and then move to the other issues. Often students want to start with the fight and how teachers can handle fights. Whatever the issue we begin with, we emphasize the processes of problem construction. We ask, for example, how else Wedman could have framed the problem the fight posed. What results might have occurred had he framed the problem in this other way?

We also evaluate the teacher's response to the fight. Were Wedman's general approach (sending the Caucasian boy to the office and leaving the Eskimo boy in the classroom) and his specific words and tone culturally appropriate and sensitive or patronizing and subtly racist? We role-play alternative ways the teacher's discussion with each boy might have been handled. Such role-plays are extremely valuable in demonstrating to education students the impact of subtle differences in a teacher's tone and manner.

In thinking about the right questions to lead the discussion of a teaching case, we have found helpful the models Christensen and Hansen (1987) provide in their analysis of case method teaching at the Harvard Business School and in the instructor's guide to *Teaching and the Case Method* (Christensen, Hansen, & Moore, 1987). Questions we have culled or adapted from these sources include:

1. What are the central issues in this situation? Which are most urgent? Which are most critical?
2. What, if anything, should anyone do? Who? When? How? Why do you think so?
3. What did the teacher actually do? With what results? At what risk? With what consequences?

4. How do you think this situation appears to other participants—students, the superintendent, parents, the school
   board? Why do you think so?
5. How did this situation develop? What, if anything, might
   alter the basic conditions that created the present difficulties?
6. What, if anything, have you learned from this case?

We ask students to prepare for a class discussion of a case by
writing a two-page paper responding to two or three of these questions. In teaching "Malaise of the Spirit," for example, we ask students to identify what they see as the main issues and to describe and
evaluate the teacher's actions. Requiring students to write this short
paper ensures that they have actually read the case and that they
come to the class prepared to present and defend their positions.

After the case discussion, we again ask students to write a short
paper on the case. This paper helps students review and conceptualize what they have learned from the case discussion. One of our
goals with "Malaise of the Spirit," for example, is to increase students' repertoire of strategies for dealing with common problems as
multicultural classrooms. Wedman, a seasoned teacher, uses an enormous number of imaginative strategies. We ask students simply to
describe and evaluate Wedman's actions in order to give students an
opportunity to add them to their own stock of strategies.

During case discussions, students often tell stories of their own.
Such personal narratives, as Hymes (1980) points out, are typically
considered inappropriate in university classes. They are mere "anecdotes," politely passed over. A case discussion makes such narratives
useful. They extend our base of dilemmas and exemplars. The
teacher can approach the student's narrative of personal experience
with the same analytic framework as that applied to the case narrative, asking the student: What were your intentions? Why did you
select this strategy? What did you consider its risks? The students'
own anecdotes help them apply the analytic framework we are trying to teach to their own experience—and learning this reasoning
process is our ultimate purpose in teaching with cases.

WHAT STUDENTS CAN LEARN
FROM "MALAISE OF THE SPIRIT"

Cases give students vicarious experience. The cases show how
someone else has faced and dealt with the kinds of problems they

themselves may encounter. In writing a case, teachers communicate more than they know—more than they can state in the form of principles and abstract generalizations. "Malaise of the Spirit" develops understandings that a list of educational purposes does not entirely capture. Nonetheless, clarity about educational purposes is important in giving a clear point to discussion of cases.

In teaching "Malaise of the Spirit," we have five fundamental purposes.

1. *Giving students vicarious experience with multicultural teaching problems—emotional, not only intellectual, preparation for an unjust world.* Novice teachers are typically abrim with energy and enthusiasm. They are eager to teach brilliantly, win friends, and receive laurels from students, parents, and principals alike. They are typically unprepared— emotionally as well as intellectually—for the problems they will face. Here we do not mean instructional problems—high school students who cannot read or subtract. Teachers expect instructional problems. What they are unprepared for is the politics of school systems and for injustice—the unfairness of principals and school boards, the attacks they may get from minorities they are struggling to help. Such injustices outrage novice teachers and consume their emotional energies.

"Malaise of the Spirit" dramatizes such injustices. It gives students the opportunity to conceptualize these problems and understand the historical and cultural contexts that have created these difficulties. Left to their own, teachers typically blame individual people for the unfairness, and their anger and frustration drain commitment to teaching.

One of the important contributions of a case literature is to give students emotional preparation for dealing with an unjust world. Cases—due to their very particularity—create opportunities to talk about those injustices that are taboo topics if raised as general problems. It is neither true nor just, for example, to claim that superintendents "buy" their boards, that Eskimo students harass Caucasian students, or that Caucasian students call Eskimo students "dumb." What a case such as "Malaise of the Spirit" offers is a particular instance of such a problem. We can talk about particular problems without making any claim that such situations are common or representative. Indeed, a great virtue of teaching cases (as opposed to case studies or ethnographies) is that they do not make general claims.

2. *Showing students how to spot issues and frame problems.* "Malaise of the Spirit" shows students how an expert teacher goes about constructing educational problems. The case shows how an expert teacher sees in small incidents, such as a fight between an Eskimo and a Caucasian student, large and significant issues.

Some of our students are able to conceptualize the interwoven issues in "Malaise of the Spirit" simply by reading the case and following the thinking of the teacher. Other students resist hard thinking. In their first papers on the case, they dismiss the complexity of the situation with a catch-all label such as "It's all politics."

After class discussion of the case, students' papers show a much greater appreciation of the way in which expert teachers frame in and reframe issues, what Schön (1983) terms "reflection-in-action:

Wedman seems to be a case study of the process of inquiry and reflecting; he identifies problems, tries solutions, modifies his understanding, and refines his approach to improve the situation.

One thing I noticed about Wedman is that his pursuit of solutions involved in-depth analysis of the problems. Often the problems were rephrased or reidentified.

Case discussion is particularly useful for those students who find it difficult to conceptualize issues and to understand the complexity of problems. It is these students who showed the most change when we compared the papers they wrote after a first reading of the case with the papers they wrote after class discussion of the case.

3. *Modeling the process of analysis and inquiry in teaching.* "Malaise of the Spirit" not only models the ways in which an expert teacher frames a problem but also the way the teacher goes about trying to understand the various dimensions of the problem. This is an eclectic, synthetic process that resembles the exploratory stage of formal research.

In trying to figure out why Eskimo students are themselves as "dumb" and the sources of his own malaise, Wedman models the practitioner's process of inquiry. As previously pointed out, he does analyses of differences between his Eskimo students and Caucasian students in patterns of tardiness, absenteeism, and test grades. He thinks about what has caused such ethnic group differences. He seeks out key informants who can give him a historical and cultural perspective on his situation. He thinks about published research he has read on motivation and identity formation and uses these conceptual perspectives to try to illuminate his particular problem.

Students reading this case become conscious of how an expert teacher gathers information and reasons from it:

> Wedman immerses himself in a vigorous analysis of the problem. He undertakes an in-depth analysis in which he attempts to discover the reasons that these problems exist. This discovery involves a search for information which is presented to the reader through a series of "clues." His actions—analysis, research, reflection—have begun to fight his apathy.

> I learned that a teacher must use his observational skills to assess "problems" in himself, his students, his peers, and his community. I hope I can learn to observe more carefully, think through the background and framework of a problem, organize possible strategies while considering negative and positive outcomes and move to address the problems in a flexible manner.

In teaching "Malaise of the Spirit," we not only conceptualize the way an expert teacher goes about framing and analyzing problems so novice teachers have available a clear heuristic. We also emphasize the emotional satisfactions of inquiry—the passion and excitement. Wedman calls the process "detective work."

4. *Enlarging students' repertoire of educational strategies.* When students discuss "Malaise of the Spirit," we are invariably amazed at the difficulty they have in identifying possible avenues for action. Novices lack a base of experience from which they can retrieve alternatives. Many students say that they can think of nothing a teacher might do in this situation. Others dredge out of their experience some inappropriate possibility—like holding an open house for parents—and then say that they realize such an action would not really accomplish anything.

A great benefit of cases is that they describe concrete strategies teachers can use to address the classroom and community problems common in the teaching situations our students are entering. Most students are impressed with the richness and variety of techniques Wedman was able to bring to the problems, and they try to remember these approaches:

> I learned from this case some great teaching techniques such as polling, speaking order, posting awards and credentials, and ways to generate an environment of success. I would repeat

many of the strategies Wedman used to initiate parental involvement in the school such as asking the Yup'ik teacher to
call homes, sending out study tips on union stationery, and
posting photographs of students doing homework around the
community.

I like the ideas Wedman came up with. I will keep most of
these in mind and probably use some of them. I really like the
idea of "student leaders" in a class where there are quiet kids.
The study skill tips sent home for parents is another great
idea. The poster and photos in the paper are tempting to copy,
but I want to be more original. These are concrete examples I
can give of what I liked that he did and I am leaving some out.

Students also learn from Wedman's errors. Wedman describes,
for example, how he unintentionally humiliated an Eskimo girl.
Having learned a few words of the local language, he proudly addressed her in Yup'ik (the native language of the region). But she
only spoke English, and the other students jeered at her for not
knowing her own language. Wedman—and our students—file this
error under "mistakes-definitely-not-to-be-repeated."

Students come away from "Malaise of the Spirit" with more
than an expanded repertoire of action strategies. They also come
away with a moral lesson: one teacher can make an enormous difference, even in an educational situation beset with a history of political
and cultural problems. Wedman managed to dissipate much of the
racial hostility in his classroom. His Eskimo students began to participate more in class, and their grades went up. His students' scores on
standardized tests improved. Community people began to speak with
approval of the teachers and the schools. Wedman's political action
committee changed the way the school board was elected and the
schools were funded in the district. When we asked students what
they had learned from this case, many echoed one student's response: "Wedman's example encouraged me to remember how much
of a difference one person can make."

5. *Stimulating the habit of reflective inquiry.* "Malaise of the Spirit" is
not a simple heroic tale. Most students are shocked to come to the
end of the case and find out that Wedman left Ruden at the end of
the year for "personal reasons." The case ends with a mystery: Why
did Wedman go?

In class discussions, we pose other nagging questions: What did
Wedman really accomplish? What do you think happened in this

school after he left? Is the "one-man-band" approach to educational change the appropriate approach? Could a personality like Wedman—someone with his intelligence, energy, and ego—have done anything else? What would you have done in the same situation?

We use cases to develop the habit of asking such questions about experience. We want students to leave the case not satisfied with a "happy ending" but aware of the complexity of situations and of their own limited understanding:

> I have made a hundred guesses as to why Wedman left, especially when things seemed to be turning around and getting better. I have speculated about his relationship to teachers, students, administration, and the community. Maybe he was too pushy. Maybe he got into the politics of the area and had to leave. Maybe the place wasn't ready to change or they view change as wrong. I do not know. The biggest lesson I have thought about from this case is what my approach should be when coming into a new teaching position.

Most students reading this case compare themselves to Wedman. They use the case to reflect on their own personalities, styles of action, commitments, and fit with potential teaching situations. The case demands not only a discussion of abstract principles—how educational change comes about and is sustained—but also a discussion of teachers as people—how a teacher with Wedman's personality responds to a problem. To understand the case, students must think about Wedman as a person—his intelligence and vitality, how he relates to others, the "spiritual" element in his commitment to teaching. Narrative methods of social research, as Polkinghorne (1987) points out, legitimize discussions of significant dimensions of human experience overlooked in other research paradigms.

CONCLUSION

After 3 years of teaching with cases, I am impressed with their benefits in the professional preparation of teachers. Students find these readings interesting and memorable. The cases, they feel, provide them with real experience in ways that traditional course material does not. Students enjoy cases.

From the professor's viewpoint, a good case can accomplish a great deal. A case can illuminate the nature of educational problems—their ambiguity and complexity, the way pedagogical, ethical, and philosophical questions merge in a concrete situation. A case can present a vivid model of how an expert teacher thinks about educational dilemmas, gathers information, shapes problems, and constructs imaginative designs for action. Like schools of law and business, schools of education can use cases to develop in novices the particular way of thinking characteristic of expert professionals.

REFERENCES

Barrows, H. S., & Tamblyn, R. M. (1980). *Problem-based learning: An approach to medical education.* New York: Springer.

Christensen, C. R., & Hansen, A. J. (1987). *Teaching and the case method.* Boston: Harvard Business School.

Christensen, C. R., Hansen, A. J., & Moore, J. F. (1987). *Teaching and the case method: Instructor's guide.* Boston: Harvard Business School.

Dewey, J. (1933). *How we think: A restatement of reflective thinking to the educative process.* Lexington, MA: Heath.

Feiman-Nemser, S. (1980). Growth and reflection as aims in teacher education: Directions for research. In E. G. Hall, S. M. Lord, & G. Brown (Eds.), *Exploring issues in teacher education: Questions for future research.* Austin, TX: Research and Development Center for Teacher Education.

Finley, P. (1989). Malaise of the spirit: A case study. In J. Kleinfeld (Ed.), *Teaching cases in cross-cultural education.* Fairbanks: University of Alaska.

Hymes, D. (1980). *Language in education: Ethnolinguistic essays.* Washington, DC: Center for Applied Linguistics.

Kleinfeld, J., & Noordhoff, K. (1988, April). *Re-thinking teacher education programs: What are the right questions?* Paper presented at the western meeting of the Holmes Group, Boulder, CO.

Polkinghorne, D. E. (1987). *Narrative knowing and the human sciences.* Albany: State University of New York Press.

Schön, D. (1983). *The reflective practitioner: How professionals think in action.* New York: Basic Books.

Tom, A. (1984). *Teaching as a moral craft.* New York: Longman.

Zeichner, K. M. (1983). Alternative paradigms of teacher education. *Journal of Teacher Education, 34*(3), 3–9.

Zeichner, K. M., & Liston, D. P. (1987). Teaching student teachers to reflect. *Harvard Educational Review, 57*(1), 23–48.

CHAPTER 3

Cases for Decision Making in Teacher Education

KATHERINE K. MERSETH

Schools and departments of education do not, like the professional schools of law, medicine, and business, have a distinctive form of pedagogy with which to deliver training to their students. Indeed, much of the coursework found in education resembles the academic coursework found in the liberal arts, even though education faculties frequently embrace the mission of training professionals for schools. This lack of a distinctive pedagogy stems in part from an ambivalence within schools of education about their role—is education a liberal or a professional endeavor?—and in part from the intellectual and capital expense of developing distinctive teaching philosophies, materials, and techniques (Merseth, 1980, 1981, 1991).

Recent debates about the reform in teacher education center not only on the structure but on the content and method of teacher education programs (see Holmes Group, 1986). These discussions naturally lead to an increased interest in alternative pedagogies for the teacher education curriculum. Cases and the case method of instruction offer one such alternative to schools of education seeking materials and teaching technique designed specifically to train practitioners.

The use and ultimate impact of cases in teacher education differ widely, depending on the purpose, content, and method of case-based instruction. Cases may be used for a variety of pedagogical purposes, including training students to analyze complex situations and to develop deliberate action plans. They can also set the stage for role playing or simulations in order to provide vicarious experiences and offer an opportunity for students to link diagnosis and action.

In this chapter, one particular form of case will be considered, along with a rationale for its use in teacher education. Next, the steps frequently followed to construct this case form are described. Unlike other case forms described in this volume, this genre of case is not written by a major protagonist in the case; rather it is a teaching document designed to present multiple perspectives that is written by a case researcher. The chapter closes with an example of a decision-making case used with preservice and beginning teachers and administrators.

DECISION-MAKING CASES

To train students to analyze complex classroom situations and to make informed decisions is not an easy task. But educators can build on the experience of other professional fields that impart similar skills. In particular, business education has a long history of case work devoted to the development of analytic skills, strategy formulation, and concrete action plans. The aim of cases in business education is to train students both to know and to act. As Christensen notes: "When successful, the case method of instruction produces a manager grounded in theory and abstract knowledge and, more important, able to apply those elements" (1987, p. 32). This form of case method seeks to combine analyses grounded in content knowledge with informed action plans to empower the manager to deal with situation-specific dilemmas.

Drawing heavily from the business education tradition, cases for decision making in teacher education satisfy the following criteria:

- A decision-making case describes a situation requiring analysis, planning, decision making, and action.
- A decision-making case is a descriptive research document based on a real-life situation, problem, or incident that is presented in an unbiased, multidimensional fashion.
- Decision-making cases are carefully crafted teaching instruments intended to facilitate discussion and analysis; they therefore contain key "trigger" issues requiring assessment and action.

Typically presented in narrative form, a decision-making case is a distillation of some real event or sequence of events that provides both substantive and process data that are essential to the analysis of the specific situation. The knowledge in question is not abstract and scientific but embodied in the particular situation under study and in the experiences that the discussants bring to it. In this way, such cases take advantage of the work of cognitive psychologists involving what Jerome Bruner calls "narrative" rather than "paradigmatic" knowing (1986).

Good decision-making cases are complex, often ambiguous, and developed from carefully crafted research designs and field work (Christensen, 1987). Although frequently disguised, these cases seek to represent as completely and objectively as possible the reality of an actual educational setting. For this reason, simulations are not included as cases. Similarly, personal recollections are not classified as decision analysis cases because of potential bias introduced by the participant.

Effective decision-making cases stimulate discussions at multiple levels of abstraction. Sometimes issues not apparent upon first reading may prove to be critical after further analysis. For example, in the case at the conclusion of this chapter, topics as diverse as classroom management, bilingual education policy, student motivation, teacher workplace issues, and sexism are present.

As participants discuss the multiple issues in complex cases, they realize that many potential actions taken to alleviate one dilemma may exacerbate another. Offered in conjunction with readings about the management of dilemmas in teaching (e.g., Lampert, 1985), this case form provides an excellent vehicle for exploring the messy complications and sometimes unsolvable dilemmas of practice.

Following the business tradition, there is no one "right" answer in discussions of decision-making cases; in fact, two discussion groups may reach quite different, but nonetheless legitimate, conclusions. Instead of conducting a Socratic dialogue, case instructors ask questions to guide the discussion—to engage the prospective teachers as vicarious participants and analysts—without a predetermined assumption about the ultimate result of the discussion.

In the case at the conclusion of this chapter—"It Ain't Fair!"—it is not clear what is the "right" thing for Laurie to do. Should she change Maria's grade or work out another arrangement with Tony? Rather, the purpose of the case discussion is to develop problem-solving and analytic skills that will offer practitioners a methodology or "way of thinking" about a wide range of problems.

A Rationale for Decision-Making Cases

Recent research on teacher thinking has broadened the conceptualization of the teacher from that of a narrow transmitter of knowledge into an individual making hundreds of daily decisions and interacting with learners in the context of particular learning situations (Calderhead, 1987; Clark & Peterson, 1986; Clark & Yinger, 1977; Jackson, 1968). In some respects, this new conceptualization of teaching has recaptured an earlier vision of teaching as much more than the application of technical skills (Dewey, 1933; Green, 1985). The work of the teacher is context-specific and constantly evolving.

While another form of cases, such as "theoretically specified" cases, may be used to "instantiate theoretical knowledge about teaching" (Doyle, 1990, p. 13), the exclusive use of this particular type of case will not provide sufficient training for teachers. Knowing a principle is of little use if the practitioner is unable to recognize the application of the principle or to spot the salient issue (Schön, 1987; Kennedy, 1987). A broader spectrum of training is required, for as Lampert and Clark (1990) note "the conventional academic pattern of producing general principles from particular cases and delivering those principles to novices may not be the most appropriate form for teacher education to take" (p. 22).

The new conception of the teacher's role and expertise means that teacher educators need a curriculum and pedagogy that prepare novices for a complex, context-dependent environment wherein knowledge is neither fixed and nor well established. Teachers need analytic and decision-making skills to make thoughtful assessments that induce appropriate action. Decision-making cases can hone these skills. They are designed specifically to develop the power to analyze a situation, to formulate action plans, and to evaluate those actions with respect to specific context variables.

The tradition of multilayered, complex decision-making cases also helps accurately reflect the reality of teaching. This genre of case affords an excellent vehicle to bring "chunks of reality" into the professional classroom (Lawrence, 1960). Carefully constructed cases and skillful instruction guard against the oversimplification of the teaching environment. This style of case also provides an opportunity to present disparate and varied teaching situations. Physically, teachers can visit a limited number of classrooms. Through this form of case presentation, a vicarious visit may be conducted to places as geographically and culturally diverse as an Eskimo village on the north coast of Alaska and the inner city of Los Angeles (Finley, 1988; & J. Shulman & Colbert, 1987).

The Construction of Cases for Decision Making

The construction of a decision-making case requires extensive planning, research, and hard work. Drawing from the experience of faculty in business education, there are five steps or stages to follow. These include case topic or site identification, gaining access and establishing leads, data collection, writing the case, and acquiring its release.

The first stage of decision-making case development is the identification of a topic that requires action, analysis, or planning. Leads from the world of practice abound for the educator and come in at least three forms: practitioners willing to be observed, interviewed, and written about who have no particular issue in mind; ideas that exist in the mind of the case developer without willing participants or sites; and, most ideally, well-defined issues with willing subjects. Case writers look for dilemmas with concrete detail and ample complexity. When assessing possible topics, it is important to keep the following questions in mind: Why is this an interesting case? Are the issues presented in this case compelling to teachers? What purpose will this case serve? Cases written without a clear educational purpose are destined to be little more than interesting stories.

The next stage is to establish leads and to assess whether the situation affords easy access to the subjects and to the site. Such access is critical in order to provide a complete picture of the context and to protect against bias. The case writer must plan ahead, anticipating potential difficulties or barriers to the data. Are all of the participants willing to be interviewed? Are relevant documents available to the researcher, either through the public domain or from participants? Can the researcher visit the site to gain valuable context information? Case writers must thoroughly understand a specific context or event in order to write an effective case about it.

Data collection for case writing is similar to data collection for research. Planning is important; having a sense of key issues and points of view will expedite the process. A variety of methods can be used to collect case data, including intensive interviewing, observation, and document analysis. It is very important to be aware of possible personal bias on the part of the writer as well as the participants. A skilled case writer will assess carefully the data and corroborate or "triangulate" the data with different methods.

The next stage includes making sense of the situation and writing a compelling case about it. Decision analysis cases contain two key components: A "trigger issue" that stimulates initial discussion and the engagement of readers and a careful "weaving" of multiple issues that will support a variety of viewpoints and levels of analysis. This type of case typically does not offer the case writer's "solution" or personal interpretation because the purpose of the case is to develop problem-solving and decision-making skills in the reader. Such skills are acquired more effectively through active participation rather than passive listening.

Finally, educators must address concerns about the use of the case. This includes permission from the participants to use the case (even if the participants and location are disguised), printing policies, and distribution control. In order for cases to be valuable and useful to the teacher education community, guidelines for successful case implementation are necessary.[1]

How Are Cases for Decision Making Used in Teacher Education?

The case "It Ain't Fair!" offers an example of a decision analysis case. It has been used in programs for preservice and beginning teachers and administrators at Harvard University and the University of California, Riverside. Many avenues for instruction are available in this complex case. For example, it supports the exploration of techniques and requirements for the successful implementation of cooperative team-learning environments. Cast in a different light, the case can help beginning (and experienced) teachers identify and articulate their own motives and beliefs regarding standards and evaluation of students. For administrators and mentor teachers, the case also stimulates discussion about systemwide accountability requirements and encourages an examination of workplace and collegial relationships. Other topics that can be explored successfully with this case include curriculum organization, the teacher's role as confidant and counselor, and the particular demands of urban education.

In the preparation of the case for discussion, the following questions are useful in focusing the thinking of preservice students about classroom groups and cooperative team-learning environments: What were Laurie's motivations for the group work assignment? How did Laurie communicate her grading standards to the students? Experienced teachers often begin their consideration of the situation by pursuing the following queries: Where can Laurie expect to get assistance with this situation? How does Laurie know whether she is doing a "good" job?

In the discussion of these issues, participants analyze the situation and suggest action plans. In such a discussion, analysis guides action. For the instructor, the most compelling and instructive questions to stimulate analysis and foster critical thinking are: Why would you do that? What are the implications of your proposed actions? Other effective discussion techniques include role playing and debates.

Summary

The successful integration of decision-making cases such as "It Ain't Fair!" and others into teacher education will take skillful planning, hard work, and courage. The teacher education community has sufficient resources and knowledge available to tackle this reform. What is exciting is that this versatile pedagogical form has the potential to serve as a transformative force in the revitalization of the teacher education curriculum.

"IT AIN'T FAIR!"

It was Sunday night. Laurie Cabot felt her stomach tighten as she switched off the TV and moved slowly down the hall toward her desk and the pile of student essays awaiting her comments. As she gazed out the window at the blinking Christmas lights, she recalled Tony's angry words before his stormy exit from her room at Gardiner High School on Friday afternoon: "How come I gotta do essays and Maria don't? Huh?? How come she gets the same grade when she don't do the work? Dumb Spic!! Huh? How come, Miss Cabot?? *It ain't fair!* Group work stinks and so does this class!!"

As Laurie looked back at her desk and the papers, she knew she needed to do something about tomorrow. Indeed, she had told Maria 2 weeks ago that she would not have to make up her missed essays; she felt Maria simply could not handle the pressure. On the other hand, Laurie was convinced Tony had talent but had never been pushed. Tony's words—"How come, Miss Cabot? It ain't fair!"—kept ringing in her head.

Laurie Cabot

After graduating with a B.A. degree in English, Laurie chose an M.A. program in teaching at Longfellow University. Laurie received her certification to teach English and joined the faculty of Gardiner High School. She felt lucky to get the job because jobs for white teachers were difficult to get in the inner city. Mandates for racial balance required personnel offices to seek minorities as new hires. Often, however, minority teachers could not be found because so few minorities elected teaching as a career. For Laurie, this meant that she got her job on Friday, August 29, and was to report to Gardiner the next Tuesday, the day before school opened on September 3.

Laurie's commitment to urban education stemmed in part from the influence of her mother, who had been a kindergarten teacher for 18 years, and from her undergraduate work in a history, literature, and urban studies concentration. She enjoyed school, loved learning new things, and had always been surrounded by others with similar values. Her father, a successful corporate lawyer, and her brother, a third-year medical student, were not so sure why Laurie had such a passion for education, and urban education at that. When Laurie visited home over Thanksgiving break, her father commented, "If you really like teaching that much, why don't you just come back to Evanston and teach at Deerfield High for a few years? You could live at home and save some money in case you decide to go back for a doctorate in a few years." Laurie often wondered if her father feared for her physical safety in an urban school or whether he simply disapproved of her use of her Longfellow education to be a teacher. She never asked him.

Gardiner High School

Gardiner High School was a large, urban school of 2,600 students, known for its superiority in athletics and its eight-story physical plant complete with escalators connecting the floors. Because Gardiner was the only high school in the city, students reflected varied social and economic backgrounds as well as intellectual talents and interests in learning.

Gardiner High was 65 percent minority, with more than 70 countries of origin and languages represented in the student body. The racial makeup of the school was 35 percent black, 30 percent white, 25 percent Hispanic, and 10 percent Asian. Gardiner had not always been so racially and ethnically diverse. In fact, the mix of students had changed dramatically over the last 10 years since the major employer, National Steel, had closed the mill. These changes in student and town demographics were not reflected in the teaching staff, who were predominantly white and over 40.

As a first-year teacher, Laurie was given four classes with three different preparations, lunch duty, and bathroom patrol. Her classes were two general ninth-grade English classes, one tenth-grade remedial English class, and a senior elective in composition for students in the vocational-technical track. Laurie knew it was a tough schedule, but she knew it was typical for a first-year teacher. Classmates at Longfellow had told her that schools often give the toughest schedules to the new teachers. Something about experience and seniority left the advanced placement classes for the veteran teachers.

Laurie was the only new hire in the English department this year. She had heard that there was also a new teacher in math and a new soccer coach who also taught health. She had never met them; they did not have the same free "prep" periods and Laurie taught in three rooms on the fourth floor, while math and science were taught on the seventh floor.

Laurie felt reasonably comfortable in the English department, with its staff of 14, even though she was more than 20 years younger than the next youngest member. Nearly all were married and had jobs after school. While most were friendly, few seemed to have the time or interest to help a rookie learn the ropes. In one of the monthly department meetings, Laurie asked if she could observe some classes. Two teachers said it would be all right, but she felt by their response that her request was an unusual one.

System Policies

The chairman of the department, Paul Kelly, talked with Laurie during the first week of classes. He gave her a tour of the bookroom (which by then was in a sorry state after the veteran teachers had taken their books) and reviewed some of the system policies. Paul informed Laurie that, according to a systemwide plan instituted the prior year, all teachers were to turn in plans every 9 weeks to the superintendent's office. The purpose of this activity was to enable administrators to know what was being taught in each class in order to conduct unannounced evaluations of teachers on any given day. In addition, teachers were required to write their objectives and class plans on the board each day. The principal of Gardiner routinely checked to see if this information was on the board. Laurie had heard a rumor that a teacher had been fired the previous spring for not having this information on his board. Finally, there were mandatory instructional activities that must be observable in every lesson, including initiating the class, stating the objective, recalling the immediate prerequisites, reviewing the study assignments, introducing new information, providing practice and feedback, and offering a closing summary.

These requirements made Laurie's head swim, but she conscientiously prepared her 9-week and daily plans, although there was precious little match between her plans and reality. "How can I know how long this essay will take?" she thought to herself. The harder she worked, the worse the results were in the classroom. This upset her; hard work in college had always produced good results for her. Being a teacher was so different from being a student. She constantly worried about her evaluations. The principal had come to her room once but luckily had been immediately called on his walkietalkie and had to leave before he could ascertain what she was teaching.

The Group Assignment

Laurie continued to work hard, spending evenings and weekends planning and preparing materials, but she was not having any success with her sophomores. The class seemed lethargic and bored, with low motivation. Many students, when they came to class, just sat with their arms folded, saying nothing. Others would mumble a response or put their heads on their desks and sleep for part of the period. It was just after Thanksgiving that Laurie decided to try something different.

Laurie stopped Paul Kelly in the hall and asked what he thought about implementing small working groups in the class. He was not enthusiastic, to say the least: "It is hard enough to control a class of sophomores with everyone doing the same thing," he warned. "Control should be your first concern. If you use a whole-class lecture approach you can concentrate on the subject. Besides, it's a lot of work to have groups, and some of your students may not like it." Laurie also knew that Paul wondered how she would incorporate the mandatory instructional activities into her lessons with students working in groups. She could sense that he was about to mention this when something interrupted them. It was clear that Paul was trying to discourage her without being completely negative.

Laurie wanted to try anyway. In her classes at Longfellow, the faculty had discussed cooperative team-learning techniques and pointed out the advantages of such an approach with individuals with low motivation and from different social classes and ethnic groups. Laurie dug out her Longfellow class notes about cooperative learning and teams. In her notebook Laurie had written, "Two important effects of cooperative learning—creation of friendships among students of different ethnic or social backgrounds and an increase in self-esteem of kids." As she thought about the way her Hispanic students sat on one side of her room and the black students in the back, she decided, "That's just what I need."

As she planned for the group work Laurie decided to give a series of essay questions about a book they were reading, J. D. Salinger's *Catcher in the Rye*. At the end of a week of writing and revising essays, the small groups were to produce a final group report that addressed the development of the main character, Holden Caulfield—the conflict he faced, how he came to realize the conflict, and how he chose to deal with it. In this assignment to the class, she stressed the importance of revisions: "Today, we'll be working in groups [groans from the students] on *Catcher in the Rye*. Each of you is to select one of five questions about Holden and write a five-page essay. Wednesday and Thursday we will read each other's essays, making comments and revisions. On Friday, you will bring the final version of your essay to class and you will meet as a group to make final comments on the essays and to plan a group report for Monday that uses everyone's work. The grade for the group report will be the equivalent of a chapter test for each of you. Now listen, while I announce the teams. Team one: Tommy Young, captain; Maria Rodrigues; Tony D'Angelo; Isa Fan; and Armando Rey. Team Two: . . ."

Laurie had put Tommy Young in charge of one of the six groups she had created for the 32 students of the class. Tommy seemed a natural for a group leader. Intelligent, articulate, interested in reading, he seemed, too, to enjoy helping other students. Laurie deliberately placed Tony in Tommy's group because she thought Tommy's good work habits might motivate him. Laurie also hoped the group experience would increase Tony's self-esteem. Laurie added Maria Rodrigues to the group at the last moment because she had entered Gardiner in October, after moving to town with her mother and two younger brothers. Maria was very shy, her English extremely limited. When she came to class, she sat near the windows and said nothing.

Maria

At first Laurie had tried to encourage Maria, holding her to the same standards as the rest of the class. Late in October, after only a few weeks in her class, Laurie sensed Maria was slipping. She asked Maria to come back after school one day, and Laurie explained that she was worried about Maria's performance. Sounding a little like her own high school English teacher, Laurie said: "Sophomore English is a significant course for you. The curriculum covers many important plays and novels. Everyone in English 10 must learn to write a good essay. The same standards for this course are applied to everyone and include meeting due dates, coming to class prepared, and submitting homework. I know you can do it, Maria. I know you can; *it just takes hard work.*" Laurie felt good about her talk with Maria. She knew it was important to have clear and high standards.

But Maria continued to slip. She would be absent 2 or 3 days each week. When she came to class, she would not have her homework, and for the in-class writing assignments she would submit a single page of poor quality. Laurie knew she had to do something. She invited Maria to come see her to go over her missed assignments. Nearly a week had passed when Maria quietly walked into Laurie's room. During the meeting, Maria told of her responsibilities caring for her younger brothers and working in a donut shop after school. Tears welled up in her eyes. The family needed her earnings, she said, to pay for groceries.

Laurie felt an ache of frustration within her. She resolved then to take certain steps to help Maria. Since the class was starting group work in 2 weeks, Laurie decided it would be a good time to make different arrangements for Maria. Feeling great sympathy for Maria, Laurie offered her a different grading system: "Maria, you don't have to complete your past essays; we'll just ignore those and I will give you a special competency exam to demonstrate your skills. When you come to class, do what you can. If you miss an assignment because you are absent, I will excuse you." Maria was grateful. Laurie decided not to press Maria. She now felt it best to accept Maria where she was.

The Response

"You wouldn't believe what happened then!" Laurie was saying to her roommate. "I looked up and Tony and Tommy were yelling and pushing each other. A desk was overturned; kids moved away, anticipating a fight. Tony said something like 'I ain't gonna take no crap from you about my essay. Who do you think you are to tell me it stinks?' Then Tommy said something like, 'But we all have to work on it for a group grade. If our group fails, it's *your* fault.' Then Tony glared at me, shook his fist, and walked to the door. 'I ain't gonna be no part of no stupid group! Besides, how come I gotta do essays and Maria don't? Huh? How come Maria gets the same grade as me when she don't do the work? Dumb Spic!! It ain't fair! Group work stinks and so does this class!!'"

NOTE

1. Business education has a helpful literature that outlines specific methodologies for the development of cases (see Leenders & Erskine, 1978; McNair, 1954; Towl, 1969; Lawrence, 1960). Information about the Intercollegiate Case Clearing House (ICCH) may be obtained from the Harvard Business School, Soldiers Field Road, Boston, MA.

REFERENCES

Bruner, J. (1986). *Actual minds, possible worlds.* Cambridge, MA: Harvard University Press.

Calderhead, J. (1987). *Exploring teachers' thinking.* London: Cassel Educational.

Christensen, C. (1987). *Teaching and the class method.* Boston: Harvard Business School Press.

Clark, C., & Peterson, P. (1986). Teachers' cognitions. In M. Wittrock (Ed.), *Handbook of research on teaching* (3rd ed.) (pp. 225-296). New York: Macmillan.

Clark, C., & Yinger, R. (1977). Research on teacher thinking. *Curriculum Inquiry, 7*(4), 279-394.

Dewey, J. (1933). *How we think: A statement of the relation of reflexive thinking to the educative process.* Chicago: Heath.

Doyle, W. (1990). Case methods in the education of teachers. *Teacher Education Quarterly, 17*(1), 7-15.

Finley, P. (1988). Malaise of the spirit: A case study. In J. Kleinfeld (Ed.), *Teaching cases in cross-cultural education.* Fairbanks: University of Alaska.

Green, M. (1985, Fall). Public education and the public space. *The Kettering Review,* 5-60.

Holmes Group (1986). *Tomorrow's teachers: A report issued by the Holmes Group.* East Lansing, MI: Author.

Jackson, P. W. (1968). *Life in classrooms.* Chicago: Holt, Rinehart & Winston.

Kennedy, M. (1987). Inexact sciences: Professional education and the development of expertise. In E. Rothkopf (Ed.), *Review of research in education* (Vol. 14) (pp. 133–167). Washington, DC: American Educational Research Association.

Lampert, M. (1985). How do teachers manage to teach? Perspectives on problems in practice. *Harvard Educational Review, 55,* 178–194.

Lampert, M., & Clark, C. (1990). Expert knowledge and expert thinking in teaching: A response to Floden and Klinzing. *Educational Researcher, 19*(4), 21–24.

Lawrence, P. (1960). The preparation of case material. In K. R. Andrews (Ed.), *Case method of teaching human relations and administration* (pp. 215–224). Cambridge, MA: Harvard University Press.

Leenders, M., & Erskine, J. (1978). *Case research: The case writing process* (2nd ed.). London, Ontario, Canada: University of Western Ontario School of Business Administration.

McNair, M. (Ed.). (1954). *The case method at the Harvard Business School.* New York: McGraw-Hill.

Merseth, K. (1980). *Case studies in educational administration at the elementary and secondary levels: An annotated bibliography.* Unpublished manuscript, Harvard Graduate School of Education Committee on School Leadership. Cambridge, MA.

Merseth, K. (1981). *The case method in training educators.* Cambridge, MA: Harvard Graduate School of Education.

Merseth, K. (1991). *The case for cases in teacher education.* Washington, DC: American Association of Colleges of Teacher Education and American Association of Higher Education.

Schön, D. (1987). *Educating the reflective practitioner.* San Francisco: Jossey-Bass.

Shulman, J., & Colbert, J. (1987). *The mentor teacher casebook.* San Francisco: Far West Regional Laboratory for Educational Research and Development.

Towl, A. R. (1969). *To study administration by cases.* Boston, MA: Harvard Business School.

CHAPTER 4

A Case Concerning Content

Using Case Studies
to Teach About Subject Matter

SUZANNE M. WILSON

Subject-matter knowledge has recently become focal in the policy, research, and practice of teacher education. Some states, for instance, have instituted alternate routes into teaching whereby individuals with undergraduate degrees in subject-matter specialties participate in brief training programs that focus on generic pedagogical skills in order to obtain their initial certification. While these teachers are required to attend additional courses throughout their first year of teaching, they are nevertheless considered card-carrying members of the profession. Other states have changed requirements for teacher education programs, increasing the number of credit hours required in subject-matter studies while decreasing those required in professional studies. Reform efforts, such as those of the Holmes Group (1986) and Carnegie Task Force on Teaching as a Profession (1986), also emphasize the pivotal role of subject-matter knowledge in teaching.

Concurrently, in a growing body of research, scholars are exploring the role of subject-matter knowledge in teaching, highlighting the nature of its interaction with knowledge and beliefs about learners, learning, and pedagogy.[1] Some scholars, among them Lee Shulman (1986), propose that there exists a kind of subject-matter knowledge—pedagogical content knowledge—that is unique and essential to teaching. This knowledge consists of understandings and beliefs about the range of alternatives for teaching a particular idea to particular students for particular reasons in particular schools. Teachers who possess pedagogical content knowledge are able to generate and use alternative representations of the subject matter that reflect various beliefs about and understandings of disciplines, teaching, learning, students, and schools. In order to do so, teachers must have deep and rich understandings of the subject matters they teach, including knowledge of the history of inquiry in a field, central concepts that scholars in that field employ and study in their work, the intellectual and technical skills necessary to generate and test new knowledge, the aspects of subject matter that are difficult to learn (counterintuitive, perhaps), and the focal disputes that have characterized debates about what is important to know.

So researchers and policy makers agree: subject-matter knowledge is central to teaching. However, teacher educators are handed the responsibility of developing prospective and practicing teachers' subject-matter knowledge and pedagogical content knowledge. This is no simple feat. More courses in content will not ensure adequate subject-matter knowledge for teaching. There has been little research on what students learn in liberal arts and sciences coursework (Ball & McDiarmid, 1990), and it is not at all clear that traditional undergraduate liberal education leads to the deep and rich subject-matter knowledge that good teaching requires. Neither will a heavier emphasis on conventional teacher education Methods courses fit the bill, for they all too often involve learning about pedagogy absent any attention paid to the specific ideas to be taught. Instead, the subject-matter knowledge required for accomplished teaching requires that we develop new methods and new content for teacher preparation.

As a researcher of subject-matter knowledge *and* a teacher educator, I feel a particular commitment to developing such methods and content. While the creation of new courses is one promising area of development, another is the development of instructional materials and method that can be used in preexisting teacher education courses. As the authors of the chapters in this book suggest, one such method worth exploring involves using cases. My interests concern how teacher educators might use cases to stimulate prospective teachers' thinking about the ways concerns for subject matter surface in the dilemmas teachers face. Such cases could be used in different types of teacher education courses, for subject-matter concerns relate to many aspects of teacher preparation.

In this chapter I present and discuss a case that I developed for use in a teacher education course I teach at Michigan State University. I begin with a brief discussion of the course in which I use the case, and my purposes for doing so. I then present a portion of the case, along with a series of questions that I use to discuss the case with my students. I conclude with a discussion of the case and mention a few issues we should consider as we begin to examine the uses of cases in teacher education.

TEACHER EDUCATION 101

At Michigan State University, I teach a course entitled "Exploring Teaching." Commonly referred to as "TE 101," the course is designed to help students interested in teaching explore the complexity of teaching and learning. An introductory course, it is the first course that all teacher education students take at the university. Throughout the class, students examine their beliefs about teaching and learning as they are presented with three questions: What does it mean to teach? How do the social, political, and historical contexts of schooling influence teaching and learning? What do teachers need to know in order to teach?[2]

For the section of the course that focuses on questions about what teachers need to know, we read a piece I wrote with Lee Shulman and Anna Richert (Wilson, Shulman, & Richert, 1987) entitled "150 Different Ways of Knowing: Representations of Knowledge in Teaching." In this piece, we discuss how teachers transform their subject-matter knowledge into instructional representations. We claim that teachers constantly think about how best to represent ideas to students by considering such issues as what their students already know, what their instructional purposes are, what else they have done during the year, the contexts in which they are teaching, and the subject matter of concern. As a result of their reasoning, teachers produce metaphors, analogies, simulations, visual representations, explanations, models, and a host of other representations that communicate aspects of the subject matter to students.

For example, an American history teacher, when considering how best to teach students about the relationship between England and its North American colonies, might use a mother-child analogy. She might use such an analogy because she assumes her students know something about the relationships between mothers and their children and that they might be able to draw on this knowledge as they develop understandings about North America. Although the relationship between England and its colonies cannot be completely accounted for with this analogy, a teacher might select it because it is at once familiar to learners and has some disciplinary authority.[3]

This analogy—mother and child—becomes a representation of an idea—the relationship between England and its colonies.

The notion of subject-matter knowledge for teaching is seductive. On the one hand, it seems sensible: teachers should know something about the subject matters they teach. On the other hand, it is complicated: teachers cannot possibly know everything, so what is most important? The issue is also complicated for me as a teacher educator because my own students—the undergraduates—believe that learning to teach requires learning about classroom management, discipline, and lesson planning. They do not believe that they have much to learn about the subject matter. After all, teachers just need to stay "one chapter ahead" of their students (McDiarmid, Ball, & Anderson, 1989), they believe. To disabuse them of this notion, I engage them in several projects that are designed to help them confront their assumptions about the role of subject matter in teaching. In addition, I use a case of a student teacher—George[4]—as an occasion to explore these issues.

Whenever I think about using a case in my teaching, I first consider the issues I want to examine, illustrate, extend, and develop with this case. I use the case of George in TE 101 because it illustrates some aspects of pedagogical content knowledge that are central to my pedagogical purposes. It is to these issues that I now turn.

WHAT IS GEORGE A CASE OF?

I wrote the case of George while working on the Knowledge Growth in a Profession Project at Stanford University (for a complete report on this project, see L. Shulman & Grossman, 1987). A central aim of this research was to explore the ways in which the subject-matter knowledge of new teachers both influences and is influenced by the process of learning to teach. George was one of 20 new teachers with whom we worked on that project, and it was through our conversations with and observations of such teachers that we generated our theoretical work on teacher subject-matter knowledge (Grossman, Wilson, & L. Shulman, 1989; L. Shulman, 1986, 1987; Wilson et al., 1987).

In that research, we found that the ability of a prospective teacher such as George to communicate his understanding was not simply a matter of mastering a few generic principles of teaching and learning that could be overlaid, like templates, on the subject matter in question. Teaching laboratory science is different from teaching creative writing; teaching Shakespeare is different from teaching the Constitution. The ability to do something with the content of instruction depended, we found, on a sensitivity to the interaction of pedagogy and content: an understanding of the ways in which the nature of the subject matter shapes the nature of the pedagogy and vice versa.

In our research, we observed that the experiences of novice teachers such as George influenced the development of their subject-matter knowledge in several ways. Not surprisingly, one type of change we observed was additive—teachers learned more about topics that they were required to teach. For example, several of the mathematics teachers we worked with had not taken a geometry class since they were high school students. Yet they were assigned to teach it during their first few years of teaching. Preparing for class, teaching students, and then talking with us about the instruction provided a powerful learning experience for those novice teachers. They knew more geometry.

While learning to teach, however, the novice teachers learned more about the content than additional names, events, concepts, short stories, or equations. They also learned about examples, metaphors, analogies, and illustrations to aid in the communication of subject-matter knowledge to students. As witnesses to the deliberations of these new teachers, we observed them transform the content, producing "representations" of the subject matter that they then used with their own students, a process that involved translating the subject matter for the purposes of teaching it.

Our analysis of the teachers' representations led us to conclude that teaching requires many types of knowledge (of content and learners and learning and curriculum and context) and skill (of planning and discussing and lecturing and managing and reflecting). This is not new news; many educational philosophers and researchers have discussed these types of knowledge and skill before (see Dewey, 1902/1956; Schwab, 1978). But we have also proposed that teachers possess a knowledge that has not been identified previously, a knowledge that is produced by the interaction of pedagogy and content, pedagogical content knowledge. Lee Shulman (1986) explains:

> A second kind of content knowledge is pedagogical knowledge, which goes beyond knowledge of the subject matter per se to the dimension of subject matter knowledge *for teaching*. I still speak of content knowledge here, but of the particular form of content

knowledge that embodies the aspects of content most germane to its teachability.

Within the category of pedagogical content knowledge I include, for the most regularly taught topics in one's subject area, the most useful forms of representation of those ideas, the most powerful analogies, illustrations, examples, explanations, and demonstrations—in a word, the ways of representing and formulating the subject that make it comprehensible to others.

Pedagogical content knowledge also includes an understanding of what makes the learning of specific topics easy or difficult: the conceptions and preconceptions that students of different ages and backgrounds bring with them to the learning of those most frequently taught topics and lessons. If those preconceptions are misconceptions, which they so often are, teachers need knowledge of the strategies most likely to be fruitful in reorganizing the understanding of learners, because those learners are unlikely to appear before them as blank slates. (pp. 9–10)

The representations our teachers generated became part of their growing pedagogical content knowledge. But pedagogical content knowledge is not simply a bag of tricks. A repertoire of representations that combine pedagogy with content in ways that are sensitive to learners and school contexts. Pedagogical content knowledge also involves a way of thinking, of reasoning through and solving problems. This process usually involves the generation of or evaluation of alternative representations of the subject matter. Called "pedagogical reasoning" (Ball, 1988a; Wilson, 1988b), this dynamic dimension of pedagogical content knowledge accounts for the ways in which teachers think through how to present the subject matter to their students, what "hooks" to use, what prior knowledge to capitalize on, what points to make. It is through this process of pedagogical reasoning that teachers are able to generate, evaluate, use, and reflect on instructional representations.

The case of George illustrates how one teacher produced a host of instructional representations: some successful, some not. In the case, we see George thinking about his teaching, drawing on his knowledge of the subject matter and his growing knowledge of students. The case, then, is one of both the development of pedagogical content knowledge and the nature of pedagogical reasoning. The analysis I present as the author of the case highlights issues about the role that subject-matter knowledge plays in teaching, for his preparation as an English major helped his pedagogical thinking but was insufficient preparation for his debut as a high school English teacher.

Before my students read the case in class, they have read Wilson and colleagues (1987) as well as L. Shulman (1986). Readers unfamiliar with the research on teacher subject-matter knowledge may wish to read those pieces prior to interpreting or using the case that follows.

GEORGE, A BEGINNING ENGLISH TEACHER

There is no pithy way of characterize George. He is a young man from Nevada who has dreams of becoming a novelist. He listens to Beethoven, Mozart, and Dan Fogelberg when driving his red pickup. He is a baseball player who loves to read Shakespeare and Kundera, Faulkner and O'Connor. He wants to be a minister some day but for now, he would really rather teach English. Like all of us, George is many different people—a writer, a cowboy, a first baseman, a teacher, an avid reader, a man in his early 20s. For the two years we worked together, I saw many of George's passions, dispositions, interests, values, and understandings influence the teacher he became. In this case I focus on his academic training and his experiences learning to teach literature.[5]

A Brief Intellectual Biography

George presents a compact figure; five feet nine inches tall, he is strong and muscular. His mischievous yet intense brown eyes shine when he talks about teaching or literature. As a young boy growing up in a small Nevada town, he read avidly, rode horses, played baseball. He left home in 1980 to attend Pine University, a private research university in California. Receiving a B.A. with distinction in English in 1984, he specialized in creative writing; however, his transcript is also filled with courses in literature, humanities, languages, and religious thought.

When I asked him to talk about his undergraduate education, George focused on his development as a writer of prose and critical literary analysis. Three types of academic experiences influenced George's development as a writer: courses that traced the development of an author or a literary genre, classes that provided an opportunity for George to write either fictional or critical pieces, and courses in which the professor used particular analytic frameworks to critique fiction.

The experience of writing papers had a tremendous influence on George as an undergraduate. In one interview I asked him to identify the classes that had had the greatest impact on him. Among the ten classes he discussed, six involved writing major papers and two others were writing classes that involved writing short fictional pieces. The experience of writing papers and prose contributed to his intellectual growth in two ways—not only did the practice of writing fiction in seminars contribute to his development as a writer, but his exposure to the "craft side" of literature also contributed to his ability to analyze critically the work of other authors.

Within the realm of literature, George was intrigued with the work of modern authors, most notably Milan Kundera. He planned his coursework in college so that he could meet the requirements of his major during his first 3 years, reserving his senior year for intensive study of modern art and literature. He valued the English classes he took prior to his senior year because he believed they provided him with the background knowledge of literature and skills of critical writing that he needed to pursue his personal interests in modern art and fiction. Summarizing his undergraduate career, George said:

> If you break it down, the vast majority of my classes are read-
> ing and English from the eighteenth century to the present.
> Renaissance literature, the history of language, Chaucer. I
> really tried to get those out of the way. I really wanted to get
> to the modern stuff, mostly because I wanted to write myself.
> That was really on my mind a lot when I was taking those
> classes. To see things like why a writer is presenting things in
> the way that he or she is. What prompts him or her to write.
> Mostly, I think, why and how the historic tradition behind the
> writer has influenced the way that he or she writes. In other
> words, why do Dickens and Eliot write these really moralistic
> novels in which real morals and real philosophical issues are
> dealt with? Why are they writing those novels and why are
> the newest authors not? Why are these new authors more in-
> terested in style where it becomes the writing itself that they
> are writing for, not writing about something?[6]

George's passion for good literature—either as a reader or a writer—was matched by a passionate commitment to his religion. A fundamentalist, George found especially important those experiences in and out of Pine University that provided him the opportunity to tie his Christian values and ideals to his academic interests, such as reading Dostoyevsky's *Notes from The Underground*, a novel that he found "had a lot of ties with my Christian background and hit me on a literary and moral and psychological level."

George's academic interests were not defined by the walls of universities or the covers of books. Indications of his outside interests and values—in sports, in religion, in art, in photography—frequently found their way into his comments about literature and writing. School subjects, as they are traditionally perceived, did not mean much to George, for he did not consider them valid representations of the organization of knowledge. As he put it, "Subject matter does fall into neat categories of history, science, and English. Rather, they're all a mix."

While an undergraduate, George toyed with several career choices. For a short period of time, he thought of pursuing a career in professional baseball. With one brother in the major leagues and some pressure from his father, it was a serious consideration until he found his participation on a university varsity team "unfun." By the time he was a senior, George had narrowed his choices to two: the ministry and teaching. He applied to a well-known seminary in St. Louis and to the fifth-year teacher education program at Pine University. Accepted in both programs, he spent considerable time mulling over his options. Taking the advice of one professor who suggested he needed to get "knocked around by the world a little" before entering the ministry, George opted to enter the teacher education program.

George enrolled in the Pine University teacher education program in June 1984, 2 weeks after graduation. In this intellectually demanding and theoretically oriented program, George was required to teach two classes of high school English during the academic year, simultaneously taking courses in English curriculum and instruction, adolescence, and educational foundations. George also took several electives in the English department.

George's teaching assignment was a paid internship at St. Francis, a parochial high school located about 12 miles from the university. During the 1984–1985 year, George taught two classes: one in composition, another in creative writing. He also helped coach the baseball team in the spring. In the spring of 1985, he was offered and accepted a full-time job teaching freshman and sophomore English in the same school. My interviews with and observations of George took place from January 1985 (midway through his teacher education program) through June 1986 (the conclusion of this first year of full-time teaching). During that time, I watched him struggle to learn to teach writing and reading in ways that at once interested his students and engaged them in rigorous intellectual work. Since George was a serious, avid, and accomplished student of literature, I was particularly interested in how he translated his passion for and knowledge of literature into educative experiences for his students.

Learning to Teach Literature

One of George's central concerns when teaching literature was how to accommodate multiple interpretations of the texts his classes were reading. This issue concerned him for both disciplinary and pedagogical reasons. As a student of literature, George was aware that the use of different analytical frameworks resulted in different interpretations of the same piece of literature. For example, he knew that a Freudian and a feminist could read the same novel and leave with different experiences, reactions, and understandings. As a student of teaching, George was aware from his curriculum instructors of the value of multiple interpretations, especially interpretations that were personally relevant to students. George left his teacher education program believing that learners apply what they read to their personal experiences and, therefore, they "are probably getting something different from the piece than we are." He also believed that it was important to allow students their personal interpretations. But what, then, of literary criticism? George wrestled with this issue repeatedly, as is reflected in one of his journal entries: "How do we 'teach' a book? Is it just reading, discussing, writing? How are we sure that we use and explore students' personal reactions to the book? What is legitimate interpretation in terms of student response?"

George believed that a teacher should start with the personal and move slowly toward the more objective, the more analytic. George conceptualized the difference between these two perspectives as a chasm, a "gap" that teachers needed to bridge:

We have to try and close that gap. Or at least try to understand what [the students] are getting out of [the book]. We can let them get that out of it *plus* what we want them to get out of it. Either that or to be able to change . . . trying to let the students go with their interpretation more than dictate mine. . . . It is at the foundation of how I teach.

When George decided to teach "Greenleaf," a short story by Flannery O'Connor, to his students, this "gap" became very real:

> I noticed when I taught the story—I taught it slowly because it's a fairly tough story—that only at the very end did I feel that they were cluing in on how important motivations were. It's real key. The whole story hinges on two characters' motivations. The students were not reading it on that level at all, and I understand the story almost exclusively on that level. So they were not understanding the flow of the story in terms of the causation of events. It was sort of a sequence of more or less unconnected events for them. Whereas, if you knew the motivations of the characters, the events were not unconnected at all. You knew exactly why what went on went on. So there was a difference, a gap there. . . . Their interpretation wasn't necessarily off, it just wasn't complete because they hadn't considered this important element. So I had them do character analyses where they had to look specifically at the passages about the characters. Then they could understand the character better. By the end, they understood the story better because these exercises helped. . . . I tried to close the gap by helping them discover those facts.

As he learned to teach his students how to read literature, George thought a lot about his own habits as a reader. As an undergraduate, he had extensive experience doing textual analyses, reading and rereading closely, tracing themes and characters. Noting important passages, George would sometimes reread one book 10 or 15 times before he really felt he "owned" it. When I asked him how he analyzed texts, he explained:

> Reading and rereading. I think that was easily the thing that was most influential . . . rereading. If it was a story, I would reread it twenty times. If it was a novel, probably two or three. Then, as I'd reread it, I would find problems. Then I would have to go back and reread in order to solve those problems. By the end, I had more or less figured out the book.

When it came time to teach novels, George tried to mold his students in his own image:

The summer was my first experience with teaching novels, which was important because I didn't know how to do that. I didn't know what that was about. I ended up talking about specific passages that I thought were important and I had them do a quote journal where I had them pull out the most important quote in each chapter, had them write it down and tell me why it was important. . . . I read with an eye toward important passages. If a page is just useless information, then I just gloss over it. But if I can see it is important, then I read it very carefully. I feel that that's a reading skill that good readers always use, and I'm hoping that I get at that thinking process.

For George, determining what was "important" involved tracing themes that authors were examining in their stories. George conceived of themes as "handles" that he could give students when they read fiction. When he talked of the things that he learned in his teaching, he frequently referred to themes he noticed in the short stories and novels he read with his students. For example, although he knew the story before he taught it to his freshmen, George explained that his knowledge of John Steinbeck's *Of Mice and Men* was enriched as a result of teaching it:

I guess there were a couple of issues that I hadn't considered, a couple of themes that are explored in the novel that I hadn't considered before. One major one that I can think of now is dreams—having a dream and trying to follow it. The reality and unreality of trying to follow that dream, which happened a lot in that setting of westward expansion and early California when people thought they were going to make big killings on various things. Thought they were going to get their own land, although it never panned out. But they chased the dream all of their lives.

These newfound insights came from a variety of sources:

I gain those perspectives by reviewing the novel itself. I form opinions and interpretations in the first reading. I'll put it down to prepare for class and another idea comes into my head. Maybe because of something that I read the day before, maybe because of a conversation that I had the night before, some other angle pops into my head when I look at that material again or I make another connection that I hadn't seen before. Or a kid says something in class that I hadn't thought of. "Okay, wow, that opens a whole new way of looking at it!" I think all those sort of contribute to my thinking. The more experience you have with a book, to a point, the better your perspective.

Although identifying and tracing themes had been central to his work as a student of literature, George noticed that he was examining literature in new ways as a teacher: "Now I read stories in a different light. I think about them in terms of how easy the themes are to trace." While George learned a great deal about thematic analysis as an undergraduate, a closer examination of his attempts to *teach* theme highlight some of the differences in knowing something such as theme for personal use and knowing something such as theme for teaching.

Teaching his students about themes was not an easy task for George. In the spring of his student teaching year, I watched him teach his students how to trace themes in short stories. While planning for the unit, he thought he might have his students do a free-writing, answering the question, "In fiction or in short stories, what is theme?" He hoped that this activity would provide him with a sense of what they already knew (or did not know) about theme. He planned to follow this up with an in-class thematic analysis of John Cheever's short story "The Enormous Radio." After this short modeling exercise, he wanted to play the first movement of Beethoven's Fifth Symphony as an illustration of musical theme: "It's just an example of what counterpoint is in music. How [the musical phrase] is repeated by different instruments, echoed, changed a little bit. You introduce this theme and then you play upon it." Finally, George planned to have the students read a few more short stories and write papers analyzing a theme in one of them.

George's choice of Beethoven to illustrate his ideas about theme was not surprising to me. Throughout the time we worked together, George frequently used analogies and metaphors in his instructional representations as well as in his conversations with me. "Interdisciplinary analogies," as he called them, were his favorites, for he enjoyed making connections between different fields of study. He also valued such bridging of disciplinary chasms because he could "see comparisons across disciplines, maybe start to discover some principles that apply outside of specific systems." He wanted to be "cross-disciplinary" in his "understanding of the world around me," and he jumped at the chance to learn more about fields that enrich the "web" of meaning that he constructed of his world. In turn, he tried to enrich the webs in the minds of his students. His comments in his journal suggest various aspects of George's web for theme:

A theme is an idea or thought that a story explores or treats. A single story may explore or treat several themes to varying degrees of depth. To be able to trace a theme in a story is to be able to recognize it at different parts of a story and to be able to compare what is said about that theme in each appearance. How is it different in each different circumstance? How is it similar?

After a theme is introduced, it is the repetition and variation on theme later on that gives it meaning. A composer does the same thing with theme in music and with the use of counterpoints. I'm thinking of stories now where counterpoint might be visible. The Bible has many: Jacob deceives his father Isaac . . . into giving him Esau's birthright. Later, on the night Jacob is to wed Rachel, Rachel's father puts Leah into the tent in the dark. Jacob has been fooled by the same means he fooled others. And here two themes emerge: blindness and deception.

I'm trying to think of an everyday example of this so as to "get into it" with the students. What things are repeated in your life but are never the same each time? Seasons, school, sunrises, meals, etc. Or what is something which had assumed a pattern suddenly changed?"

For example: A baseball game has a pattern that we can anticipate—nine, three-out innings. However, it is how that pattern is varied in each of its nine repetitions that gives a game meaning, that tells who wins or loses. We know that a school year has a planned pattern that gives the school year meaning for you and for me. What is in those semesters, those quarters. . . .

So a theme is a thought or idea that gets special treatment in a story. The treatment is special because the story gives the idea a specific place and circumstance to exist and the story examines that idea in the light of that place and those circumstances. In a sense, a story forces us to look at an old thing (theme, idea) in a new way. It prompts thought and exploration. . . .

I guess I'm trying to reveal to students how to read a
story through a certain lens. To see that a theme is one thing
a story treats, and if you re-read a story looking for that
thing, that theme, you see it differently, and you see what a
story is saying about a certain thing, and not necessarily what
a story as a whole is "saying." (It is always debatable if stories
ever do that.)

The conclusion George reaches at the end of his journal entry—
the idea that a theme is a lens through which the reader reads a
story—is one that he discussed later on with me in an interview:
"Actually, in a lot of ways, from a critical perspective, a theme is a
lens through which you see a story. If you decide that there's this
theme, you read through that theme. You read [the story] in expectation that things refer to that theme."

When he presented the concept of theme to his students,
George started the first lesson with an exercise in which he gave his
students a parable from the Bible, analyzed the theme for them, and
had a class discussion about the process he had engaged in. George
did not believe that modeling was the best way to "hook" his students, so he presented the analogy of the baseball game and its
innings that he discussed in his journal. Unfortunately, the students
did not respond well to the analogy. Reflecting on the lesson, George
recalls:

What frustrated me with the lesson from Tuesday was the inability on my own part to connect the repetition and pattern
of a theme and the image I tried to use of the innings in a
baseball game. I was trying to show that themes are general
ideas that take on new meanings when placed in specific character and setting circumstances of a story. In other words,
treating a theme in a story is looking at something old in a
new way. Just like we know that a baseball game has nine
innings and 27 outs, we know how we see a theme as it appears generically—whether it be honesty, jealousy, loneliness,
or whatever. What gives the game and the time meaning,
however, is how it is worked out in the game itself, the story
itself. Anyway, my frustrations led me to look for a better
image, a better metaphor that I could give the guys for tracing
and understanding a theme. What I came up with was the
trailing of a wounded animal by a hunter. Here the hunter
disregards all or most of the information. The scene before

him represents and concentrates only on that which pertains
to the animal he is searching for. Now, some of the clues
might be from the animal itself—blood or hair—just as the
word or words of a theme might appear outright in any given
passage. But also a hunter must see the broken grass, the
hoofprint, the signs that are the indicators. A story can deal
with a theme indirectly also, by association, juxtaposition, and
other evidence. So we read a story through again, looking for
that theme, searching for that game. This is the kind of reading that opens a story up because, if the theme being traced is
a major one, close reading makes one realize the intercon-
nectedness of the whole story.

In his attempts to teach theme, George failed to separate two
very different issues. He wanted his students to understand the
concept of theme and to be able to answer the question, "In fiction,
what is a theme?" He also wanted them to be able to trace a theme.
He searched for analogies and metaphors, using examples in the
students' lives that would give them "structures to hang these ideas
on." But his analogies were confusing: in class he interchanged
explanations of theme with thematic analysis, leaving it to the students to distinguish between the concept and the skill. The metaphor
of the hunter trailing an animal, for example, is one way of talking
about thematic analysis; the reader must pick up clues in the text to
understand fully the ways in which an author is developing a theme.
However, this analogy is not a definition of theme, George's original
purpose. The students were left wondering what the topic of discussion really was.
    George also had his students read through the short stories in
the unit, "The Enormous Radio" and Flannery O'Connor's "The Life
You Save May Be Your Own," several times, reading for different
themes. This aspect of the unit resembled George's own undergraduate experience, where a professor would discuss the relevance of a
particular theme and the students would have to find evidence for
that theme in the story.
    While the unit, on the whole, was confusing for his students *and*
for George, he did have a few successes. On the day he played
Beethoven's Fifth, the students all heard:

> the basic "da-da-da-dum!" musical theme that Beethoven in-
> troduces right from the start. The repetition and counterpoint
> are quite clear. Also, early on [there] is a pastoral part of the

piece where the theme is not recognizable, so they got the idea that the theme appears more clearly and concisely at some points than at others.

As an observer, it appeared to me that his students responded well to this part of the lesson; the conversation was animated; comments by several students suggested that they recognized how the same piece of music could manifest itself in different ways throughout the composition. Students also were making many connections between themes in literature and counterpoint in music. George ended the lesson with a thematic analysis of several prints by Escher, for he believed Escher's emphasis on ideas such as time would help students see how themes were present in stories, music, and art.

The victory was brief; George was disappointed with the quality of the students' papers that closed the unit. He felt he had failed, for his students seemed unable to either recognize a theme or analyze one. But how is it that George, a skilled, experienced writer of critical literary analysis and a concerned, enthusiastic educator, had so much difficulty teaching his students how to identify and trace themes in short stories?

ANALYZING THE CASE

As I mentioned earlier, I use the case of George in TE 101 to illustrate the constructs of pedagogical content knowledge and pedagogical reasoning. I use this case because George is an excellent example of someone who has a thorough, rigorous liberal education. Yet this education is not sufficient preparation for teaching. On the other hand, we can also see how George's knowledge of the subject matter is essential to his thinking, for the instructional representations he is able to generate depend on his knowledge of literature, art, music, and literary criticism.

The concepts of instructional representation, pedagogical content knowledge, and pedagogical reasoning are difficult ones for my prospective teachers. They are not used to thinking about the representation of knowledge, primarily because many of them hold a view of knowledge and learning that involves the absorption of inert facts. The idea that knowledge is constructed and interpretative is new to them. Thus the notion that teachers serve as filters and interpreters of knowledge is also novel. When they enter my class, my students assume that a theme is a theme and the teacher's job is to tell students what a theme is. Students then imprint this definition on their brains.

Yet we can see in this case of George that it is not a simple matter of telling students about theme. Certainly, he could have read them a dictionary definition: "a subject or topic of discourse or of artistic representation" (Webster's, 1981, p. 1200). But George was committed to helping his students grapple with how the abstract idea of theme is manifested in actual prose. Each of George's representations highlighted a specific aspect of theme: its variations, its structure, its repetition, its role in interpretation. Many of my students have never thought about ideas like theme as having multiple facets, multiple configurations. The proposition that teachers consider these facets and then construct representations of them involves rethinking the assumptions my students make about knowledge, about teaching, about learning. Rethinking these assumptions is at the heart of TE 101, and George, as a case, offers a concrete, illustrative example for me to use in discussions about the assumptions we make about what it means to know and to teach a subject.

George knew a great deal about the concept of theme and thematic analysis. But teaching this unit to his class meant that George had to, for the first time in his life, make public his private, tacit understanding of theme. His experiences teaching theme required him to explicate his knowledge. It was difficult; no teacher had ever defined what a theme was or the steps involved in doing a thematic analysis. He told me:

> I had never been given a definition of theme or had seen a professor trace a theme to any great extent. In some ways, in lectures you do. You trace a symbol or you trace what a character does and, sometimes, a specific theme. But in terms of having one defined or having a theme followed through a story, I never saw that done. But I had done that in my own papers.

It is interesting to note that George did not simply teach theme "the way he was taught." By his account, his tacit understanding of theme had been developed through a kind of intellectual osmosis: professors had made reference to themes in lectures, George had been required to do thematic analyses for course papers, and he had noticed a number of themes in his reading of literature.

However, when George chose to *teach* theme, he started with a free-write about the definition of a theme, then moved on to trying to provide students with a definition of theme, both through analogies such as counterpoint and baseball games, but also through modeling thematic analyses in class. Finally, he had students do their own thematic analysis. He did not leave it up to the students to find a way to understand theme through the process of osmosis that he had experienced; he tried to facilitate the development of an understanding in a more direct way, an admirable goal despite his lack of success. One can trace this decision to the heavy emphasis that George's teacher education program put on such activities and concerns.

But what George's teacher education program had never done was teach him what theme was, nor about the match or mismatch between different instructional representations of theme and its meaning to literary critics. In my discussions of this case with students, I try to point these issues out and get them to explore the complex relationship between subject-matter knowledge and subject-matter knowledge for teaching. As with the literature that George teaches his students, however, there is no one right interpretation of this case, no single point to be made about pedagogical content knowledge, subject-matter knowledge, or pedagogical reasoning. Rather, there are many theories embedded in the story, and the one I choose to pursue with each class depends as much on what my students see in the case as what the focus of our discussions has been prior to the introduction of this case.

After my students have read the case, I ask them to meet in small groups and do the following analysis:

- List and describe the alternative representations of theme that George generated for his teaching.
- Analyze each representation. Describe what you believe George wanted students to learn from each representation. What are the individual strengths and weaknesses of the representations that George generated?
- Why do you think that George had so much difficulty teaching his students about theme?
- Why do you think that George's students did not learn about theme by the end of the unit?
- How did George's experiences as a student influence his teaching of theme?

- How did George's knowledge of the subject matter—of themes and thematic analysis—influence how he taught his students about theme?
- Do you think that George understood what a theme was?

After they have met in their small groups, our large-group discussion meanders through the territory their small-group analyses explored. Sometimes we talk about the nature of disciplinary knowledge, for George lets us think about the role that interpretation plays in subject matter. At other times we talk about the types of knowledge teachers need, for George also shows us that he is gradually accumulating knowlege of how his students think and react to his various representations. We can also examine the assumptions that George makes about what students care and know about, as well as how he factors those beliefs into his pedagogical deliberations. As a case, the story of George allows us to pursue multiple paths. Determining which I will pursue with my students involves thinking about where our conversations have been, where they are going, and what ideas seem critical at this juncture.

A CAVEAT OR TWO: LESSONS ABOUT CASES

I enjoy using cases like that of George, as well as other cases. Like the videotapes we watch, such cases allow us to "look" inside the minds and classrooms of teachers and to observe and consider aspects of teaching and learning. But the more I use these cases, the more I understand the complexity of their pedagogy. My experiences with using this case have helped me think about two issues related to the pedagogy of cases. I discuss each briefly.

The Content and Complexity of Cases

One issue involves the content and complexity of the case one uses. George's is a highly analytical case. It is not mere description of a teacher's experiences. Rather, it is my interpretation as a researcher of what George knew and what he did. In this way, it differs substantially from other types of cases that remain more descriptive, leaving the analysis as something for students and teachers to do in discussion. Indeed, I use such cases in this class and others that I teach. But the type of case one uses depends on the pedagogical purposes of the case's use.

In TE 101, when teaching about representations of knowledge, my purposes require that I use an analytic case about pedagogical content knowledge. Instructional representations and pedagogical content knowledge are not natural phenomena that are readily and easily observable. Instead, they are theoretical constructs used by researchers and teacher educators to think about the nature of teaching and teaching knowledge. When my students encounter these ideas in TE 101, they need to learn how to do two things. First, they need to learn to look at instances of teaching through these conceptual lenses. Second, they need to learn how to think about the products of such analyses—specific instructional representations and processes of pedagogical reasoning—and consider the lessons we can then learn about teaching and teacher knowledge. In TE 101, that is, I am trying to help my students learn how to "see" pedagogical content knowledge and instructional representations in an instance of teaching. But I am also trying to get them to interpret what we learn from such analyses. Requiring that they do both the analysis and interpretation is overwhelming initially, and I use the case of George as a short cut. Because it already contains an analysis of George's thinking and teaching in terms of instructional representations, students can focus on interpreting what such an analysis contributes to our collective understanding of teaching. In other situations, when I want them to learn how to do such analyses themselves, I use other pedagogical tools; I do not hand them an analysis that someone else has done. However, because they have seen such an analysis, I can use it as a model for them as they think about how to do their own.

When and What Students Learn from Cases

A second lesson I have learned about the use of cases grew out of an experience I had with an earlier version of this case. I began developing this case when I was working with Vicki LaBoskey on a project in which we were teaching preservice teachers to write cases (LaBoskey, 1989; LaBoskey & Wilson, 1987). I used excerpts of my case of George to demonstrate what a case might look like, how one uses data to support claims, how one searches for meaning in the behavior and talk of teachers and students.

The student teachers in the program hated George. They did not simply hate the activity of examining the case or reading the data; they despised George. One student, Joseph, was particularly adamant. A published author himself, he explained to me that George should not have been allowed in a classroom. He did not care about students, he did not know his subject matter, he did not know anything about teaching.

I was heartbroken. Not only did the students appear to miss the point of the case—that there are fundamental differences between knowing the subject matter and knowing how to teach the subject matter—but they also disliked George, a man whom I had come to admire, respect, and care about. With tail between my legs, I retreated, eventually regrouping and finding other ways to discuss with students how to write a case.

But my story does not end there. Several months later, after the George-haters had been teaching for several months in their own classrooms, Joseph's supervisor approached me in the hallway, smiling. She had just returned from observing Joseph teach. And what should the subject matter of the lesson be but themes and thematic analysis! Poor Joseph—he had failed miserably at his attempts to communicate his notions of theme to his students. Seeing that he was frustrated and unnerved afterwards, Joseph's supervisor tried to help him figure out why the lesson had failed. Suddenly he looked at her, eyes widening. Slapping his forehead, he exclaimed, "Oh my God! I'm George!" Subsequently, using George as an example, they went on to discuss the differences between knowing something personally and being able to develop that understanding in students as shared knowledge and experience.

Revenge is sweet, and I thanked the supervisor for sharing that experience with me. I felt vindicated. But it is not the vindication that is important here; it is the host of lessons I took from that experience. Cases are fruitful ways of talking with practicing and prospective teachers about teaching. Joseph and his supervisor were able to use George and the case of his teaching theme to make sense of Joseph's own experience. The case provided them with a way of framing the problem Joseph encountered as well as a way of analyzing it.

But we cannot expect too much from our cases. Joseph was not ready to see what I wanted him to see in the case of George until after he had wrestled with some of the same issues. Thus my case did not work as a *substitute* for field experience, a story of instruction that allowed prospective teachers to discuss an important issue without going into the field. Rather, my case of George acted as an *enhancer* of experience, helping Joseph and his supervisor critically reflect on Joseph's personal experience.

When I developed this case I focused on the question: What will my students learn from this case? But it is equally important, when thinking about the use of cases, to consider the question of when students will learn from our cases. The answer is simple: they will learn when they are ready, and what they learn depends on what they are able to see. As we begin to think about the use of cases in teacher education, we must also pursue these related issues, reflecting not only on the methods we use to teach cases and the cases we choose to develop, but on issues of when to introduce cases, how and when to revisit cases and explore new issues with students or old issues in a new light, and how to insure that when they are able to learn, there will be someone—like Joseph's supervisor—there to help them.

NOTES

1. This is a rapidly growing body of research, which I cannot do justice to here. However, readers may want to consider the work of Ball (1988a, 1988b, 1990, in press a, in press b), Ball and McDiarmid (1990), Grossman (1988, in press), Grossman and colleagues (1989), Hashweh (1987), Lampert (1985, 1987, 1989, 1990), Leinhardt and Greeno (1986), Leinhardt and Smith (1985), McDiarmid and colleagues (1989), Peterson, Carpenter, and Fennema (1989), L. Shulman (1986, 1987, 1990), Wilson (in press a), Wilson and colleagues (1987), Wilson and Wineburg (1988), and Wineburg and Wilson (1988).

2. I have written about teaching this course elsewhere (Wilson, 1990, in press b), as have my colleagues who also teach the course (Ball, 1988 b; Feiman-Nemser, McDiarmid, Melnick, & Parker (in press); McDiarmid, 1990). Also see collected essays by instructors of the course in Feiman-Nemser and Featherstone (in press).

3. The familial metaphor was a common one in the colonial world. Gross (1976) notes that colonial magistrates were often referred to as "father" and England as a "tender parent." In his pamphlet *Common Sense*, Thomas Paine turned this metaphor on its head: "But Britain is the parent country, say some. Then the more shame upon her conduct. Even brutes do not devour their young . . . the phrase 'parent' or 'mother country' has been jesuitically adopted by the king and his parasites with a low papistical design of gaining an unfair bias on the credulous weakness of our minds. Europe, and not England, is the parent country of America" (Paine, 1776/1953, p. 21).

4. George, the name of his school, and name of his university are pseudonyms.

5. The case presented here is an abbreviated version. For the longer case, see Wilson (1988a).

6. All quotations are unedited and taken directly from interview transcripts, field notes, or George's journal entries.

REFERENCES

Ball, D. L. (1988a). *Knowledge and reasoning in mathematical pedagogy: Examining what prospective teachers bring to teacher education.* Unpublished doctoral dissertation, College of Education, Michigan State University, East Lansing.

Ball, D. L. (1988b). Unlearning to teach mathematics. *For the Learning of Mathematics, 8*(1), 40–48.

Ball, D. L. (1990). The mathematical understandings that prospective teachers bring to teacher education. *The Elementary School Journal, 90*(4), 449–466.

Ball, D. L. (in press a). Halves, pieces, and twoths: Constructing and using representational contexts in teaching fractions. In T. Carpenter & E. Fennema (Eds.), *Learning, teaching, and assessing rational number concepts.*

Ball, D. L. (in press b). With an eye to the mathematical horizon: Dilemmas of teaching. *Elementary School Journal.*

Ball, D. L., & McDiarmid, G. W. (1990). The subject matter preparation of teachers. In W. R. Houston (Ed.), *Handbook for research on teacher education* (pp. 437–449). New York: Macmillan.

Carnegie Task Force on Teaching as a Profession. (1986). *A nation prepared: Teachers for the 21st century.* Washington, DC: Carnegie Forum on Education and the Economy.

Dewey, J. (1956). *The child and the curriculum.* Chicago: University of Chicago Press. (Original work published 1902)

Feiman-Nemser, S., & Featherstone, H. (Eds.) (in press). *Exploring teaching: Adventures of teachers and students in an introductory teaching course.* New York: Teachers College Press.

Feiman-Nemser, S., McDiarmid, G. W., Melnick, S., & Parker, M. (in press). Changing beginning teachers' conceptions: A study of an introductory teacher education course. *Journal for the Education of Teachers.*

Gross, R. A. (1976). *The Minutemen and their world.* New York: Hill & Wang.

Grossman, P. L. (1988). *Sources of pedagogical content knowledge in English.* Unpublished doctoral dissertation, Stanford University, Stanford, CA.

Grossman, P. L. (in press). Subject matter knowledge and the teaching of English. In J. Brophy (Ed.), *Advances in research on teaching: Vol. 2. Teachers' subject matter knowledge and classroom instruction.* Greenwich, CT: JAI Press.

Grossman, P. L., Wilson, S. M., & Shulman, L. S. (1989). Teachers of substance: The subject matter knowledge of teachers. In M. Reynolds (Ed.), *The knowledge base for the beginning teacher* (pp. 23–36). New York: Pergamon.

Hashweh, M. Z. (1987). Effects of subject-matter knowledge in the teaching of biology and physics. *Teaching & Teacher Education, 3,* 109–120.

Holmes Group. (1986). *Tomorrow's teachers: A report of the Holmes Group.* East Lansing, MI: Author.

LaBoskey, V. K. (1989). *Using cases in the education of reflective teachers.* Unpublished doctoral dissertation, Stanford University, Stanford, CA.

LaBoskey, V. K., & Wilson, S. M. (1987, April). *The gift of a case study "pickle": Using cases in teacher education.* Paper presented at the annual meeting of the American Educational Research Association, Washington, DC.

Lampert, M. (1985). Mathematics learning in context: The voyage of the Mimi. *The Journal of Mathematical Behavior, 4,* 157–167.

Lampert, M. (1987). Knowing, doing, and teaching multiplication. *Cognition and Instruction, 3,* 305–342.

Lampert, M. (1989). Choosing and using mathematical tools in classroom discourse. In J. Brophy (Ed.), *Advances in research on teaching* (Vol. 1) (pp. 223–264). Greenwich, CT: JAI Press.

Lampert, M. (1990). When the problem is not the question and the answer is not the solution: Mathematical knowing and teaching. *American Educational Research Journal, 27,* 29–64.

Leinhardt, G., & Greeno, J. G. (1986). The cognitive skill of teaching. *Journal of Educational Psychology, 78,* 75–95.

Leinhardt, G., & Smith, D. A. (1985). Expertise in mathematics instruction: Subject matter knowledge. *Educational Psychologist, 77,* 247–271.

McDiarmid, G. W. (1990). Challenging prospective teachers' beliefs during an early field experience: A quixotic undertaking? *Journal of Teacher Education, 41*(3), 12–20.

McDiarmid, G. W., Ball, D. L., & Anderson, C. W. (1989). Why staying one chapter ahead doesn't really work: Subject-specific pedagogy. In M. Reynolds (Ed.), *The knowledge base of the beginning teacher* (pp. 193–205). New York: Pergamon.

Paine, T. (1953). Common sense. In N. F. Adams (Ed.), *Common sense and other political writings.* New York: Liberal Arts Press. (Original work published 1776)

Peterson, P. L., Carpenter, T., & Fennema, E. (1989). Teachers' knowledge of students' knowledge in mathematics problem solving: Correlational and case analyses. *Journal of Educational Psychology, 81,* 558–569.

Schwab, J. J. (1978). The practical: Translation into curriculum. In I. Westbury & N. Wilkof (Eds.), *Science, curriculum, and liberal education: Selected essays* (pp. 365–383). Chicago: University of Chicago Press.

Shulman, L. S. (1986). Those who understand: Knowledge growth in teaching. *Educational Researcher, 15,* 4–14.

Shulman, L. S. (1987). Knowledge and teaching: Foundations of the new reform. *Harvard Educational Review, 57,* 1–22.

Shulman, L. S. (1990, April). *The transformation of knowledge: A model of pedagogical reasoning and action.* Paper presented at the annual meeting of the American Educational Research Association, Boston.

Shulman, L. S., & Grossman, P. L. (1987). *Final report to the Spencer Foundation*

(Knowledge Growth in a Profession Publication Series). Stanford, CA: Stanford University, School of Education.

Wilson, S. M. (1988a). *George, a beginning English teacher* (Knowledge Growth in a Profession Publication Series). Stanford, CA: Stanford University, School of Education.

Wilson, S. M. (1988b). *Understanding historical understanding: The subject matter knowledge of U. S. history teachers*. Unpublished doctoral dissertation, Stanford University, Stanford, CA.

Wilson, S. M. (1990). The secret garden of teacher education. *Phi Delta Kappan, 72*(3), 204–209.

Wilson, S. M. (in press a). Mastodons, maps, and Michigan: Exploring uncharted territory while teacher elementary school social studies. *Elementary School Journal*.

Wilson, S. M. (in press b). Thinking about teaching, teaching about teaching. In S. Feiman-Nemser & H. Featherstone (Eds.), *Exploring teaching: Adventures of teachers and students in an introductory teaching course*. New York: Teachers College Press.

Wilson, S. M., Shulman, L. S., & Richert, A. E. (1987). "150 different ways" of knowing: Representations of knowledge in teaching. In J. Calderhead (Ed.), *Exploring teachers' thinking* (pp. 104–124). Eastbourne, England: Cassell.

Wilson, S. M., & Wineburg, S. S. (1988). Peering at American history through different lenses: The role of disciplinary knowledge in teaching. *Teachers College Record, 89*, 525–539.

Wineburg, S. S., & Wilson, S. M. (1988). Models of wisdom in teaching history. *Phi Delta Kappan, 70*, 90–98.

CHAPTER 5

On Becoming a Consulting Teacher

Overcoming Role Conflicts
and Misperceptions

SUZANNE E. WADE

Joan Baker relaxed into her chair and sighed, "This is the first chance I've had to sit down all day." Enthusiastic shouts and running steps of the students could be heard through the window of her small office off the library. It was the end of school on a Friday afternoon, the first balmy day of April. Joan got up to pour herself a cup of coffee, then stood staring out the window. After several moments of reflection as she sipped her coffee, she turned and leaned against the windowsill.

"Well, you want to know what it's like trying to get content-area teachers here to take some responsibility for teaching reading and learning strategies in their classes. It's been an exercise in futility. I think the teachers here are too lazy to really change much. Many have been teaching for 20 years—they're worn away, burned out. They have no incentive, except for a few individuals, and since no new teachers are coming in because of the freeze on hiring, there's no competition. Their focus isn't on how much the kid has learned any more, it's on going through the motions of doing the job; they get no respect from the community, little pay; the kids are rude. Why should they change?"

This chapter presents a case of a reading specialist who is attempting to work with junior high content-area teachers in a new role—that of consulting teacher. This role involves collaboration with teachers to provide instructional support to help academically at-risk and learning-disabled students succeed in the regular classroom where possible, rather than be placed in remedial pullout

90

programs. However, in this case, Joan was not a successful reading consultant. Analyzing the case helps students understand the problems that specialists and regular education teachers may experience as they attempt to work together. More broadly, the case illustrates some of the problems any educator may face when attempting to change role expectations and collegial relationships in schools.

The chapter is divided into six sections. The first provides some background to the idea of the consulting teacher, including what it is, what it is designed to accomplish, how it represents a change from past practice, and how successfully it has been implemented in schools. The second section describes the purpose and origin of the case. The third section, "Teaching the Case"—written to the instructor rather than to students—describes how the case can be used in reading, special education, and teacher education courses, and includes specific suggestions and activities. The fourth section—written to students—introduces the case by providing an overview and questions to guide their reading. The fifth section is the case itself, entitled "Through Different Lenses." This section consists of descriptions of events from the point of view of both the specialist and the three content teachers with whom she attempted to collaborate. Hearing from all the participants enables students to see the situation from different perspectives. The sixth section is a commentary written by Dixie Huefner, a professor of special education who has written extensively in this area (c.f., Huefner, 1988). In her commentary, she describes a number of prerequisites—both individual and organizational—to successful implementation of the consulting teacher model and discusses how lack of these prerequisites adversely affected Joan's efforts. The chapter concludes with some thoughts about the strengths and limitations of cases in teaching and research.

THE CONSULTING TEACHER: SOME BACKGROUND

The idea of collaboration between teachers and specialists is a relatively new one, particularly at the secondary level. Traditionally, these two groups have had little to do with one another. Content-area teachers have tended to see their job as teaching the knowledge of their disciplines—not reading—whereas reading and learning disabilities (LD) specialists have taught in remedial pullout programs, separate from the regular school curriculum. However, remedial programs have come under fire because they have failed to help students make the transition back into the regular classroom (Reynolds, Wang, & Walberg, 1987; Will, 1986). As an alternative, some educators have advocated the idea of integrating reading instruction into the content-area curriculum (see Herber, 1978). This means that content-area teachers would be responsible for teaching students how to read and learn from the textbooks and other written material that are used to teach subject-matter knowledge.

Advocates of an integrated approach to reading—who tend to be special educators and reading specialists, not content-area teachers—offer the following arguments in favor of this idea. First, students with mild-to-moderate learning disabilities could remain in regular classrooms, which is consistent with the idea of *mainstreaming*. The goal of mainstreaming is to place students in the least restrictive learning environment—ideally, the regular classroom wherever possible. Advocates argue that the chances of success for such students would be greater in regular classrooms because they would learn how to learn in the setting and with the materials they will eventually have to deal with. They would also escape the stigma of being labeled as different or learning-disabled. Second, fewer students would be placed in remedial programs, which would enable special educators to better serve students who have more severe learning disabilities. Third, regular education students at all grade levels would also profit from instruction in reading strategies because most need to learn how to organize information in ways that make it meaningful and memorable, relate examples and details to generalizations, and draw generalizations from facts. Finally, reading strategies instruction involves many of the same methods as teaching content knowledge—that is, modeling, demonstrating, explaining, and practicing. Thus strategies can and should be taught using regular classroom materials, not easier materials or special skill books.

Although their arguments seemed compelling, advocates of an integrated approach to reading soon realized that the idea was not enthusiastically embraced by either experienced content-area teachers (Ratekin, Simpson, Alvermann, & Dishner, 1985) or undergraduates preparing to become content-area teachers (O'Brien & Stewart, 1990). Therefore advocates began to plan an implementation strategy. The result was the idea of the consulting teacher, which represents a new role for specialists. Instead of only teaching remedial reading with small groups of students in separate classrooms, specialists would also work with teachers as a resource person—consulting, diagnosing, and recommending instructional ideas as well as modeling them in the regular classroom.

Despite its potential as a kind of individualized on-the-job training to help content-area teachers integrate reading instruction into their curriculum, the idea of the consulting teacher has met with little success in many schools (Bean, 1979; Pikulski & Ross, 1979). Teachers have been especially resistant to the idea of specialists coming into their classrooms to team teach or model innovative teaching practices—the kinds of activities that have the most potential for changing instructional practice. Regular education teachers do not want specialists to share any of the teaching responsibilities in their classrooms, believing that the proper role for specialists is remedial instruction in pullout programs, thereby removing the students whom content-area teachers do not want to deal with.

Resistance to the idea of mainstreaming and the consulting teacher is not surprising, since both involve profound changes in the roles and responsibilities of teachers and specialists. Only by understanding the concerns, needs, and perceptions of teachers and specialists can such changes be successfully carried out. The case that follows provides an opportunity to analyze how Joan and the three content-area teachers with whom she attempted to work as a consulting teacher view their interactions and to think about how Joan might have been more successful.

PURPOSE AND ORIGINS OF THE CASE

This case can be used in both preservice and inservice courses in reading, special education, and teacher education. For example, in reading and special education courses, such as Methods for Teaching Reading in the Content Areas or Principles of Collaboration in Schools, it can be used alone to introduce the role of the consulting teacher, which many reading and special educators will be expected to assume at some time in their careers. In teacher education Methods classes that cover a wider range of topics, including classroom management and teacher decision making, it can be used with other cases in this book. The issues raised in this case are important to regular education teachers who may someday want to use the services of resource personnel or who may become teacher leaders, as advocated by the Carnegie Forum on Education and the Economy (1986) and the Holmes Group (1986). The purpose of analyzing the case is to give students experience in dealing with some of the policy and role issues, such as mainstreaming and educational consulting, that they are likely to encounter in the future. Analyzing the case will help them frame problems, understand events from the different perspectives of the participants, and evaluate alternative courses of action.

The case is based on findings of a larger case study, which analyzed the attempts of a reading specialist to work in a junior high school as a consulting teacher (Wade, 1984). The study involved 4 months of observations, meetings, conversations, and interactions that I had with the principal, the reading specialist, and three content-area teachers in the school who had agreed to participate in the study. These interviews and observations provide data for understanding the events and issues from multiple points of view. To illustrate how participants held misconceptions about one another and disagreed on some fundamental issues, the case had been written to let participants voice their own interpretations of the situation.

Although based on this research, the case itself has been written with some literary license. The major change is that the specialist's account is a composite of both her and my own experiences working at the school in the role of the consulting teacher. Although the incidents are true and most of the opinions expressed by the specialist and teachers are direct quotations, all names are fictitious in order to maintain the confidentiality of the participants.

TEACHING THE CASE

I typically use this case toward the end of a course. In courses with a field-based component, it is presented after students have covered topics of immediate, practical concern to them as they prepare to work in classrooms. Once students have had some experience in teaching we move on to the policy and role issues covered in this case.

First I have students read the material included thus far in this chapter. This gives them some background to the case itself and the issues involved. Then I begin a general discussion by asking class members to describe any experiences they may have had with mainstreaming, team teaching, and other kinds of collaborative work with colleagues in schools. Some questions I ask are: How successful was it? What were the reasons for its success or failure? What could have been done differently to ensure success?

When I distribute the case, I ask the students to reflect on the problems from the point of view of both the specialist and the content-area teachers. It works best to have students read it outside of class and to write an analysis of the case. In this analysis, I ask students to examine the evidence, frame the problems, understand the motivations and concerns that explain participants' opinions and behavior, and develop a plan of action with a description of the possible risks and consequences involved. I also ask students to pay close attention to the specialist's and teachers' perceptions of one another and their concerns, such as how confident they feel about their ability to teach and carry out their new responsibilities, whether they are concerned about collaboration as a threat to their autonomy, and whether they believe that the goals and rewards of collaboration are worth the time and effort that is required. Questions related to these issues are provided in the introduction to the case to guide students in their analysis.

Then, to initiate discussion of the case after students have read and analyzed it on their own, I begin a role-playing exercise by having one person represent Joan, the reading specialist, and three others represent the content-area teachers—Mary, Harold, and John. Each of these actors begins by summarizing some of the points made by the person they are representing. They are then free to defend their position and counter the arguments made by the others. Besides developing audience interest, role playing provides a summary of the main problems in the case and initiates a dialogue among the participants and other class members.

After several minutes of role playing, I have class members form small groups to identify problems that prevented collaboration from occurring and to analyze the underlying concerns of the reading specialist and content-area teachers. The whole class then convenes to discuss the case, beginning with the contradictions and misconceptions that the specialist and teachers have about one another. The instructor may want to use some of the ideas presented in the commentary to guide discussion and ensure that all relevant issues are covered.

For a final activity, students develop a plan of action that they could employ as a consulting teacher or teacher leader. This assignment can be accomplished as a small-group or individual research project. Then, either in small groups or as a whole class, students share plans of action and evaluate them in terms of the risks they entail, their possible consequences, and their chances for success.

After they have analyzed the case, I give students the commentary that follows it. The commentary is useful because it allows students to compare their own analysis, particularly their plan of action, with a person who has studied the conditions that are necessary for successful implementation. Students can then revise their plan of action in terms of how they would get their plan off the ground, who they would work with initially (e.g., volunteers), how decision making would proceed among participants, the goals and focus of their work together, and the kinds of organizational support that would be needed.

INTRODUCTION TO THE CASE

The case begins with the grievances of Joan, the reading specialist, who is frustrated in her attempts to work as a consultant and collaborator with the content-area teachers in her school. Despite support of her efforts by the well-respected principal, most of the teachers in the school have not volunteered to work with her. She feels that the three who did—Mary, Harold, and John—are not really cooperative, and she distrusts the motives of some of them. Is she right? Are they resistant to change? Could she have interacted with them differently? After reading Joan's side of the story, you will then hear from the three content-area teachers, who interpret some of the events quite differently.

As you read and analyze the case, you should consider the events and relationships described in it as prototypes of problems inherent in any kind of planned educational change that affects individuals' roles, responsibilities, and interactions. To help in analyzing the case, think of how you would answer the following questions:

1. How do the participants in the case differ in their perceptions of one another and the situation as a whole? Specifically, how does Joan perceive her role and the reasons she has not been successful? How do Mary, Harold, and John evaluate Joan's work? In what ways do the perceptions of Joan and the teachers conflict?
2. How do you make sense of the conflict? In what ways do the stated intentions of the participants in the case differ from their behavior? What are the underlying concerns and needs (expressed and unexpressed) of each participant?
3. What are the prerequisites to successful collaboration? For example, what skills, knowledge, and attitudes does a con-

sulting teacher need to be successful? Under what conditions might the teachers have been more receptive to change?

Whether you are (or are planning to be) a specialist or content-area teacher, you may someday be asked to work as a consulting teacher or teacher leader. After you have read the case and thought about answers to the questions above, think of a plan of action you might follow if you were expected to work as a consulting teacher in a situation similar to Joan's.

- How would you recruit teachers initially?
- What would your goals be?
- How would the team make decisions and work together?
- What kinds of organizational support would you need?

THROUGH DIFFERENT LENSES

The Setting

Located in an affluent suburb of a large city in the Northeast, Wellington Junior High is a modern two-story building, serving approximately 500 pupils in grades 7, 8, and 9. Class size ranges from 22 to 26 pupils. The faculty are older and have had more years of teaching experience than was the norm for faculty in the past. Because of a decreasing student population and the consequent freeze on hiring, few new faculty members have been hired in recent years.

The policy of the school is to randomly assign students to classes without regard to ability, except in math. This policy of mainstreaming was designed to avoid stigmatizing students by exposing them to the regular curriculum wherever possible. However, this policy has resulted in frequent complaints from the faculty about the difficulty of dealing with the wide range in reading ability that can be found in every classroom—from nonreaders to those who are able to read college material.

At the time, the school had one full-time reading specialist (Joan) and two part-time LD specialists. Joan's responsibilities included administering diagnostic tests to reading-disabled pupils, teaching remedial reading to individuals and small groups of students, administering achievement tests to all classes on a yearly basis, conducting inservice workshops in reading, and acting as a consulting teacher to the regular classroom teachers in the school. The sole responsibility of the LD specialists was to work directly with the most disabled pupils several times a week, either individually or in small groups.

Joan Baker, Reading Specialist

Before coming to Wellington Junior High, Joan had been a reading specialist for several years in another state. She was now completing her third year at Wellington, which made her one of the youngest and newest members of the faculty. However, because of continuing budget problems in the district, she was not sure whether she would have a job there in the fall.

Joan enjoys working directly with individuals or small groups of students in her office. She feels that this gives her an opportunity to get to know the students well and to observe rather dramatic improvements in their reading skills. She also likes the freedom of choosing reading materials that match their reading levels and interests. But she realizes that tutoring and small-group work is a luxury that the school can no longer afford. Providing direct services to only 30 or 40 students a week is doing little to alleviate reading problems in the school as a whole. As she says, "Many kids here are barely making it. Because their problems aren't severe and they're not disruptive, they're falling through the cracks." So becoming a consulting teacher to help regular teachers provide reading and learning strategy instructions in their classrooms is a role that she wants and needs to assume. However, despite her efforts and her principal's support, Joan feels that she has met with only limited success in this role. As she speaks, she presents a story of frustration—a "history of futility," as she puts it:

> When I came here I found that lots of kids in this school don't show growth and can't deal with schoolwork. The first thing I did was pretest in order to get to know the teachers. We talked about test scores and the kids I was concerned about. That worked well. A lot of teachers were willing to talk about individual kids. But I don't think they followed any of my suggestions, like giving different assignments or having them read material they could handle.
>
> When I suggested to teachers that I work with small groups of remedial readers in the regular classroom, teachers had wanted them removed. For example, Mary Calley, one of

the history teachers, wanted to raise the class average on exams and so was willing let me work with her. But she viewed my role as remedial and separate from the classroom. She asked me to take out a small group of pupils who were having difficulty and work on organizational skills such as summarizing and finding the main idea.

She was insistent that I use regular classroom materials—which meant the textbook—and that was fine with me. Students in the small group were really cooperative, and we covered the chapter thoroughly in preparation for the upcoming exam. They not only developed outlines and diagrams for short essay questions, which Mary said would be the format of the exam, but also wrote questions they thought might be on the test. Unfortunately, not many of the students did very well on the exam. Not surprising! Without telling me, Mary dropped her original idea of having essay questions and used exclusively multiple-choice items.

Mary also wouldn't let students take the textbook home or even use it in study hall. Somehow she hoped it would get students to develop strategies other than committing the text to memory—to learn to quickly pick out the generalizations instead of getting bogged down in details. These are worthy goals, but she never taught the students these skills. This is where I could have helped, but she wouldn't consider my working with the class as a whole. And her tests emphasized factual-level material, which requires memorization of the text and lectures.

Joan feels that she has had some minor successes. One was a workshop on readability, which the principal required teachers to attend. The principal had told her to keep her lecture to 12 minutes, followed by hands-on activities for the remainder of the hour. As a result, Joan felt she had gained some credibility and was then able to begin to work as a consulting teacher with a few content-area teachers. But in Joan's description of her work with the teachers, her frustration as she encounters what she sees as teachers' irresponsibility and evasiveness becomes clear:

I helped them develop unit and lesson plans and made suggestions about how to deal with remedial readers in the regular classroom. I suggested things like preteaching vocabulary and using study guides and chapter summaries before reading an assignment. I had the most success with those least in need of change; they already had good teaching skills. I was able to do a few observations in classrooms, saying I wanted to watch particular kids. But mostly, I worked as a teacher's aide, and even a substitute teacher! I'll give you one example. Harold Whitmore, another one of the history teachers, agreed to collaborate with me on developing some innovative lesson plans and then trying them out in his classroom. I think he only agreed because the principal had personally suggested this to him to improve his teaching, which consisted mainly of lecture and questioning. The principal is right! Harold has a structured routine, distributing a weekly schedule of assignments and classroom activities. His style is not a reflection of his dedication to teaching but rather of doing the same thing every year.

The first problem I ran into was in scheduling planning meetings because of his many outside commitments. And he'd often forget appointments when I *was* able to schedule them. But we did eventually get together and decide on the lessons that I would prepare. Although he wouldn't agree to my observing him teach, he said he would observe and evaluate demonstrations of lessons I'd teach in his classroom. I was pleased with that because I felt that I had my foot in the door. If he liked the lessons, he might be willing at some point to try them out himself. But when I began to teach the first day, he left the room as soon as he had introduced me to the class and did not return until 10 minutes after the demonstration had ended, when he was supposed to take over! So I found myself essentially being a substitute teacher, which would hardly bring about any change in his teaching. Well, I talked to him about how I needed his feedback on the lessons, and so he did stay in class after that. But he was never willing to teach any of the lessons himself, at least while I was there. I can't say that working with him had any effect on his teaching.

I had even less success working with another teacher that the principal had pressured into collaborating with me— mainly because this teacher was having a lot of classroom management problems. This was John Peterson, an eighth-grade science teacher, who, surprisingly, seemed willing not only to let me observe his classes but to work together on lesson planning and teaching. Our discussions together concerned the need to find ways to teach a classroom of students who vary greatly in ability—to individualize instruction and deal with students who lack decoding skills.

Although I had no trouble scheduling meetings with him, trying to observe in his classroom was another matter. Once when I showed up for a previously scheduled observation, he said it was not a good day because he was going to go over a test and show a movie rather than introduce a new chapter in the textbook as planned. In fact, he told me that he often changed his plans like that. When I tried to schedule a time to observe a textbook-related lesson for the following week, he told me he doesn't plan far enough ahead to be able to say what would be a good day.

By sheer persistence, I managed to observe a couple of times and found that he really did have poor control of his classes. Although he had a fairly good rapport with students, his general passivity often resulted in wasted time with students, who just mill about the classroom. But the worst problem was the lack of textbooks. I couldn't have one to plan lessons with! I never did develop lesson plans or demonstrate them in his classroom. Instead, I just administered some informal diagnostic tests to some of the students. I doubt that the recommendations I made for these students were ever followed.

You know, the teachers here really are resistant to change, extra work, and evaluation. Even those who have been willing to work with me—and they are few and far between—are vulnerable, defensive, and unwilling to put much time into additional projects.

There's a lot of suspicion toward specialists in general, especially among older teachers. The personality of the reading specialist is crucial. You have to be friendly, bouncy, but not pushy. And you have to be careful to deal with teachers with delicacy, tact, and flattery. Most important, you have to be willing to accept a subservient role. The key is to gain their trust and convince them that you are part of the group. You have to view yourself as a service. That means you do it all.

Mary Calley, History Teacher

A 15-year veteran of the history department at Wellington, Mary teaches eighth-grade American history. She had recently completed a doctorate in education, which focused on the role of women in history. Mary also has a strong interest in issues related to reading. She believes that the problem for most students is their inability to distinguish important from unimportant information and to draw generalizations from details: "There's a tremendous range in every class, from those who read at the third-grade level to students who can read almost anything. But most aren't good at abstracting material—they're very literal-minded. When they're working with the text, they can't organize the information into a framework; instead they wallow around in all the details and facts."

Mary wants to develop in her students a sense of history that expands their awareness and helps them become critical thinkers. She does not think this can be accomplished with her textbook, which she had no voice in selecting.

"The text is a piece of junk, filled with every American platitude. It has a fair amount of super patriotism, which is dangerous. It also has a cardboard approach to historical personages and question-answer regurgitation. Most texts have been through so many different revisions that there's practically nothing left. Parents need texts more than pupils. My preference is to work with outlines."

Mary also wants to help students learn to organize information and abstract generalizations, but she is not sure of how to do it. Constant repetition by the teacher doing the generalizing, she guesses, is needed. Mary tries to individualize assignments and reading materials for the reading-disabled in her classes to some extent, although she is worried about stigmatizing students in front of their peers. Most individualizing, she feels, has to be done outside of class—handled privately. This is where she sees the reading specialist fitting in. Mary believes that the role of the specialist should be remedial and separate from the classroom:

> A reading specialist can best work with content-area teachers by taking groups of students out of the classroom, but still using the content materials, to teach organizational skills such as summarizing and finding the main idea. The reading teacher should try to keep tabs on who's getting what and what kinds of problems particular students are having. This is an almost impossible task for the classroom teacher.

Mary views the problem Joan faces in trying to work with content-area teachers as one of resistance to change on the part of both the specialist and the teachers at the school. She readily acknowledges that most teachers in the school had been resistant to

Joan's efforts to work with them in their classrooms. As she puts it, "Teachers prefer to be islands and are generally resistant to anything forced on them." At the same time, she sees Joan as having little interest in the resource role. She describes specialists in general as preferring the easier role of remediation, which isolates them from classrooms and teachers:

> Reading specialists want to stay isolated in their cubicles, working on a one-to-one basis instead of getting into classrooms. That's much easier than having to deal with 30 kids in every class. This is one reason they have trouble developing working relationships with content-area teachers.
>
> I'm against the use of special or easier reading materials. This is one of the main reasons why there's a clash between content teachers and specialists. After the kid has been in a resource room for a while, the specialist will now say that he can handle regular classroom materials and assignments. But she's made this assessment based on the kid's handling of specially adapted materials, not the textbook. Then, when the kid is put back in the classroom, he still can't handle the work. So he becomes discouraged and quickly withdraws.

Harold Whitmore, History Teacher

Harold is another eighth-grade American history teacher, with about 20 years of teaching experience. He is actively involved in a number of extracurricular activities. Directing play rehearsals, for example, occupies a great deal of his time, not only after school but also during his planning periods. Although appearing to be perpetually busy, he does like to talk about his teaching, once he sits down and relaxes. Like Mary, he would like to help students develop critical thinking skills—"being able to think for themselves rather than parroting back information." He believes that to accomplish this, the teacher needs to be good. "It's the humanness and flexibility of the teacher rather than any one technique or philosophy of teaching that's responsible for learning." Given the fact that he has a part-time job as a car salesman, it is not surprising that he views teaching as selling: "A good teacher is a good salesman—good at establishing an intense, short-term relationship with the objective of getting a person to say, do, or feel something they wouldn't do on their own."

Despite his concern with developing critical thinking skills, which he shares with Mary, Harold's teaching style and use of the textbook are radically different. Whereas Mary covers a few topics in American history in great depth, with role-playing activities and primary source materials, Harold covers the entire textbook, relying primarily on lecture, questions in the textbook, and quizzes. He describes the structure of his course in this way:

"I like to follow a basic routine each week. The activities and homework are always outlined in detail on a handout that I give each week. On Monday, I'll introduce a chapter. I also have students read a column in the local newspaper for interpretive work with current events. On Tuesday, I test them on the newspaper column and have them complete the check-up questions in the first part of the textbook chapter. Wednesday, I finish lecturing on the chapter, which students have been assigned to read at home. Thursday, they work on all the end-of-the-chapter questions, and on Friday, I give a test on the chapter and check the questions they have completed."

Harold finds that his students have two problems in reading: a limited attention span and the inability to understand the main points of the text. To some extent, he believes that his teaching is affected by the wide range in reading ability in his classes: "It makes me more aware of their needs. I try to individualize by personal contact and by suggesting additional or alternative materials. But because the textbook [the same one Mary uses and one he helped to select] is so superior, I don't find its use a problem."

Harold says that he welcomes the idea of collaboration, and he advocates an aggressive approach on the part of specialists. In contrast to Joan's negative attitude toward him and her belief that she has had little effect on his teaching, he describes Joan in positive terms and expresses the opinion that she has important things to offer content-area teachers:

> The specialist should not wait for the teacher to generate ideas, but rather should approach the teacher with ideas and try them out. We won't know if they work unless we try them. It's best handled by an aggressive attitude. As a classroom teacher, I used to have guilt feelings about not using resource people. But I didn't use them because they never approached me. Don't wait to be asked—come to me and ask if I've tried different things. Those who do wait around become a glorified teacher's aide to one or two teachers. You should assume that the content teacher is very busy and can't give up planning periods. We don't have time to set up elaborate reading programs—that's the responsibility of the reading person.

I see reading specialists now as being part of the wood-work. They need to come into the classrooms. The specialist should begin by finding a cluster of teachers to work with. When these teachers tell of what they are doing, others will be envious and start to fall in. My stereotype is a little old lady sitting in a room with one student. Another part of the stereotype is people who use elaborate obfuscating instruments in irrelevant ways, as razzle-dazzle. No teacher likes to be overwhelmed by statistics.

But none of this is true of Joan. She's an exception to the stereotype—the model reading teacher. She's pleasantly aggressive and touches base with everyone at least once a month. Because she shows such an interest, the teacher is moved to put himself out. I like her approach to reading in the content areas. She has never attached reading to English. Instead, she sees reading as underlying all content areas. I also like her pre- and posttesting. She uses one simple test and doesn't try to impress us with jargon and numbers.

John Peterson, Science Teacher

A relative newcomer, having been at Wellington for only 3 years, John is a young eighth-grade earth science teacher. Like the other teachers, he would like his students to acquire both course-specific information and a way of thinking that they can apply to their everyday lives.

"This is the only time they'll take an earth science class, so I'd like them to get some basic knowledge of the earth they live on. For a lofty aim, I'd like them to understand the scientific method—a way of problem solving—and apply it to everyday situations.

"Students learn best by doing. Especially as a science teacher, I agree with the saying: 'I hear and I forget; I do and I understand.' But because of the realities of the classroom, I can only give them hands-on experience during lab periods. During the rest of the week, I have to rely on the textbook, worksheets, and lectures. I also use films fairly frequently and occasionally show filmstrips and slides on such topics as rock formations."

John identified several types of reading problems in his classes, including vocabulary and comprehension for a few, and study skills for most. And he talked about what he sees as the best role for a reading specialist. He reveals below several clues that explain the evasiveness that Joan found so frustrating:

I'm not sure what a reading specialist could do working in my classes, because you have to know the material. Joan was originally trained as a social studies teacher, so I think she could help out in those areas. But to teach science, you have to be trained as a scientist. Another problem is that I don't like to plan more than a few days ahead. Scheduling lesson plans with someone else just won't work for me. What I would really like is to have the lowest ones—the learning-disabled students, who are reading around the third-grade level—out of my classes all together because I don't have the time and attention to give them. That's how Joan could be the most useful.

Commentary

Dixie Snow Huefner.   The consulting teacher model is not an easy one to implement. It demands of its participants high degrees of commitment, solid preparation and training, and skilled communication. Different kinds of organizational support and some additional consulting skills would have helped make Joan's intervention more successful. Here are what I see as some of the prerequisites for successful implementation of the model.

The first is willing participation. Since the role of the consulting teacher is sometimes viewed by regular teachers as suspect, I would not work in this capacity with any teacher who had not *volunteered* to participate. In one way or another, Harold, John, and Mary were all reluctant participants who viewed Joan's role differently than she did. Mary, for example, did not believe that individualization inside the regular classroom was possible, an attitude that threatens the success of the consulting teacher model from the onset. Harold did not want to team teach, and he especially did not want to give up his planning period. He just wanted the reading teacher to take over some of his responsibilities. John was skeptical about the usefulness of anyone not trained in the sciences. Pleasant comments about the reading teacher notwithstanding, none of these teachers was eager to work with another teacher. Experience teaches us that reluctant or coerced participation is an invitation to failure.

The second prerequisite to success is inservice training as a team. I would encourage inservice training of the consulting team prior to the initiation of the model. The primary purpose of the training would be to reach consensus about the team's goals and its commitments of time and energy to the model. Pitfalls could be anticipated and strategies for their minimization discussed prior to experiencing them firsthand. A facilitator experienced with the model could be useful in helping the team to develop its own procedures, as could visits to successful consulting teams and classrooms. Role playing, simulations, and videotapes of consultation sessions could help the team anticipate problems and might suggest models for their resolution. The team should agree on the general stages of model implementation—for example, observing and identifying students to be served by the team, identifying the regular teachers' and consulting teachers' strengths that are appropriate for that child, changing the teaching interventions, and establishing mechanisms for evaluating the progress of each child accepted for consultation. The team could also design, in advance, procedures for sharing frustrations and rewards with one another. What emerges from the inservice preparation should be the team's own plan for their consulting teacher model and a willingness to share accountability for the measurable progress (or lack thereof) of each child served.

A third ingredient for success is placing the focus on individual children rather than on the classroom in general. That is, the consulting teacher should focus on the child or children about whom he or she is consulting, not on the classroom teacher's control and effectiveness with the class in general. Similarly, the classroom teacher's focus should be on the child, not on the consulting teacher. Thus the goal of collaboration is to achieve consensus on what strategies are worth implementing and to decide who does what in order to implement them. Teaching new skills to one another is not the primary purpose of the model but only an incidental means to an end. Therefore I would resist pressure to use the consulting teacher model as a covert way to improve the teaching or classroom management skills of a teacher whom the principal wants "beefed up." Teachers know how to read such motivations and resist them. It was Joan's perception that the principal saw Harold and John as weak teachers and encouraged Joan's presence in their classrooms as a way to help them improve their overall teaching. If a principal believes that a teacher needs help, the principal should communicate that information to the teacher directly and be responsible for the remediation. A consulting teacher is not a teacher remediator in disguise.

One of the greatest concerns teachers have about collaboration is the time it will take. Teachers cannot consult in their "spare" time. Harold did not want to give up his planning period but was happy to be freed from the classroom while Joan was there. John changed his class schedule without informing Joan. Mary changed the ground rules on her tests without notifying Joan. Each of these behaviors reflects the reality that most teachers are busy and their time is precious and limited. Lack of time for consultation is a serious problem that must be addressed if the consulting teacher model is to succeed. Somehow, additional time must be set aside each week for planning and feedback sessions. In all likelihood it must come from time that would otherwise be spent with students. This issue is a serious one and not addressed well in the education literature.

Another prerequisite to implementation of the consulting teacher model is training in communication skills. Although highly desirable for all involved, it is particularly necessary for the consulting teacher, who is the potential "interloper." Any implied (or explicit) criticism of the regular teacher is likely to be counterproductive. The consulting teacher initially must be able to identify what is going right and what the regular teacher's goals are and then must build on both. He or she must also be able to describe the observed needs of the child in a straightforward, nonjudgmental manner and to suggest alternative means to meet those needs, acknowledge that they may not succeed, make joint decisions about which to try first, and agree on the time period for giving them a chance to work.

All participants have to minimize their own needs in the interest of solving the child's needs. It is difficult even for mature and skilled teachers to do this, since all of us feel vulnerable and inadequate at times. It cannot be stressed enough that the consulting teaching model is *not* one of a person with superior skills entering a classroom to help someone whose skills are inadequate. Rather, it is one of a person, whose training and skills may be different and whose involvement may be more detached, coming in to *team* with a teacher—a person who must help determine and critique the strategies used and who appreciates someone else's perspective and can tap another's willingness to lend a hand.

Realistically, one should not expect too much from the model. The expectations must be manageable, and an incremental increase in the rate of progress in individual children is a sufficient goal. Spillover effects of success, if any, to the classroom as a whole are incidental, not the primary focus. Finally, I would like to suggest that some schools and teachers will be unable to implement a consulting teacher model successfully, even if district leadership supports it fully. Communication and trust among equals are at the heart of this model; any one participant can undermine its success simply by not communicating his or her thoughts and feelings, by not treating others as peers, by not following through, or by any number of other means. Part of the role of school administrators is to know when *not* to attempt to implement the model.

CONCLUSION

As a result of analyzing this case, we can learn a great deal about the conditions that facilitate or inhibit educational change in general and implementation of the consulting teacher model in particular. First, it reveals the kinds of skills and knowledge a specialist will need before assuming the role of consulting teacher. Second, it should help us understand how the climate of a school and teachers' concerns, needs, and beliefs, affect their attitudes toward change. And third, it should help us develop realistic goals and plans of action, which a consulting teacher could use as a starting point to initiate and maintain collaborative relationships.

However, as useful as cases are in learning, there is the possibility that they can be misused. The main concern with using this case, as with any case study in research, is the question of generalizability. Case studies, like experiments, are generalizable only to theoretical propositions, not to populations (Yin, 1984). In other words, as vivid and memorable as the individuals in the case may be, they are not representative of all reading specialists or content-area teachers. Furthermore, the conditions under which these individuals worked and interacted are unique to their situation. What a case study does produce is a picture of some phenomenon in its real-life context, which enables us to understand and perhaps explain events, processes, or decisions; but it does not enable us to predict the underlying motivations or behaviors of individuals.

REFERENCES

Bean, R. M. (1979). Role of the reading specialist: A multifaceted dilemma. *The Reading Teacher, 32,* 409–413.

Carnegie Forum on Education and the Economy. (1986). *A nation prepared: Teachers for the 21st century* (Report of the Task Force on Teaching as a Profession). Hyattsville, MD: Author.

Herber, H. L. (1978). *Teaching reading in the content areas.* Englewood Cliffs, NJ: Prentice-Hall.

Holmes Group. (1986). *Tomorrow's teacher.* East Lansing, MI: Author.

Huefner, D. S. (1988). The consulting teacher model: Risks and opportunities. *Exceptional Children, 54,* 403–414.

O'Brien, D. G., & Stewart, R. A. (1990). Preservice teachers' perspectives on why every teacher is *not* a teacher of reading: A qualitative analysis. *JRB: A Journal of Literacy, 22,* 101–129.

Pikulski, J. J., & Ross, E. (1979). Classroom teachers' perceptions of the role of the reading specialist. *Journal of Reading, 23,* 126–135.

Ratekin, N., Simpson, M. L., Alvermann, D. E., & Dishner, E. K. (1985). Why teachers resist content reading instruction. *Journal of Reading, 28,* 432–437.

Reynolds, M. C., Wang, M. C., & Walberg, H. J. (1987). The necessary restructuring of special and regular education. *Exceptional Children, 53,* 391–398.

Wade, S. E. (1984). *A case study of reading in the content areas.* Unpublished doctoral dissertation, Harvard University Graduate School of Education, Cambridge, MA.

Will, M. C. (1986). Educating children with learning problems: A shared responsibility. *Exceptional Children, 52,* 411–415.

Yin, R. K. (1984). *Case study research: Design and methods.* Beverly Hills, CA: Sage Publications.

CHAPTER 6

Toward a Cognitive Conception of Classroom Management

A Case of Teacher Comprehension

KATHY CARTER

> I think what you have to learn is how to deal with mental jumbling. You have to learn how to manage the . . . excuse the term . . . "mental mess" provided by all the action in the classroom and how to stay in control of yourself and the situation in such a way that it continues to be a productive learning situation. (Third-grade teacher from the University of Arizona Cooperating Teacher Project)

As this experienced teacher suggests, teachers engage in many sense-making activities each day in their classrooms. There is, in classroom life, simply so much that goes on, so much to monitor, so much to see and study, so much to interpret and comprehend.

Yet until recently research on classroom management has not focused on these intricate mental processes that teachers use to achieve and maintain conditions of effectiveness over long periods of time in classrooms. Rather, the focus has often been on discovering the discrete behaviors of teaching that are exhibited by effective teachers and on summarizing these behaviors into a set of principles for practice that teachers could utilize in planning for and organizing their classrooms. This research has been successful in identifying a number of characteristics common to the well-managed classroom and has been helpful in providing a base technology for teaching. It has not, however, been able to provide the more broad and fluid sketch of teaching that is necessary to convey the richness of teacher knowledge captured in the introductory quote of this chapter. The case presented in this chapter is an attempt to paint such a picture, a picture that emphasizes the careful thinking required of teachers as they manage classrooms.

This case is one of six cases I have developed to describe the different ways teachers understand their task of managing classrooms. These cases represent a deliberate effort to move away from describing fundamental actions for teaching and toward the representation of teaching as fundamentally a cognitive act. The cases, then, describe teachers' *comprehension* of classroom events and suggest that the different ways teachers interpret classroom events influence their actions, students' actions and reactions, and ultimately classroom histories in powerful ways.

CASE DEVELOPMENT

Each of the teacher comprehension cases was originally developed as a research activity that was part of a larger effort to understand how classrooms are managed. The teachers described in these cases were selected from a sample of 17 English teachers who participated in the Junior High Classroom Organization Study (JHCOS) conducted at the University of Texas R&D Center for Teacher Education. The data for each teacher consisted of 10 to 14 detailed narrative observations in each of two class periods. Observers were instructed to focus on classroom rules and procedures and on how activities were conducted. Observations were made throughout the year, with a concentration on the first 3 weeks of school.

Prior to the development of these cases of teacher comprehension, the entire sample of teachers in the larger JHCOS study were rated on selected indicators of management success (i.e., student success, amount of inappropriate behavior, amount of disruptive behavior, and task-oriented climate). Because success in management was a known quality for each of the teachers in the cases, it has been possible to formulate case descriptions about the patterns of activity management associated with "successful" cases compared with those discovered for the "less successful" managers.

STRUCTURE OF CASES

The written cases are presented in three sections. First, I provide a general description of the structures and processes in each of the teacher's classes. In this section of the case, I ask readers to move quickly into the daily life of the classroom teacher and his or her students and provide them with an analysis of typical activities, routines, and actions of the teacher. This description, which is the result of my analysis of hundreds of pages of narrative records, is the written picture of important patterns and trends that occurred in a particular context with a particular teacher and with a particular set of students. This contextual grounding is necessary for the careful study of the case. This description provides some clue to the question, "What instructional activities, routines, and teaching procedures were selected by the teacher, in part, to solve the problem of classroom order in this particular context?"

Next, I describe the teachers' reaction patterns as they go about carrying out their work of teaching amid the contingencies of everyday classroom life. This description provides a window to teachers' understandings of how they act in classroom environments to solve the problem of order when faced with the spontaneous and surprising events that sneak into everyday life in classrooms. This description, then, potentially uncovers for the reader the way a particular teacher views the problem of classroom management and reacts to unforeseen situations in light of that view.

Finally, I employ metaphor in the concluding section of each of the cases. Because recent studies on teaching have suggested that metaphors structure our thinking and affect our behavior (see, e.g., Carter, 1990b; Marshall, 1990; Munby & Russell, 1990; Tobin, 1990; Weade & Ernst, 1990), I have chosen metaphors as the vehicle to represent different ways the teachers comprehended their task of managing the classroom environment. These metaphors carry with them the opportunity to explore the functional value of different ways of thinking about classroom management.

It is important to note that the analyses in these particular cases are not separate from the cases themselves. In fact, the analysis *is* the case. The work of readers of the case, then, becomes to examine the analysis that has been presented in the cases, to use this analysis to reflect on their own understandings of classroom management, and to explore how different ways of comprehending classroom events might result in very different scenarios for daily life in classrooms.

CASE USE

Since the spring semester of 1987, I have used written cases of teacher comprehension in a graduate-level course I teach, the Supervision of Student Teachers (informally called the Cooperating Teacher course), offered in the Division of Teaching and Teacher Education at the University of Arizona. The course, which meets weekly for approximately 2½ hours, was originally designed as a part of an endeavor funded by the Office of Educational Research Improvement (OERI). My major goals for the course are to help cooperating teachers analyze their craft and reflect on their own knowledge of their teaching tasks, reveal to novices the complex decisions that are made in teaching, and suggest positive ways of thinking and acting in classrooms.

These course goals run parallel with the broad goals of case use recently being espoused for teacher education (see, e.g., Carter & Richardson, 1988; Carter & Unklesbay, 1989; Doyle, 1990; J. Shulman & Colbert, 1989; L. Shulman, 1986) as well as my earlier (Carter, 1990a) stated goals for the other cases of teachers' comprehension of classroom management that I have developed to date. Each semester the Cooperating Teacher course has been offered, I have devoted class sessions to the presentation and analysis of these cases. To date, I have asked students to read the cases prior to designated class sessions and to be prepared to use these cases as stimuli to unpack publicly, through talking aloud with colleague teachers, their own understandings of the task of classroom management. Specifically, I ask students in the course (who are all practicing teachers) to discuss the cases of classroom management and to try to call up and capture, through the use of metaphor, their own ways of thinking about classrooms. Finally, the cases are used as models by these course participants/practicing teachers in the development of their own written cases of their student teachers' models of comprehending classroom events (see Carter, 1990b, for a more complete description of cooperating teachers' development of cases using metaphor).

It is important to note that prior to assigning the cases for study, I provide some guidelines to course participants about how a case should be read. This has been necessary because students in the course have indicated that responding to a classroom-based case is radically different from the tasks typically required in other college courses.

I carefully caution course participants against reading the cases in order to find "right answers" to recall on tests. Rather, I ask them to view the cases as pedagogical puzzles, puzzles that grow increasingly more complex as they are reread and analyzed. I ask participants to read the cases with a critical but objective eye, an eye that is keen to explore what different events may mean to the participants described in the cases.

I also ask readers to bring to the study of these cases both heart and mind. I ask them to consider not simply what they might *do* in the contexts described by the cases, but additionally and especially how they might feel and think about the problems that the teacher in the case confronts over the course of the schoolyear. As readers come to know the teacher through the text, I challenge them to ask themselves how different teachers' personal understandings of classroom situations may lead to very different effects on the quality of classroom life.

Similarly, I preface the subsequent discussions of the case materials with guidelines about the desired kind of quality of classroom conversations about the cases. Specifically, I ask participants to monitor any inclination to reduce the discussion to judgmental statements about what teachers in the cases "should" have done in those circumstances, simplify teacher or student behaviors to emotionally laden labels, or offer a quick-fix solution to the problem of classroom order (even if they are "research-based" solutions). The focus of the discussion, then, is on understanding the nature of classroom management and on asking why teachers may have reacted in the ways they did to problems that presented themselves regularly in their classrooms. This demand for analytical discussion requires viewing the study of teaching as an intellectual activity and calls upon students to become conversant with the growing literature of research on teaching. I will provide more specific details about the way case discussions are framed following the presentation of the case in this chapter.

THE CASE OF MS. ROBIN

The case that follows is a case of a teacher who was known to be an effective manager. But as I have suggested, this case is not meant to be an illustration of "good" teaching behaviors. Rather, the case provides both a close-up look at the dilemmas a successful teacher faced and an analysis that illustrates how her actions can be connected to a way of comprehending the task of classroom management.

Background Information

As has been noted, data for Ms. Robin suggested that she was an "effective" manager and teacher. She was given a high overall rating of 5 on a 5-point scale for her management ability, and students in both her classes were able to improve their academic standing. Observers in this teacher's classes regularly commented in their narratives on the warmth, caring, and "sweet tone" that characterized her style and on the general feeling of mutual respect between the teacher and her students.

Observations were made in two of Ms. Robin's seventh-grade classes, a fourth-period low-ability class and a sixth-period low-ability class. While some variations between classes were occasionally noted in observations, there were many more similarities than differences in the management of these two classes.

Format and Routines in Ms. Robin's Classes

On a representative day, Ms. Robin would clearly signal the beginning of class even *before* the tardy bell rang by warning, "The bell is about to ring," "It's nearly time for the bell," or, "You should already be in your seats because the bell is about to ring." As soon as the bell *did* ring, Ms. Robin would typically greet the class as a group and quickly announced that she was checking roll. If students continued to talk, she would let them know verbally or nonverbally that she was "waiting" until they were quiet to proceed with roll call. If students still persisted with their talk, she would say "timing" and begin to watch a large wall clock (which she claimed kept perfect time) until students were quiet. Students learned quickly that "timing" meant they would have to remain after class for whatever amount of time the teacher had to wait for them to get quiet. If worksheets or papers needed to be distributed, Ms. Robin would generally ask two students to do so as she checked attendance.

Ms. Robin emphasized the importance of getting to class on time and being prepared to work. If she herself was ever late to class or spent, in her words, "too long" in checking roll, she profusely apologized to students for using up "this valuable time."

As I will soon demonstrate, Ms. Robin demanded high levels of student participation during work activities, regardless of their type, and used a number of techniques to insure that students proceeded efficiently through what appeared to be a carefully planned course of action. Ms. Robin's voice signaled when activities would start and stop, and transitions generally lasted 1 minute or less.

Ms. Robin did not often allow students to cease work prematurely in her classes. By winding down most class sessions with a teacher-led oral review, she positioned herself to be directly in charge of class closings. In several records, the observer noted that the teacher detained students for a few seconds following the bell in order to terminate the question/answer sequence typical of her oral reviews.

Ms. Robin exhibited a preference for keeping students focused on the content of the curriculum during all activities. Order problems did present themselves daily, but she appeared to focus her energies on guiding students through the curriculum. Inappropriate and disruptive incidents were cautiously downplayed, terminated, or sometimes ignored until they did not challenge the instructional activity. Ms. Robin often reacted to behavioral incidents by publicly renewing her push to get work done in a specified time period. Rather than focusing on students' behavior, she would remind students of the work they needed to complete. She might also accelerate the pace of oral activities or ask nonengaged students to show her their products during seatwork activities.

When reprimands *did* occur in Ms. Robin's classes, they were typically brief (e.g., "Bonnie" or "Dave," "waiting" or "timing") or took the form of rhetorical questions ("Gentlemen, are you listening?")

Ms. Robin also used a pattern of reprimands which conveyed her sentiments that students' behavior was quite disappointing to her and was "absolutely unbelievable in my classroom" (e.g. "Larry, the idea!!!"; "Class, this noise is unbelievable and unacceptable"). Reprimands were most severe when students were threatening the progress of the class as a group, when students arrived to class tardy, or when students were resisting work involvement and, to the teacher's mind, wasting valuable time.

Activities Established by Ms. Robin

Previous research has indicated that the behavior of students and teachers is affected by characteristics of different activities (see Doyle, 1986). In both of her classes, Ms. Robin organized work chiefly into three activity types:

1. *Oral content development,* wherein the teacher mixed content presentation with question/answer interactions about the content
2. *Seatwork activities,* wherein students were required to practice skills or apply concepts from the preceding oral activity
3. *Oral review activities,* wherein the teacher appeared to try to

gauge the level of students' understanding and provide them
with additional practice or explanations

Together, oral content development and oral review activities
accounted for 31 percent of observed class time in Ms. Robin's
fourth-period class and 22 percent of observed time in her sixth-
period class. Seatwork activities accounted for 41 percent and 45
percent of observed time in fourth-period and sixth-period classes,
respectively. Comparatively small percentages of time were spent in
other activity types.

Oral Content Development. Ms. Robin typically began each class
session by initiating an oral activity in which she intertwined content
presentation with question/answer interactions with students. Ms.
Robin consistently initiated these activities by moving to her overhead projector (located near the center, back of the room) and turning on its lamp. She quickly called students' attention to material on
the projected transparency ("Class, I'm going to write a sentence
here; watch this") or stood in silence while giving nonverbal cues to
suggest she was waiting for students to stop talking and give her
their attention. If students continued to talk, she initiated her "timing" routine (see previous discussion).

For all topic areas included in these oral activities (e.g., parts of
speech, history of the English language, mythology, grammatical
rules), Ms. Robin used the overhead projector to call students' attention to key ideas and to special information she wanted them to
remember. Especially at the beginning of the schoolyear, she issued
constant reminders that students should attend to the information
she wrote on the overhead transparency. On several occasions, she
asked students to copy material from the overhead and, in addition,
to circle or underline selected words or phrases that she felt would be
particularly important for them to know. If she felt students were
not attending well or were not understanding the material, she
would often attempt to "stop the action" just long enough to refocus
students' attention on her explanation ("Put your pencils down and
look").

When Ms. Robin called on individual students to respond to
content questions, she appeared to be unwilling to terminate the
interaction until she had some sense that the target student understood and was able to answer correctly. This meant that she often
persisted in order to get an answer from students whose first response was "I don't know" or who made several incorrect "guesses."

She occasionally provided heavy prompts to these students if their struggling slowed the pace of the activity and often asked them or the entire class to repeat in chorus the concept or grammatical rule on which the desired answer was based.

In an illustrative incident, Ms. Robin attempted to reinforce a previously taught rule about a word and a certain part of speech. After having called on Jessie, who was unable to recall what part of speech *is* is, Ms. Robin had the class repeat *"Is* is always a verb" a number of times. Students chanted along with the student, *"Is* is always a verb, repeat, *is* is always a verb, repeat, *is* is always a verb, repeat . . ."* until Ms. Robin appeared satisfied that they would remember this piece of information. Interestingly, later in the year, when a different student was asked during a review to identify the part of speech for the word *is*, his answer was, *"Is* is always a verb, repeat."

Ms. Robin clearly orchestrated the pace of these oral activities so that they were characterized by regular movement. She managed these activities in such a way that disruptions or interruptions were minimized. She made it quite clear that she expected students to participate in oral activities and that she was unwilling to tolerate interruptions or student comments that would take them away from the content they were covering.

This unwillingness to spend time in directions other than those she planned can be seen in an example from a February narrative describing Ms. Robin's fourth-period class. In this activity, she was attempting to demonstrate rules about possessive forms. When the possessive of *Zeus* was in question, students suggested they were more interested in talking about the myth of Zeus than about possessive forms. Having tolerated a few callouts of this order, Ms. Robin said, "I don't want to talk about the myth; I want to talk about *this*" (pointing to the examples of possessive forms on her transparency), and quickly proceeded to the next example.

Unexpected interruptions were quickly handled as well. Ms. Robin consistently focused her attention on the group's movement and directed the flow of events so that individuals were quickly brought into the group. For example, when Walt entered the room while an oral activity was in progress, the teacher said, "Sit down unobtrusively, Walt, and put the note on the desk," and continued, without pause, her discussion of the content being considered. Ms. Robin seemed publicly to celebrate the effect of reprimands and the minimal amount of time she had to take to monitor inappropriate or disruptive behavior. When reprimands "worked" (and they generally did), Ms. Robin often paused momentarily and said "thank you," signaling the end of an unwanted interruption. She then moved easily again into academic interactions with students.

Seatwork Activities.   Seatwork activities were installed with considerable efficiency by Ms. Robin. In fact, it was often difficult to observe actual endings of oral activities because Ms. Robin would use the same patterns of question/answer interactions observed during oral activities to illustrate to students how to accomplish the first few examples of the written work they were to do. Ms. Robin would work through these examples with students and would then announce, for example, "I'm very pleased; let's go on from there"; "You're on your own, now"; or "The rest are yours." However, it should be noted that the teacher did not simply turn the work over to students; rather, she hovered over these activities and guided their flow and direction. After seatwork activities were underway, she would generally announce a timeframe for their completion and would issue "status checks" about where students should be in reference to the passing time.

Ms. Robin was visible throughout seatwork activities and regularly circulated to check students' work and progress and to comment on the neatness of their papers or their handwriting. In general, she seemed to prefer private contacts with students during seatwork activities, especially if the contact concerned a student's work or individual instances of misbehavior. However, she regularly made comments directed to the whole class if seatwork activities were going particularly well ("Look at all this work that is getting done"; "We're really clipping along now"; "Y'all really have a handle on this; I'm just sure we can move on to adverbs.") *or* if seatwork activities were becoming sluggish or student engagement appeared to be at undesirable levels ("I take it by all of this talking that all of you are through"; "Only 1½ minutes, so keep busy.")

Students were not allowed to hand in their work if they finished early. Ms. Robin spotted early finishers quickly and suggested that they either review their papers, check them for neatness, place them in the appropriate place in the notebook they were required to keep, or solve a "seek-and-find" puzzle that she would give them after they had shown that the written assignment had been completed. She let students know that she would call for all of their papers at the same time.

In summary, oral content development activities and seatwork activities in Ms. Robin's classes were tied closely in content and in theme. Skills required for task accomplishment were typically routine or recall, and work was characterized by continuity and efficiency. Students in both of Ms. Robin's classes tended to chatter during seatwork activities, but she was able to push students through the curriculum by her attention to the content and to accountability for accomplishing work within a specific time frame.

Oral Review Activities.   Ms. Robin directed the close of seatwork activities so that there was a type of natural progression into oral review activities. Oral review activities were brief and were typically the last activities installed in the class session. When several students began to complete their written work in the previous seatwork activities, Ms. Robin would begin to issue time warnings to let students know that it would soon be time to check their work. As the time to terminate seatwork grew closer, these time warnings became more frequent and more explicit ("only 1½ minutes"; "60 seconds"; "31 seconds"). When time was up, Ms. Robin returned to her overhead projector, projected a replica of the students' worksheet or assignment, and called on students to supply correct answers. Answers generally took the form of "right" or "wrong" answers, and the teacher directed these activities so that their pace was rapid and interactions were brief. Ms. Robin would frequently ask, "Let me see hands—how many got that right?" or "Did anyone miss that one?" or "Any problems here?"

Ms. Robin seemed successfully to time these activities so that they terminated seconds before or after the bell to end class. In the latter case, Ms. Robin required that students remain in their seats until she ended the review and officially dismissed them.

In summary, the three common activities Ms. Robin chose to initiate were tied together both substantively and procedurally. In each activity Ms. Robin carefully pursued a program of action (see Doyle, 1986) that promoted progress through the curriculum and minimized the effect of interruption and competing interests.

TEACHER REACTION PATTERNS

In the previous section I described the overall structures and programs of action that Ms. Robin established to solve the problem of order in her classes. I now turn attention to an analysis of how this teacher reacted to specific events that occurred as she created and maintained these structures and action programs. The focus, in other words, is on what Ms. Robin reacted to and talked about as she tried to hold activity systems in place in her classes. As I will attempt to illustrate in the final section, knowledge of these reaction patterns is especially useful in constructing comprehension models that account for the "solution strategies" that Ms. Robin used.

The data suggest that Ms. Robin achieved order primarily by concentrating on a program of action that maintained activity flow and kept the group of students moving through the work. Much of what this teacher did can be interpreted as reactions to (1) sluggishness in the work system, (2) unevenness in the production of the work, and (3) persistent digressive student behaviors (i.e., those behaviors that did not easily coexist with the teacher's intended program of action and that, if unchecked, could threaten its durability).

Sluggishness in the Work System

Ms. Robin's actions suggest that she was acutely aware of signs that suggested a loss of group vigor or energy in work progress. Her reactions suggest that she saw slow progress as a serious threat to the life of the work system she attempted to establish and maintain. She watched for early signs of students' nonengagement of passive participation and appeared to react especially to signs that individual off-task students might "link" with other nonengaged students. In these cases, she attempted to pull such students back into the work system by reminding them to "keep busy," by alerting them to the passing time, or by asking if they were having problems she could help them with.

Unevenness in Production

Ms. Robin also attended to signs that students were covering the content or accomplishing the work at uneven rates. In both oral and seatwork activities, she regularly reminded all students alike exactly what they should be focusing on or approximately where they should be in their work or thinking. By continuously supplying such strong signals as "Class, look at this!" or "Students, what is the title of this selection?" or "Everybody, circle this phrase on your papers" or "Put down your pencils until I can see that we're together," Ms. Robin clearly exhibited a preference for orchestrating movement at a group level. In an illustrative incident (one of several similar ones), Ms. Robin clearly informed a student that she was quite unhappy with him when he was proceeding without the group and ignoring her explicit direction to begin ("I think you're being extremely rude today; I haven't told you to start yet").

Persistent Digressive Student Behaviors

Ms. Robin consistently created an either/or work setting for students. *Either* students were attending to the academic work she set up and secured in activity systems *or they were not.* Because she typically set up activities so that only one specified and sanctioned set of actions should exist at a time, participation requirements were consistently clear-cut. A few students, however, periodically resisted Ms. Robin's attempts at group movement and cohesion and would attempt to carry out their own competing agendas (by calling out about unrelated matters during oral activities, asking side-issue questions during seatwork activities, and the like). Initially, Ms. Robin reacted to these students indirectly—by emphasizing the work and reclarifying what students were supposed to be doing. She appeared to monitor but ignore these students until she felt that their actions or behavior might seriously threaten the activity system. It was then that her reactions became quite public and direct. For example, during an oral activity, Gary, a visible student, called out a number of times before Ms. Robin stated, "No, Gary, I'm sick of being interrupted." During a seatwork activity, a student's chatter had been allowed to exist until it apparently reached levels intolerable to Ms. Robin, and she stated, "All right, just notice, Michael isn't doing anything." Interestingly, Ms. Robin did not consistently reprimand individual students for breaking classroom rules like sharpening pencils or throwing away trash during class time (items that were to be handled *only* before or after the bell rang to start or end class) *unless* these infractions took place when an academic activity was being initiated or was already underway. Students could "break the rules" during brief transitions or on those rare occasions when the teacher allowed free time, but they were severely reprimanded for infractions that occurred when work was being accomplished.

ORGANIZING PRINCIPLES
IN UNDERSTANDING CLASSROOMS

Ms. Robin's broad understanding of the task of classroom management can be summarized in terms of an organizing metaphor and several principles consistent with that metaphor. When coupled with the previous description of how order was achieved in her classes, I believe this metaphor provides a rich picture of her comprehension processes.

Much of what Ms. Robin does appears to reflect a conception of her role as pathfinder and pacesetter. These metaphors carry with them a sense of directed group movement, regulation, and tempo. In addition, these metaphors suggest that the teacher viewed herself as someone guiding an entity separate from herself, that is, the classroom activity system. This is consistent with the teacher's emphasis on directing and sustaining work along planned programs of action.

At least five general principles would seem to follow from this perspective on management.

1. Classrooms are places where competing agendas must be resolved.
2. Resolving these competing agendas requires the teacher to soften or subdue competing interests in order to get the group moving together.
3. Paths through the curriculum are best selected by the teacher, and movement along these paths is accomplished through his or her constant direction and guidance.
4. Order does not ever completely come about; it is a daily task that must be deliberately managed with attention to pacing and forward movement.
5. An uneasy tension often exists between content coverage and classroom order. When this tension appears, a teacher must be prepared to pull digressive students into the group, to set the pace to ensure progress, and to make public the ground that is being/has been covered.

In summary, Ms. Robin seemed to understand the classroom as a problem space where order must be achieved so that progress can be made and work systems can operate. She appeared to plan for, attend to, and react to signals that students were not proceeding along the pathways she prescribed or moving at the pace she desired.

It is important to note that Ms. Robin's preoccupation with activity flow and group movement sometimes meant that the cognitive demands of the work students did were reduced and emphasis was placed on routine and recall responses. Keeping the group moving together often meant heavy prompting, selective attention to lower-order tasks, and "slippage" in the demands of the academic work. Moreover, students' individual reflections and comments or thoughts about the work had to be downplayed in an effort to focus on group interests and the production system.

FRAMING THE DISCUSSION OF THE CASE OF MS. ROBIN

At this point, it may be helpful to provide more detail about the way case discussions of teacher comprehension are framed for the Cooperating Teacher course. I typically devote a 2½ hour class session to the analysis of each case, organizing case discussions around four tasks:

1. Assess the utility of principles of practice that might be extracted from the case (or that might be derived from the effective-teaching literature and applied to the case)
2. Critique how well the selected metaphor fits the case description
3. Generate and discuss alternate metaphors that might illustrate different ways of thinking about classroom management
4. Role-play conversations with student teachers in which cooperating teachers attempt to convey, through their own metaphors, their understandings of the task of classroom management

In this section, I will briefly discuss each of these four tasks with reference to the case of Ms. Robin.

1. *Assess the utility of principles of practice.* Typically, I find that participants in the course are quite eager to identify practices that they felt contributed to a teacher's managerial success or downfall. For example, in discussing the case of Ms. Robin, I ask cooperating teachers why they thought this teacher was successful as a classroom manager. Teachers quickly point out Ms. Robin's "waiting" and "timing" routines, her efficiency in checking attendance, her consistency in taking clear control of the pacing and sequence of activities, and her careful control of class dismissal. As responses are put forward, I attempt to avoid judgments (although I will sometimes ask for clarifications) and prompt participants with the question, "Anything more?" As long as responses are forthcoming, I attempt to record them on the chalkboard.

Once nominations of "successful practices" are exhausted, I ask the teachers to discuss other research-based practices for classroom management and to make a case for how they might be helpful to the teacher in the case in solving the problem of order. I then ask teachers to examine the utility of these practices as exemplary practices for other teachers to follow. During the discussion, I ask participants to make statements about how fully these practices account for Ms. Robin's managerial success. Moreover, I ask them to explore the degree to which principles for action or prescriptions for practice sufficiently convey the task of classroom management and the means by which teachers solve the problem of order. It is generally at this juncture that the conversation takes some interesting turns, and the initial enthusiasm for listing practices is lessened as teachers begin to point out the caveats around each possible prescription that might be drawn from the data. For example, cooperating teachers often pose problems that would be encountered if they or their student teachers attempted to emulate Ms. Robin's practices in their own classrooms. In addition, the teachers are able to draw upon their own teaching histories and situational knowledge to present other interesting contingencies. As the class carefully explores their list of effective practices in light of these contingencies, a case that may have initially seemed straightforward becomes increasingly complex. Typically, teachers come to argue that classroom management is "more than a matter of doing things, anyway" and that Ms. Robin's "success'" was largely due to a conception she had of how a classroom could be run with efficiency. It is here that I pose a turn in the conversation, asking the class to consider the utility of the metaphorical model of the teacher's comprehension in order to try to capture some of the cognitive aspects of classroom management.

2. *Critique how well the selected metaphor fits the case description.* Because the cases of teacher comprehension have been developed from the theory that action and behavior generally follow from one's problem representation and situational understandings, I ask the teachers to critique the selection of a particular metaphor as a model of a particular teacher's understandings of classroom management. The teachers are told that while more than one metaphor might fit the data, their immediate task as students of the case is to determine, through their analysis and discussions, whether or not there is a good fit between the selected metaphor and the case data. This portion of the conversation is a way to challenge the teachers to logically connect a teacher's explicit actions to his or her implicit

understandings. In many ways, this dialogue serves as a "dry run" for the teachers' examination of how their own actions are connected to their understandings of the task of classroom management.

3. *Generate and discuss alternative metaphors for teachers' comprehension of classroom management.* Next, I ask the teachers to extend their analogical thinking beyond the particular case under study and to suggest other metaphors that would communicate alternative conceptions of the task of classroom management. This portion of the conversation is generally quite lively. Importantly, I ask the teachers to hold one another accountable to "a thorough rendering" of the metaphor, including the understandings the creator of the metaphor hopes it communicates and the patterns of action one would expect to observe if a teacher understood the task of classroom management in the manner modeled by the metaphor. As different metaphors are posed, I (as well as the teachers in the course) use questions to provoke thinking about whether a particular way of comprehending classroom management is uniformly functional even when different goals for teaching are specified. For example, in the case of Ms. Robin, the teachers often come to argue that her way of understanding classroom management was clearly quite functional for gaining and sustaining the cooperation of students and for moving students efficiently through the curriculum, but probably would be considerably less functional if a teacher wished to gear the students' cognitive responses to more generative and creative thinking or wanted to socialize students into controlling and constructing their own learning. Importantly, as we study additional written cases of teacher comprehension, these cases are also referenced and discussed so that planned comparisons can be carefully made to explore alternate ways of understanding classroom management.[1]

4. *Role-play conversations with student teachers.* Finally, I ask participants to role-play conversations with their student teachers. Specifically, I ask the teachers to construct metaphors that they feel represent their own understandings of the task of classroom management and to practice carrying out a conversation aimed at communicating their comprehension of classroom management to a novice. Cooperating teachers find this task both difficult and useful, with practice, most note that they find the conversations somewhat less difficult to design. They also report communicating richer information about classroom management than they feel they have been able to provide

to novices in the past. As has been noted, over the course of the semester cooperating teachers also develop written cases of their student teachers' comprehension of classroom management and use these cases with metaphor to engage student teachers in an analytical conversation about classroom management (See Carter, 1990b, for an exploratory evaluation of using case with metaphor in mentor-novice conversations).

POSSIBILITIES AND PROMISE IN THE USE OF CASES

Rarely do teachers have the opportunity to examine their own thinking and to talk about their understandings with other teachers. Rather, the focus of much of staff development, personnel evaluation, and talk about school improvement is often on changing teacher actions rather than considering how teachers' conceptions of teaching are connected to what they do in classrooms. It is hard to imagine that teachers can improve their craft, as many wish to do, if they are not provided the opportunity to examine different ways of thinking about their problems. It is equally hard to imagine that this can be accomplished if the work of teachers is continually reduced to the rhetoric of prescriptions for practice and not regarded as an intellectual activity, that must be supported and sustained by the profession (see Conley & Bacharach, 1991; Griffin, in press; Richardson, 1990).

Cases may be a way for smart conversations about teaching to emerge within the ranks of practicing teachers and also a way to engage novices in an understanding of the contingencies and complexities of teaching. In the long run, studying cases of teacher comprehension of classroom processes such as management may enable teacher educators at preservice and inservice levels to present classroom practices as an organized system of thinking and acting, analyze more systematically the practices they observe in classrooms, and confront the preconceptions teachers have about how classroom order and learning are established and maintained.

NOTE

1. The planned comparison case for Ms. Robin is the case of Ms. Dove, a teacher who had serious problems with classroom management. The metaphor used to model Ms. Dove's comprehension of classroom manage-

ment, "gentle persuader and arbiter of adult conscience," attempts to capture Ms. Dove's understanding that the classroom is a place where the teacher must work hard to "win over" students with soft persuasion and must reason with them as individuals so that they behave as adults. Interestingly, this way of thinking was reflected in Ms. Dove's concerted attempts to help individuals adopt more adult-like attitudes. Indeed, Ms. Dove's efforts to help individuals got carried out to the extent that the classroom group rarely moved cohesively through any part of the intended curriculum. (See Carter, 1991, for the presentation and discussion of this case.)

REFERENCES

Carter, K. (1990a). Teachers' knowledge and learning to teach. In R. Houston (Ed.), *Handbook of research on teacher education* (pp. 291–310). New York: Macmillan.

Carter, K. (1990b). Meaning and metaphor: Case knowledge in teaching. *Theory into Practice, 29,* 109–115.

Carter, K. (1991). Creating a teacher work environment for the development of classroom knowledge. In S. Conley & B. Cooper (Eds.), *The school as a work environment: Implications for reform* (pp. 43–64). New York: Allyn & Bacon.

Carter, K., & Richardson, V. (1988). Toward a curriculum for initial year of teacher programs. *Elementary School Journal, 89,* 405–419.

Carter, K., & Unklesbay, R. (1989). Cases in teaching and law. *Journal of Curriculum Studies, 21,* 527–536.

Conley, S., & Bacharach, S. (1991). From school site management to participatory school site management. In S. Conley & B. Cooper (Eds.), *The school as a work environment: Implications for reform* (pp. 127–140). New York: Allyn & Bacon.

Doyle, W. (1986). Classroom organization and management. In M. C. Wittrock (Ed.), *Handbook of research on teaching* (3rd ed.) (pp. 392–431). New York: Macmillan.

Doyle, W. (1990). Case methods in the education of teachers. *Teacher Education Quarterly, 17,* 7–15.

Griffin, G. (in press). The future of teachers and teaching: Imperatives and possibilities. *Peabody Journal of Education.*

Marshall, H. (1990). Metaphor as an instructional tool in encouraging student teacher reflection. *Theory into Practice, 29,* 128–132.

Munby, H., & Russell, T. (1990). Metaphor in the study of teachers' professional knowledge. *Theory into Practice, 29,* 116–121.

Richardson, V. (1990). Significant and worthwhile change in teaching practice. *Educational Researcher, 19,* 10–18.

Shulman, J., & Colbert, J. (1989). Cases as catalysts for cases: Inducing reflection in teacher education. *Action in Teacher Education, 11,* 44–52.

Shulman, L. (1986). Those who understand: Knowledge growth in teaching. *Educational Researcher, 15*, 4–14.

Tobin, K. (1990). Changing metaphors and beliefs: A master switch for teaching. *Theory into Practice, 29*, 122–127.

Weade, R., & Ernst, G. (1990). Pictures of life in classrooms, and the search for metaphors to frame them. *Theory into Practice, 29*, 133–140.

CHAPTER 7

Teacher-Written Cases With Commentaries
A Teacher–Researcher Collaboration

JUDITH H. SHULMAN

Recently I received a phone call from a chemistry professor at a major university. She asked if I would read some cases and journals that she had collected from teachers as part of a 2-year grant to provide support for "crossover teachers" into science. The intent was to produce a casebook written by participating teachers that could be used as a training tool for other institutions. It was now the end of the first year, the teachers had recently submitted their long-awaited cases, and the staff had read them—with much disappointment. Since there was time to make changes in the program for the next year, the external evaluator had suggested involving me as a consultant.

After reading sample narratives, I knew why I had been asked to help. Though the project's case-writing guidelines had been adapted from materials I had created for one of my casebooks (Shulman & Colbert, 1988), these narratives were superficial, sparse, unfocused, and boring. Moreover, it was difficult to find any particular value in them for prospective *science* teachers. The teacher-authors rarely embedded their narratives in a particular event or series of events as the guidelines suggested. And when they did, there was not enough detail or complexity to learn from or to stimulate a discussion.

When I conveyed my impressions to the principal investigator, she was not surprised. She too thought the narratives were superficial and had concluded that the problem lay with these particular teachers—they simply could not write. As we examined the circumstances under which the teachers wrote their narratives, however, she realized that she and her staff had to assume much of the responsibility. They had provided no support or feedback to the teachers during the entire year.

I begin this chapter with the above story because it highlights two contradictory misconceptions among teacher educators about who should write teaching cases. The pessimists argue that teachers are unsuitable as authors because they cannot write narratives complex and compelling enough to be used for teaching purposes. The optimists, like the professor in the above story, believe that teachers can just sit down and write appropriate teaching cases without much assistance.

Our experience in editing casebooks by teacher-practitioners suggests that the optimists and pessimists are both wrong. Many teachers can write compelling narratives that can be used as teaching cases, but they cannot do it alone. Teacher-authors need the continued support and guidance that comes from regular interactions with researchers and other teachers. They need to produce successive drafts, a process that helps them clarify the issues in the case, make explicit the implicit understandings and rationales, and discover ways to add or expand on details to make their narratives more vivid. When such collaborations occur, the writing process becomes a powerful learning experience for the authors. But more important, the resultant narratives are truly tools that can inform and educate new and experienced teachers.

What are the processes and skills involved in helping teachers write good teaching cases? How do you build layers of commentary that add richness to the original narratives? What can be learned from analyzing cases and commentaries? Who benefits from using cases? In what contexts? These are the questions addressed in this chapter.

I will argue that teacher-written cases can and should serve as an important part of the curriculum in preservice, inservice, and graduate teacher education, as a way of understanding the wisdom of practice from the "insider's" perspective. The past few years have brought an increasing awareness of the importance of hearing "the teacher's voice" (McDonald, 1986; Shulman, 1989; Munby and Russell, 1990). Yet, with few exceptions (e.g., Allen, 1990; Ashton-Warner, 1963; Paley, 1979; Shulman & Colbert, 1987, 1988; Shulman & Mesa-Bains, 1990), teachers' voices are generally heard in researchers' and, occasionally, veteran teachers' translations (see Kleinfeld, Chapter 2, this volume) through the medium of case studies.

The case presented at the end of this chapter is written by an intern teacher. It is one in a series of cases I have published by new and experienced teachers (see below). I will excerpt these other cases when I examine both our collaborative process of developing cases and our procedures for building layers of commentary. Before we get to individual cases, however, I will offer a brief history of our project.

BACKGROUND

For the past several years, I have been working on an evolving conception of teacher-authored cases as a way to contribute to the literature on teaching. It began when I used research-based vignettes about mentor-colleague relationships (Shulman, Hanson, & King, 1985) with mentors and administrators during staff development meetings. I found that they served as powerful catalysts to stimulate discussion about issues concerning the new role of mentor teachers.

This experience prompted a new scope of work at Far West Laboratory (FWL)—a close-to-the-classroom casebook series with narratives by practicing teachers. The initial volume would focus on mentor teachers. We felt that teachers could contribute to the literature on teaching if they were given proper support and that teacher writings had the potential to be even more powerful than those of researchers. After looking at teaching cases in professions such as law, business, and medicine, I could not find any that were written by practitioners. So I set out to create a mentor-written casebook without a clear conception of what a casebook was.

The resulting volume, *The Mentor Teacher Casebook* (Shulman & Colbert, 1987), represented a collaboration between a district resource teacher, Joel Colbert,[1] 22 mentor teachers from the Los Angeles Unified School District who were taking a course from Colbert, and myself. The volume was intended to improve the district's 30-hour mentor training program. I was particularly interested in focusing on the relationship between a mentor and his or her colleagues. But because of the collaborative nature of the project—mentors would help determine the narrative's topics—the casebook provides a much broader perspective on the complexity of the mentor role (see Shulman & Colbert, 1989, for a description of this project).

During the following year, Colbert and I embarked on a new project, *The Intern Teacher Casebook* (Shulman & Colbert, 1988). We wanted to develop a book that included cases written by new teachers who were each assigned a mentor. This book had a more structured organization than the first. Unlike the mentor casebook, we knew what kinds of dilemmas we wanted this casebook to illustrate. Thus, rather than rely on a collaborative process with the teacher-writers to select appropriate topics, we wrote guidelines for five different kinds of cases that describe specific situations that confront all novices. Themes ranged from problematic instructional events to problems with individual groups of students. The authors were asked to describe the events, to reflect on their mishaps, and to consider alternative approaches for future teaching situations (see Shulman, 1989, for a discussion about this casebook). This book also added a new dimension—novices, mentors, teacher educators, and scholars wrote interpretive comments both on the original cases and on one another's comments.

In my most recent project (Shulman & Mesa-Bains, 1990), I worked with a group of veteran teachers to write cases about the challenges of working with diverse students. Reactions to each case by at least two other educators follow each account. This project has represented our most challenging endeavor so far, because of the complexity of both the nuances of how veterans handle issues of diversity and the delicacy of some of the issues described.

THE PROCESS OF INTERACTIVE CASE DEVELOPMENT

My experience with these books has helped me to understand the processes associated with practitioner-written case development. In this section, I will address questions such as the following:

- What steps are involved in creating a casebook?
- How does a researcher stimulate a group of teachers to become committed and invested enough to spend long periods of time out of their busy lives writing compelling narratives, an activity alien to many practitioners?
- What does researcher-teacher collaboration mean in an effort like this?
- What kinds of support do teachers need as they draft their cases?
- In short, what goes into producing good teaching cases?

Perhaps the most important decision for each book was in the selection of a school-based collaborator to co-edit. Both Colbert and

Mesa-Bains are active professionals, highly regarded by both teachers and district officials and enthusiastic about the potential contribution of teacher-authored casebooks. Their "insider's" perspectives helped me understand some of the sensitive issues described in the narratives, and their status in the district proved invaluable during the sometimes delicate discussions with district officials about some of the questions raised in the cases (see Shulman, 1990, for a discussion of ethical issues). They were involved in every stage of development.

First, we developed a set of guidelines for case writers on how to write their cases, incorporating a series of writing prompts that would help the teacher-authors illustrate a problem, grounded in a particular event or series of events. (These prompts differed depending on the theme of each casebook). We also provided guidance on how to construct their stories into compelling narratives so that, for example, a reader could identify immediately with a given problem and be drawn into its intrigue. Moreover, the authors were asked to analyze what happened in their narrative and to describe what they would do differently if the situation were to occur again.

Next, we carefully planned the initial meeting for the prospective teacher-writers in order to gain their commitment for the project. We tried to pique their interest with the carrot of publication, describing how their cases would be used both in their own district and in other staff development and teacher education programs. We also stipulated strict requirements for participation, however, including attending several meetings and making time to both write and revise their cases. This was to ensure that the participants understood the level of commitment necessary for contributing to this kind of project.

This meeting had several goals. We wanted the teachers to understand the purpose of the project and the collaborative nature of our working relationships—they were definitely partners in creating each casebook. We also wanted to clarify what a problem-focused case is. It always helped to distribute a sample case. Our third goal was to enable participants to achieve a good start on writing their case.

One strategy for accomplishing the latter is to engage teachers in a reflective writing exercise, selecting as their starting point one of the prompts in the guidelines. The exercise entails writing nonstop on a problem for 8 minutes, stopping to read and underline key ideas for 3 minutes, and then writing on one of these ideas for an additional 5 minutes. When they finish, we ask the group to pair off and present their account to each other. The listener's role is to ask clarifying questions, so as to help the presenter see what kinds of information must be added to help a reader understand the situation's nuances. Finally, each person presents his or her case to the larger group, receiving not only additional input but also some ideas on how to frame the account in an interesting narrative.

Most educators with whom we have used this exercise respond positively and report that they benefited from their case presentations. It has definitely proven a good introduction to our case-writing task. Teachers often expand their exercises into full cases. Some may choose another topic, but they report that participation in the exercise has clarified some of their concerns about writing cases. Perhaps most important, however, is an unanticipated outcome: the beginning of trust-building and development of a support group among the case writers.

The collaborative process generally begins after the authors complete their first draft. We provide extensive feedback, both in writing and in person, on issues that need clarification. We also plan meetings for all of the contributors to present their cases to one another and receive collaborative input. During the last project, we also distributed these drafts to all the contributors, so that they could ask questions and make suggestions from the written as well as oral presentation. This appeared to increase the collaborative spirit that the teachers felt about helping one another with their cases.

A few of the teachers had to write multiple drafts of their cases to address questions that were raised as we received more input. Some came from outside experts who were asked to comment on the cases; others came directly from the process of writing successive drafts. It was fascinating to watch how the narratives of the teachers' subjective experiences evolved into "teaching cases." At the beginning, it was unclear to all of us what these experiences were cases of. Case writing itself became the reflective phase of the original experience. The next section provides selected examples from successive drafts of three cases, so that readers can begin to understand how we helped teachers make explicit their implicit understandings of a situation.

TEXT REVISIONS AS A RESULT
OF COLLABORATIVE EXCHANGES

The excerpts presented below are taken from first and final drafts of three cases in our most recent casebook, *Teaching Diverse*

Students: Cases and Commentaries (Shulman & Mesa-Bains, 1990). Summaries of discussions that stimulated these revisions are also provided. I present these examples to highlight the interactive and iterative quality of the collaboration needed to develop teaching cases that deal with sensitive issues on teaching diverse students.

Facing Bias and Prejudice

In one of the cases, a veteran, middle-class, white teacher looked back on her first year of teaching as she described her initial reaction to four particularly disruptive black high school students. In her first draft, she wrote the following after vividly describing her first meeting with these students:

> During those first nightmarish days, I felt I had run into the worst of everything I heard about the ghetto: crude, foul language, rudeness, low achievement, blatant sexuality, continual talk of violence, guns, drugs—the works. What saved me from indicting all the students was the obvious fact that in my first two classes I had wonderful students of all ethnic groups who defied these stereotypes.

When I talked to this teacher about the incident, she told me that she had censored her true feelings about the initial meeting with these students because they were difficult to put in writing. As she talked about her case, she admitted, "All I could see was black, Judy!" After much encouragement from me, the teacher added the passage in italics to her final draft:

> . . . continual talk of violence, guns, drugs—the works. *These students would have been a fearsome group in any color, but their blackness seemed at first to be a barrier. I was not sure what really to expect from them. Were they truly capable of decent behavior? Did they need some other kind of schooling?* What saved me from indicting all the *black* students was the obvious fact that . . .

We felt that this kind of addition was important, because it might stimulate other teachers to question their own personal feelings of bias and/or alienation from students who have different skin colors from themselves.

A Case of Hurt Feelings Becomes a Policy Case

Another case describes the devastation and guilt that an Asian teacher felt after a group of parents signed a petition requesting that their children—her students—be placed in a different classroom for the following year. In her first two drafts, the teacher expanded on reasons for her hurt feelings and began to explore possible personal and curricular reasons for their request:

> The letter indicated that they had concerns about my math curriculum. They felt that I had not adequately taught their children the basic concepts, that the children were allowed to play with manipulatives too often, and that they were not bringing home enough paper and pencil homework and math worksheets.

Our discussons with this teacher were illuminating. She had found the case cathartic to write, both because of her personal feelings of devastation about this incident and because these parents, particularly the PTA president, continued to spread their "poison" to other faculty as the account was being written. Moreover, I discovered that the incident involved much more than she had described in her case. Copies of the petition had been sent to the board of education and to other district officials, the principal eventually lost her job, and several faculty meetings were called to discuss how to respond to the parents' intervention. The teacher and I worked together on the first draft to decide how to clarify certain issues while at the same time maintaining the privacy of the school and the author. In later drafts, she deleted some descriptions of her own personal disappointment that we felt were redundant and added examples of parental interventions. These changes followed our collaborative realization that the case we wanted to create was not one merely of personal disappointment, but rather one of faculty/parent confrontations. The following reminiscence, added to the final draft, surfaced during one of our debriefing conversations:

> My mind raced back to a visit I'd had with one of the mothers early in the year. She had come to me holding a stack of ditto sheets that her daughter had completed in first grade. "Look how much more she was learning last year," the mother had said.

A Case of Flawed Pedagogy Becomes a Policy Case

A third case, by a Chicano/Filipino male, describes his shock and dismay when a group of 12 fourth-graders, part of a large Latino group of youngsters bused into Chinatown, tried to sabotage his instruction during a pullout Spanish bilingual program. The students were not only hostile but also refused to speak Spanish. In the original draft, the author provided scant information on his teaching strategies, which were in general quite poor, and did not include any reflective comments on why the students behaved belligerently.

We had several discussions about this case—with the other teacher-authors, with staff at FWL, with our advisory group, and with prospective commentators—and each conversation produced additional questions. For example, one discussion with the teacher-authors stimulated this writer to add information about his instructional plans and their consequences with the students, as well as interpretive comments about why they may have responded so poorly. Other discussions with our advisory group and officials in the district's bilingual department prompted questions about the compatibility of the district's consent decree (which specifies that all classrooms should be integrated) and the state's bilingual program (which mandates native-language instruction for students who are designated limited-English proficient, or LEP). We wondered, for example, why these 12 students, whom the teacher described as rather fluent in English, were being given native-language instruction. And if they were in fact LEP, why were they integrated into a Chinese bilingual classroom? Legally, only fluent English speakers—who do not qualify for native-language instruction—are supposed to be placed in bilingual classrooms.

As I probed deeper into the case, I raised such questions with district officials. One deputy superintendent said, "We've definitely opened a can of worms here." I spent hours going back and forth between teacher-author and district officials. Because of the delicacy of the situation, we had to ensure that the details in the case were described accurately. In fact, the case writer was unable to answer some of our questions and had to seek additional information (e.g., If these students spoke English fluently, why were they given special classes?). We also had to make some ethical judgments about how much ambiguity to leave in the account to stimulate analysis of the issues, and whether such ambiguity could embarrass the district. (See Shulman, 1990, for an analysis of ethical issues in publishing teacher-authored cases.) During these deliberations, we realized that what had begun as a case of flawed pedagogy had become instead a policy case. In the end, we decided to leave most of the ambiguity in the text, because it raised important issues for teachers and administrators, and to solicit commentaries that would both speak to these questions and provide a balanced picture. The topic of commentaries leads us into our next section.

BUILDING A CASE WITH LAYERS OF COMMENTARY

I started experimenting with commentary on selected cases in the mentor casebook and have been a proponent of its importance ever since. The commentaries I solicit do not provide answers to questions raised in each case, as in a teaching note.[2] Rather, they often raise more questions and provide multiple lenses through which to analyze the issues raised in each case. We solicit commentaries from a variety of educators—new and experienced teachers, administrators, teacher educators, and educational scholars. Each adds an important perspective to the "conversations" that follow each case. In this section, I delineate three reasons that commentaries are important.

1. *Commentaries can provide multiple perspectives on the same issue.* For the last case described above, we commissioned commentaries from three different points of views: from a teacher who is also one of our case writers, from a scholar in bilingual education, and from a researcher who has evaluated bilingual programs in California for the past 10 years. Each commentator looks at the case through a different lens and adds different information. Each one's purpose is to add grist to analysis and deliberation, not to give "correct" answers.

One issue that I encountered early was how harsh to let the commentator be toward the case writer. If a commentary seems unduly damning, should it be published nonetheless? What we have learned is that it is a judgment call. Sometimes we work with a commentator to depersonalize his or her comments. On other occasions, we consider soliciting another commentary. One of the cases from *The Intern Teacher Casebook* (Shulman & Colbert, 1988) provides an example of the latter. A new teacher described her honest initial perceptions of her students in a narrative about a particularly difficult teaching situation:

It's hard to describe the shock I experienced during my first weeks of school. Many students were loud, vulgar, poorly dressed and many had obvious physical problems, such as extremely crooked teeth, which in almost any other environment would have been taken care of by doctors. My heart went out to these kids, but at the same time they made me very angry. Every day I tried to get control of my classes. Every day it was an effort. (p. 53)

The teacher went on to show how the implementation of a management system using redeemable tokens to reward good behavior helped her to gain control of the class and "begin teaching."

One experienced teacher wrote an empathic response on the strengths of this teacher in the midst of a very difficult teaching situation. Another took a radically different position. She maintained that the teacher's description of her initial contact with students "fosters segregation and discrimination."

When I received this commentary, I was initially distressed. I thought it was unfair and considered not publishing it. After consulting my collaborator, however, I decided to use it, but also to commission a reaction from a teacher educator, Pam Grossman. Grossman's commentary welcomed the honesty of the teacher's descriptions and challenged the teacher education community to rethink how to prepare new teachers for culturally diverse classrooms.

2. *Commentaries can link cases to research.* A final commentary to the above case is by Jere Brophy, whose lens is that of a scholar on classroom management. Brophy not only reacts to the author's teaching strategies but also points to and elaborates on relevant research that deals with the issues raised in the case. He picks up on such instructional issues as the low-level, possibly inappropriate, seatwork this teacher assigned, which decreased the student motivation to finish assigned tasks. He then proceeds to describe the specific research that addresses these issues with references for additional reading.

3. *Commentaries can suggest alternate strategies for action.* In another case from *The Intern Teacher Casebook*, a new teacher described a disastrous two-week unit on the five-paragraph essay. He went on to analyze his mistakes. In accompanying commentaries, a fellow novice described a similar "disastrous unit," then proceeded to examine how he successfully modified the unit for his class. Two other expe-

rienced teachers provided additional teaching strategies that the case author could consider.

In summary, I believe that commentaries enrich, rather than stifle, opportunities for analysis, as long as they provide multiple perspectives on each case. For discussion purposes, they can be used in different ways. Some teacher educators report that they first ask their students to discuss the cases without the commentaries and then provide a second opportunity with the commentaries. Others use the case and commentaries simultaneously. They feel that pre-service teachers may be naive about the crucial questions at issue and that time could be wasted "rapping" about the case rather than engaging in constructive deliberation. We have no rules of thumb about this matter. We make our decision on a case-by-case basis depending on the nature of the commentaries and our purposes for a particular discussion.

INTRODUCTION TO THE CASE

The case presented here is by an intern teacher who was unprepared to deal with the curricular and management problems she encountered during her first few months of teaching. It is followed by two commentaries—one by David Berliner, a teacher educator and scholar, the other by Don Kemper, a veteran mentor teacher—that offer conflicting interpretations about why these problems may have occurred. I present additional information in an epilogue.

This case is excellent for preservice and first-year teachers because the writer—who teaches two high school classes as part of a fifth-year masters/credentialing program—experiences many of the same problems that all first-year teachers face during their first few weeks of teaching. The case and its commentaries are excellent discussion pieces for teacher educators, university supervisors, and mentor teachers because of what they can teach us about the readiness of this new teacher to learn and apply principles of management before teaching real students. I have used this case with a group of university professors. They uniformly agreed on its appropriateness for their advisees and then deliberated at length about how they could help new teachers like Beth.

What can teacher educators expect interns to learn from a course or two on classroom management? Is it reasonable to assume that becoming knowledgeable about theories of management in a teacher preparation program will enable a new teacher to use them effectively during her first few weeks of teaching? My epilogue at the end of the case should shed light on such discussions.

LOSS OF INNOCENCE
Beth Touchette, Intern Teacher

The funny thing about novice teachers is that we think we already know how a classroom works. After all, we have been in school ourselves for 17 years! Only by actually standing in front of the classroom, however, can anyone realize just how complex and demanding teaching is. Like many new teachers, I learned early—and painfully—that one of the profession's unappreciated arts is classroom management.

I grew up in a small town in rural Colorado and earned my B.A. in environmental sciences from U.C. Berkeley. I really enjoyed my experiences teaching sixth-graders ecology and adults algebra, so in the summer of 1988 I enrolled in a private university's teaching credential program. I had no idea what an intellectual and emotional challenge teaching high school every day would be, nor could I predict the self-exploration it would initiate.

I now know that my own mixed feelings on power and authority worked against my early classroom management strategy. I do not like bossing people around. I wanted my high school students to be like my college peers: enthusiastic, voluntary learners who cause no disturbances. If students have something better to do—like getting rid of hormonal build-up or hanging out in the mall with friends— why force them to learn science? Can I really believe that my lessons are more important to them than sharing intimacies with their friends, even if they do so during my class? My idealism abounded. I felt that I could make my class so interesting that I would never have to worry about disruptions. I was wrong.

I am an intern, teaching Geology 1 at a high school in an affluent northern California community. Geology is an elective. Unlike any of the other science courses at this school, it is composed of mixed-track seniors. I have students who have taken three advanced placement science and math classes, along with students who hate science and are taking the class to satisfy a lab requirement. Most are bright and motivated, but the advanced ones master the material quickly and get bored while those at lower levels remain apathetic and confused.

Several cocky 17-year-old males seem to be the source of most of my management problems.

Geology 1 started out well. In early September we went through simple written rules, emphasizing courtesy to me and each other. I thought I "passed" the tests my students gave me. What I did not realize was that their testing had barely begun.

My written rules and my actual behavior turned out to be two different things. I did not feel comfortable directing the classroom—and my students knew it. I distinctly remember one day in late September when I planned to reassemble the class after a lab but was unable to do it. The students were not listening to me. I reacted like some drivers do when they first suspect they are lost. I denied it. Instead of stopping to look at a map, I accelerated, hoping to find recognizable territory.

This phase lasted only until my instructional supervisor (IS) observed me. The class was inattentive and rude as I yelled instructions in a computer lab. Papers and hacky-sacs flew through the air. My IS told me he was on my side and would help me get rid of any troublemakers. But he expressed dismay at the way I had started class and outlined an assertive discipline program for me. Forced out of denial, I became angry—with myself and my students. I spent the weekend revamping my rules, writing letters to parents, and creating lots of quizzes and worksheets. I also scanned the newspapers for one-way airfares to Europe!

Throughout the following week, my IS continued to observe me. He timed me on starting class each day. On Monday I cracked down on the tardy problem with a tardy quiz—only students sitting in their seats before the bell were eligible. I then gave a 10-minute lecture on my unhappiness with their behavior, followed by 2 minutes of silent thought with the lights off. I outlined my new rules, explaining assertive discipline, negative oral participation points, parental calls, and detention. In that day's debriefing, my IS said I acted too parental. He was right, I thought. The parental authority model is the only one I have extensive background on.

For several days, however, I continued my crack-down. I rarely turned my back on the class, and I assigned lots of worksheets due at the end of the period. Anybody who disrupted class had his name written on the board. With the second violation, the student received an automatic 15-minute detention—a strategy that cost me credibility with 17-year-old seniors who could not accept it. Meanwhile, my new assertive role made my lack of confidence even more obvious.

And my IS's daily observations were beginning to wear me down. I began to doubt that I could survive until June.

During Spirit Week, my university supervisor observed me. Because of the festivities, I was more relaxed than usual. My lecture went well, and my students enjoyed the mineral discovery lab in the second half of the period. I circulated among them, giving them tips and commenting on their clever costumes. In our debriefing, my supervisor suggested requiring students to write down my directions and take notes during lectures. He commented on how much more comfortable I seemed (had this supervisor come earlier?) and how I was letting more of myself through. I realized that enjoying myself in the classroom worked better than my previous combat mode.

Over the months I observed several other teachers to get some classroom management ideas. I saw an amazing diversity of styles. The other geology teacher was very informal. His classes were almost solely lecture/discussions, and students did not have to raise their hands to speak. He dealt with disruptions quickly and with humor. His amazingly strong presence and dynamic teaching style prevented chaos. A physics teacher had a classroom that ran like clockwork in a Madeline Hunter–like format. A biology teacher kept control with tight planning, continually keeping the students busy. The only thing these teachers had in common was the ability to maintain controlled, productive classrooms. They had picked management styles that fit their personality, subject, and students.

I soon dropped my formal strategy of assertive discipline, continuing to search for a management style suitable to me. Eventually I gained control of my class, but by then the damage was done. My students had lost respect for me and enthusiasm for the subject.

My own losses from that experience were necessary ones. I lost my idealistic expectations. High school students, I now know, are not automatically interested in geology, me, or my clever lesson plans. They have many other things on their minds, including thoroughly testing all authority. I cannot simply present my subject matter—I have to "sell" it.

I also lost my adolescence. I had wanted my students to see me as a knowledgeable friend who would expose them to the joys of science. When they disrupted my class, they were violating our friendship and hurting me personally. I have learned that good classroom management involves relating to students as a mature adult who will comfortably use her authority.

Commentaries

David C. Berliner.   I wonder if there are any physicians who are prepared by their medical schools in such a way that they leave for their first job fully convinced that "If you believe hard enough in the power of positive thinking, and the benefits of genuine caring, your patients will get well." Many physicians, particularly the best of them, hold and communicate those beliefs. But they are not sufficient to insure a beneficial program for the patient. If the physician I visited had not learned the latest technical information and associated procedures for addressing my medical problems, I would seek another. And if the physician tried to treat me more with his or her beliefs and less with the technical competence that I seek, I would ask the licensing agency in my state to audit the instructional program at the college this physician attended.

In the same way I think it is unconscionable that today a teacher can be educated and trained somewhere in this country, judged competent to teach normal high school youngsters, and be as unprepared as Beth. She was armed with her beliefs, beliefs that are certainly a prerequisite to becoming an excellent teacher, but beliefs that are simply insufficient for managing the ordinary classroom. Even now Beth talks of the "art" of classroom management, as if it is mysterious and unknowable except by the few—the artists, the lucky ones with natural ability. Why did her teacher education program not provide her with management principles that were derived through scientific observation and then experimentally validated? Why had she apparently not heard of Kounin (1970) and his management concepts?

These have sparked a score of studies that resulted in confirmation of the importance of the technical vocabulary that he developed (*withitness, timing and targeting errors, smoothness, momentum,* and so forth). And his observations resulted in training programs that have been proven to work. That is, these programs help teachers be proactive in their management and provide them with a sense of control of their classes.

These methods usually work (e.g., the studies on classroom organization and management by the Texas R&D Center, such as Evertson, Anderson, Anderson, & Brophy, 1980; Evertson et al., 1981; Emmer, Evertson, Sanford, Clements, & Worsham, 1982), though they do not work for all of the teachers all of the time. But, then, most prescribed drugs also do not work well for all people all of the time. Similar programs to learn classroom management have been field tested by the AFT in the New York area, a tough proving ground, and found to work. Why would a state licensing agency allow a novice teacher out into the world without requiring the novice's training institute to provide all prospective teachers extensive practice in management procedures that seem to work? How long would a school of medicine stay open if its novice physicians could not perform procedures that work, particularly when those procedures have been working well elsewhere? I feel sorry for Beth. It was not her artistic talent that was lacking, it was her training program.

But then there is the good news. Beth's problem resulted in her visiting other classes, with a focus for her observations. There are no better ways to learn about the variety of teacher behaviors that are useful in management. She seems to have extracted what she needs from this experience, though her observations could have been helped a great deal if she had been exposed to the body of research that exists on this topic. Beth now needs to be helped to see that she can still be a knowledgeable friend who can expose students to the joys of science, but it will not be with every student in every class. For the others, Beth needs to understand that fair, sensible, reasonable, consistent management provides students with the proper models for participation in social events in schools, clubs, and employment.

Some students may not like her science, but they may forever be touched by a person who is articulate, motivated, respectful toward her students, and caring of them. To accomplish that may require more effort and be worth more to society than all the earth science these kids could digest. Perhaps Beth did not lose her innocence so much as gain her maturity.

Don Kemper.   The funny thing about novice teachers is that they are novices. My experience as a 20-year veteran science teacher and as a mentor teacher of both licensed and emergency credentialed new teachers has caused me to believe that novice teachers generally are all too naive about the complexity of teaching—whether they are products of good teacher preparation institutions or have had only a 6-week crash course in the summer. Beth is no exception. Teaching requires more than subject mastery and enthusiasm.

Beth's description of her students does not lead me to believe that she was saddled with hard-core behavior problems. After all, "cocky 17-year-old males" only describes the species! Heterogeneous classrooms, in terms of ability level, are the rule not the exception and are not the cause of behavior problems. It is my feeling that Beth's main problem was more pedagogical than managerial. The mastery of good teaching requires experience and close assistance and supervision regardless of the quality of teacher preparation.

Beth's observations of other teachers was a sound idea. However, if she had also asked those same three teachers to observe her in the classroom and then provide feedback, she would not have misinterpreted what she observed. She concluded that the three teachers she observed had nothing in common except the ability to maintain controlled, productive classrooms. I would contend that they had far more in common. They all planned appropriately for their daily classes, taking into consideration a variety of students. They all executed those plans in a manner that was acceptable to their students. The activities in all of these teachers' classrooms were aimed at the students and not at the teacher, and the students were eager participants in what they perceived to be meaningful work. Good teaching requires more than enthusiasm (although it is a requisite ingredient), and good teaching eliminates behavior problems or reduces them to only minor irritants.

The advice she received from her instructional supervisor was less than adequate. It focused solely upon management and not on good teaching techniques. Beth did not need to learn about assertive discipline at that point because her problems were not with discipline. Indeed, the increased "cracking down" only exacerbated her problems.

Beth should be reminded that students do not need to like a subject in order to excel in it. Let's face it! The more difficult subjects in school would generally be avoided if they were not required. Yet thousands of reluctant learners master chemistry, physics, calculus, and English literature each year. And they do not do it screaming and shouting the whole way.

Beth cannot give up on the desire to be viewed as a knowledgeable friend of her students. That will come naturally as her skills as a teacher grow. This growth, however, will not come naturally; it will need to be gained by consultation with mentors, by her observations of mentors and their observations of her, and by exploring in the classroom with her students new ideas for presentation of material.

With her increased personal involvement with her students, she will discover that they are not without compassion. She will be able to explain to them the depths of her feelings for them and how they can violate the friendship and hurt her personally. She will be amazed at the tender response this will evoke from even the cockiest of 17-year-olds.

I believe that Berliner's analogy to medical training is misplaced in this case. A medical school diploma does not make a physician able to practice competent, consistent medicine. Medical education culminates in a system of paid internships and residencies as well as state board exams. Our profession is only on the verge of such a system—anywhere. Beth describes herself as an intern. She is really at the beginning of her postgraduate teacher preparation work, with her teaching assignment as part of that preparation. Beginning medical interns do not treat patients without direct supervision, and because of the nature of the supervision they are not held responsible for their errors in judgment or knowledge except to their supervisors. Where, in our profession, is there anything comparable?

Studying Kounin's management concepts or the studies by the Texas R&D Center are indispensable for a beginning teacher's professional preparation. Practicing them sufficiently to make them your own is another matter. Does Berliner propose extending teacher education a few more years before permitting interns to teach on their own?

Epilogue

Judith H. Shulman.   I called Beth after receiving both commentaries and asked if she had studied classroom management theory during the teacher education program's 8-week summer quarter before her teaching internship. She said that her professors had taught lots of theories on management, but she had not paid much attention to them. She was sure that such problems would never happen to her.

CONCLUDING REMARKS

I have argued in this chapter that teacher-written cases can and should be an important part of a teacher education curriculum. I examined a variety of ways, based on my experience, of providing collaborative support for case writers as they craft their accounts into teaching cases. Finally, I described how to enrich potential case analyses by following each account with layers of commentary.

The case presented above provides an excellent example of this genre of teaching cases. The narrative is a poignant story of a new teacher's painful discovery that good teaching is a complex set of skills and understandings, not something that can be accomplished merely by enthusiasm and knowledge of subject matter. As a narrative, it is well-written, rich, and "rings true." It is also a paradigmatic case, because it illustrates the recurrent problems of many idealistic, naive neophytes who approach their craft with the belief that good teaching rests on a combination of personal commitment and content knowledge. As Beth says in the beginning of her case, "I felt that I could make my class so interesting that I would never have to worry about disruptions. I was wrong."

Beth wrote this case at the end of her intern year. As with most of the teachers with whom we have worked, the act of writing her case had a profound impact on her conception of teaching. When she submitted it, she wrote the following in a note:

> This case was cathartic for me to write. I did not expect that I would have so many problems in teaching, and writing this case helped me understand what happened. But it's interesting to see how far I have come since those first few months. I am sure that I will not make the same mistakes next year.

As I read the narrative, I found myself smiling, remembering several of my own advisees at Michigan State University who experienced many of the same problems. I felt that this would be an excellent case for preservice teachers, to help them begin to add complexity to their naive view of teaching. The case as submitted was unusual, because it needed very few revisions; Beth was a gifted writer.

When I thought of prospective commentators, I was immediately drawn to my friend David Berliner because of his scholarship on classroom management and his work with teachers. Yet when I received his eloquent commentary, I was faced with a dilemma. Though he nicely linked his reaction to the research on classroom management, I felt he was unduly harsh on Beth. Moreover, his comments purposely overstated a view held widely by both laypersons and teacher educators. The view that research-based coursework and classroom management should adequately prepare novice teachers for the pressures of classroom organization demanded critical examination from another perspective, preferably from a veteran practitioner. Thus I asked Don Kemper, a mentor teacher who had contributed to the mentor and intern casebooks, to react to both the case and its commentary. His response addressed new facets of the case and offered a contrasting perspective on what can be expected from courses on classroom management.

This chapter exemplifies the active and continuing role of the case editor in all phases of case writing. The editor solicits the case from an appropriate writer; collaborates in crafting the case by raising key questions that yield new information and perceptions as the case develops over successive drafts; and carefully glosses the case by inviting commentaries likely to be contrasting and provocative. Without such editorial activity and support, teacher-written cases and commentaries are unlikely to achieve the clarity and power they deserve and their audience requires.

NOTES

1. Colbert is currently an associate professor of education at California State University, Dominguez Hills.

2. The Harvard Business School supplies teaching notes for all of its cases. These notes raise questions and provide answers for all of the issues embedded in the case. It also provides a suggested outline for the instructor to follow during his or her discussion.

REFERENCES

Allen, A. W. (1990). Cross-cultural counseling: The guidance project and the reluctant seniors. In J. Kleinfeld (Ed.), *Teaching cases in cross-cultural education* (No. 7). Fairbanks, AK: Center for Cross-Cultural Studies, University of Alaska.

Ashton-Warner, S. (1963). *Teacher.* New York: Touchstone/Simon & Schuster.

Emmer, E., Evertson, C., Sanford, J., Clements, B., & Worsham, M. (1982). *Organizing and managing the junior high classroom.* Austin: Research and Development Center for Teacher Education, University of Texas.

Evertson, C., Anderson, C., Anderson, L., & Brophy, J. E. (1980). Relationship between classroom behavior and student outcomes in junior high math and English classes. *American Elementary Research Journal, 17,* 43–60.

Evertson, C., Emmer, E., Clements, B., Sanford, J., Worsham, M., & Williams, E. (1981). *Organizing and managing the elementary school classroom.* Austin: Research and Development Center for Teacher Education, University of Texas.

Kounin, J. (1970). *Discipline and group management in classrooms.* New York: Holt, Rinehart & Winston.

McDonald, J. P. (1986). Raising the teacher's voice and the ironic role of theory. *Harvard Educational Review, 56*(4), 355–378.

Munby, H., & Russell, T. (1990). Metaphor in the study of teachers' professional knowledge. *Theory into Practice, 29,* 116–121.

Paley, V. G. (1979). *White teacher.* Cambridge, MA: Harvard University Press.

Shulman, J. (1989). Blue freeways: Traveling the alternate route with big-city teacher trainees. *Journal of Teacher Education, 40*(5), 2–8.

Shulman, J. H. (1990). Now you see them, now you don't: Anonymity versus visibility in case studies of teachers. *Educational Researcher, 19*(6), 11–15.

Shulman, J. H., & Colbert, J. A. (Eds.). (1987). *The mentor teacher casebook.* San Francisco: Far West Laboratory for Educational Research and Development.

Shulman, J. H., & Colbert, J. A. (Eds.). (1988). *The intern teacher casebook.* San Francisco: Far West Laboratory for Educational Research and Development.

Shulman, J. H., & Colbert, J. A. (1989). Cases as catalysts for cases: Inducing reflection in teacher education. *Action in Teacher Education, 11*(1), 44–52.

Shulman, J. H., Hanson, S., with King, R. (1985). *California mentor teacher program case study: Implementation in the Waverly unified school district, 1984–85.* San Francisco: Far West Laboratory for Educational Research and Development.

Shulman, J. H., & Mesa-Bains, A. (Eds.). (1990). *Teaching diverse students: Cases and commentaries.* San Francisco: Far West Laboratory for Educational Research and Development.

Part II

CASES AS
LEARNING TOOLS

CHAPTER 8

Writing Cases

A Vehicle for Inquiry
into the Teaching Process

ANNA E. RICHERT

Recently teacher educators have become concerned with their role in the ongoing support for beginning teachers as these novices leave the university and enter the classroom full-time. Helping novice teachers acquire and develop skills that facilitate learning from experience within the classroom context is one aspect of teacher growth that warrants consideration. This chapter explores the use of a case methodology as a way to assist novice teachers in the processes of reflective problem solving in areas of professional concern. By writing cases about dilemmas they face in their work, novice teachers develop skills such as establishing collegial relationships, articulating educational problems precisely, and defining problematic issues and potential solutions. All of these skills support the teacher in the short run and enhance the teacher's potential for professional growth in the long run.

This chapter reports on one attempt to use the writing of cases with a group of 11 credentialed novice teachers enrolled in a master's degree program. Included in the chapter are

- The rationale—why write the cases and why write about professional issues or dilemmas
- A description of the context—the instructor and the college where the case method was implemented
- A description of the actual course assignment and class procedures surrounding case creation and use

- Two examples of student cases written to complete the assignment, including an introduction that highlights points of commonality between the two
- A brief reflection on the process of writing cases as part of the teacher education curriculum

RATIONALE

Writing cases to be shared with colleagues defies several norms embedded in the culture of teaching as work. The first is writing. Teaching is a "doing" profession. In my experience working with teachers, even with teachers who are enrolled in programs of higher education, I find many resistant to writing about their work. Writing requires time—a preciously rare commodity for most teachers. It also requires having something to write about and a way of thinking that is typically not part of the professional training of teachers. Teachers have little time or opportunity to talk about what they know, let alone to write about it. Yet articulating what they know is important to teachers. Without the opportunity to articulate what they know teachers are cast into a role of dispensers rather than creators or definers of knowledge (Richert, 1987b). At one extreme, without the capability to think, talk, and write about their work, teachers are left feeling void of knowledge that is valued, legitimate, or worth sharing with colleagues. But teachers are not void of such knowledge. They know an infinite amount about their work in classrooms with children. Cases written by teachers provide an opportunity for the profession of teaching to create a record of what teachers know about their work and how they know it.

While the product of case writing is good for the profession, and important for that reason, my focus in using cases in my teacher education class was on *the teachers themselves* and the opportunity for learning from experience that writing the cases offered. My goal was to create an assignment that would help the teachers in my class focus their attention on something they know a lot about and could write about and share with colleagues in the form of a case. I chose the topic "professional issues and dilemmas" for reasons of process and substance combined. First, since I anticipated resistance to the writing part of the case assignment, I wanted to minimize the difficulty with which specific topic selection would be made by each teacher. Finding a problem, issue, or dilemma about which to write, I thought, would be relatively easy. I found this true. In a posttask discussion of the process, the teachers reported that identifying the problem was not difficult, although precisely defining the problem in later stages was. All teachers are faced with issues and dilemmas that require their consideration and solution. Choosing only one issue or one dilemma rendered that aspect of the project—topic selection—relatively unproblematic.

A second consideration in choosing this focus for the cases was to demonstrate the complexity of the problems faced by teachers and the care that is necessary in articulating them clearly in the problem-solving process. While the initial identification of an issue is not difficult for teachers, defining it clearly and precisely is. In the culture of any profession there is considerable tacit knowledge that facilitates communication among colleagues. Relying only on tacit understandings among colleagues, however, creates trade-offs. One is that we become less precise in our thinking and less careful and thorough in our problem solving. Tacit understandings, while necessary, are not sufficient for professional communication. Given teachers' knowledge and intelligence, they can move their profession forward if they are better able to talk about what they do and what they know. Writing about a professional issue or dilemma in a clear and precise form, and then sharing that case with colleagues who will consider it with them, is thus conceived of as a step toward professional development.

The sharing aspect of the written case assignment challenged another norm of the profession: remaining separate and somewhat isolated in one's work. While teachers consistently say they would like to talk about their teaching with colleagues, the culture of teaching does not support their doing so. Time for talking with colleagues in schools is rare if it exists at all. There is also an issue of safety. Implicit in the process of discussing one's work in teaching is evaluation. For many teachers, the only opportunity they have to discuss their work is when they are being evaluated on it. Discussion of the substance—of such questions as why, how, and what we teach—is rare. Teachers fear judgment as a result of their profession's low status and high accountability. Evaluation is built so deeply into the educational system that many teachers avoid contact with colleagues for fear of being judged negatively about what they do or do not know, or what they do or do not do.

I designed the case method described in the following pages to address a number of teacher education concerns. My goals were to have the novice teachers reflect on some aspect of their work that they found problematic and then share their reflections with their colleagues. The process involved developing the skills of problem identification and definition, as well as communication in both written and verbal forms. My work is motivated by a belief that teaching is fundamentally an intellectual task. Helping teachers acknowledge what they know by talking about it, writing about it, and sharing it with one another moves not only the individual teacher forward, but the profession forward into the domain where it is defined and owned by the people who do it.

CONTEXT

The Teacher Educator

My enthusiasm for writing cases as a vehicle for learning about one's work is born of considerable experience writing cases myself. For my doctoral dissertation (Richert, 1987a), I wrote 12 case studies about 12 student teachers who were reflecting about their field experiences in schools. The focus of my study, and of the cases, was on reflection in teaching and the facilitation of reflection in teacher education. Each student teacher reflected under different structural conditions that were built into a teacher education program. I wrote the cases to examine the reflection processes and outcomes as they were experienced and discussed by each individual.

I found this experience of writing cases important to my conceptualizing of the teacher education case method discussed in this chapter. Equally important were the results of my dissertation study, which were informative about how reflection contributes to the process of "learning from experience." My findings indicated that student teachers reflect about different things and in different ways when they reflect under different circumstances. If we want novice teachers to reflect about the broad range of teaching issues—from content, to context, to students, to curriculum, and so forth—we need to provide a broad range of opportunities for them to do so. Case methods in all of the forms discussed in this volume provide fertile ground for facilitating reflection in teaching.

The written case assignment described in this chapter is an extension of my work on facilitating reflection in novice teachers. For example, in reviewing programs of professional education in disciplines other than education, I was able to identify two factors— one or the other of which was characteristic of all program structures designed to promote reflection in novice professionals. The two features are *social* and *artifactual*. Through both social and artifactual means, professional educators attempt to facilitate reflection by enhancing memory and offering opportunities for collaborative thinking. In teacher education, social means for facilitating reflection include various techniques of people working together: partners, small groups, supervisors, seminar discussions. Artifactual aids to reflection include ways in which the work done is represented by some kind of tangible evidence: teaching portfolios, videotapes, journals. According to the findings of my study, each way of facilitating reflection enhances the process.

The written case method described in this chapter combines the features of the social and the artifactual means of facilitating reflection in teaching. The written cases are artifactual in that the teachers first gather evidence in creating them and then document that evidence in a case that is written and tangible. They are social in that they are discussed with colleagues first in the process of writing them and again when they are complete. My work on reflection in teaching and learning from experience, therefore, provides the theoretical basis upon which the teacher education method described in this chapter is based.

The Teacher Education Course

The context in which the teachers wrote their cases was a course in a postcredential master's degree program for practicing teachers. The course, Inquiry into the Teaching Process, meets 1 night a week for 2 hours. The 11 students in the class were credentialed, practicing teachers with 5 or fewer years of teaching experience. There were two exceptions. One person was a novice substitute teacher, and the other was a novice high school administrator (though an experienced teacher). Both secondary and elementary teachers were in the group. I made no attempt to distinguish among the elementary and secondary teachers for any aspect of the assignment.

The written case assignment was given during the second semester of a two-semester course. The course was experimental in its use of case methods. The written case assignment was one of three forms of casework done in the class. It was the only one of the three with a written case product. The focus on professional issues and dilemmas was different from the other case assignments, which were focused on the learner and on instruction.

The Assignment: Conduct and Guidelines

In planning the casework I scheduled 3 weeks of class time for the project. As the class progressed through the steps, however, 4 weeks of class time were consumed in completing the work. How to organize the amount of time needed depends on both the number of students and the number of times the class meets each week.

In the first week I introduced the case assignment by discussing what cases are, how we might learn from casework in education and teaching, and how teachers are an important source of case material if we are to move in the direction of using case knowledge of teaching. Spending time introducing the ideas and the terminology was extremely useful for the teachers who had little or no previous experience with cases. Having a common language to talk about cases was helpful as we continued the introductory work and as we moved into subsequent discussions.

The remainder of the introductory session focused on how to get started writing a case. I distributed a set of guidelines describing the case assignment and process to the students. After discussing the purposes of the assignment as they are outlined in the guidelines, we proceeded to think about the *content* of the cases—the issues and dilemmas we all face in our work as teachers. In a brainstorming session, the teachers raised problems and dilemmas from their teaching, which I recorded on the board, clustering them in categories whenever possible. Problems having to do with students—for example, student absenteeism, student diversity, and student lethargy—were clustered into one group. Contextual problems or issues having to do with the school structure, such as not enough time, too much uncertainty with the new principal, and inadequate resources, were grouped together as well. This brainstorming of ideas seemed to "break the ice" for the teachers. Each person in the class had a lot to contribute, and there were many opportunities for them to commiserate with one another about the circumstances of their work. The process also provided ideas about topics they might choose and a sense of confidence that getting started on this project would not be too difficult.

To make a transition from the identification of problems to the writing of the case, I used examples of brief cases (or vignettes) from Far West Laboratory's *The Intern Teacher Casebook* (J. Shulman & Colbert, 1988). I distributed two separate cases that we discussed as a group, first from the point of view of the case itself (e.g., What was it describing? How do you feel about it? Is this something that you have experienced in your teaching?), then from the point of view of the writing (e.g., How does this case read? Do you understand it? Is the writer's point clear? Is there enough/too much detail?). The use of examples from *The Intern Teacher Casebook* was helpful. The teachers found the vignettes intriguing; they generated considerable discussion of both their content and their form.

The teachers left this first session knowing that they were to bring four copies of their two-page case draft to the next class meeting. I had expected to have time during the first class to have the teachers free-write about an issue they had mentioned during the brainstorming session. Since we spent so much time talking about issues and dilemmas, and about the cases used as examples, we did not have time to do the in-class free-writes. In retrospect I think the writing is an important part of the introductory process. If they had had the opportunity to try writing about an idea I think they would have had less anxiety about the writing they did for the first draft.

I designed the second class of this sequence to focus on writing and collegiality. I explained to the class that the session was devoted to helping one another think about the cases they had written, thinking about both problems they had identified *and* about ways they had written the problems. Working in groups of three or four, the teachers read and responded to one another's cases one by one. First one person's case was distributed by the teacher who wrote it. This person facilitated the "case conference" in the same way that she might conduct medical grand rounds if she were presenting a case in that setting. The teachers read the case and before discussing it wrote a reaction to its content.

Following the written reactions the students discussed the case—both the content and the writing. In observing and participating in this process, I noted that the discussion of the content of the case drafts illuminated several significant writing difficulties. There were a number of instances when the discussion took a turn in response to the written material that was very different from what the teacher had intended. Often the difficulty lay in the writing: the ideas were not clearly developed or sequenced; too many details confused the readers; extraneous contextual information was provided, or else no contextual information was included when that information would have been helpful. In any case, according to the discussion we had at the end of the process, the teachers found the draft experience—writing it, talking about it with colleagues, and thinking through both content and writing—the most exciting part of the assignment (Richert, 1989).

For the third week students prepared second (and final) drafts of the two-page cases. They arrived in class with four copies of their cases to be used for a second case conference. The groups were rearranged so that the teachers were working with different colleagues the second time. Once again the cases were considered one by one. The teacher presenting the case distributed and introduced the written material. Immediately upon reading the case, the other teachers wrote reactions that will be considered commentaries for the casebook we are developing as a result of this course. The written reactions forced the teachers to focus when they read the cases. They also provided a good springboard for the discussion about the case that followed after the written reactions were all completed. The purpose of this culminating experience with the written cases was to have a collegial case conference in which colleagues joined heads to think and talk together about the issues and dilemmas of their work in schools.

INTRODUCTION TO THE CASES

Following are two cases written by students in the class. A secondary mathematics teacher wrote "The Dumping Ground"; an elementary teacher wrote "Team Teaching with AT&T." Other students in the class wrote the commentaries that follow each case. Both cases were written using the two-draft process just described. The commentaries were written as an immediate and informal response to the case as the first step in the case conference process. In reviewing the cases, it is interesting to note several general shared characteristics:

• In both instances the teachers chose topics about which they felt passionately. This passion was transformed, they told me, when they wrote their cases and were required to explore their dilemma on levels other than the emotional. The writing helped them move beyond their feelings to the source of those feelings. It helped them clarify their response and focus their thinking, which, in turn, helped them generate solutions that were then useful in solving the problem.

• The process of writing the cases also put the teachers in contact with their colleagues as sources of validation and clarification. When committing their ideas to paper the teachers felt compelled to check them out more thoroughly. As a result the teachers turned to colleagues at their school sites to discuss the issue, gather evidence, and construct their arguments. Though totally independent of the class project, both teachers took their finished cases back to their school sites and used them to open a discussion with school administrators about the dilemma presented. They were joined in this effort by the colleagues with whom they had discussed the case as they were writing it.

• A third common response to the case had to do with the "context" section of the assignment. Including "context" as a required part of the case underscored the idea that teaching concerns are neither context- nor content-free. There is an interesting tension in writing cases between having the reported instances, on the one hand, represent accurately the particular circumstances of the case described, and, on the other, be open to more general interpretation and abstraction. The teachers were surprised in their analysis of the experience about the relevance of contextual factors—context played a larger part than they had thought it would. In general, first-draft attempts were weak in their consideration of contextual factors influencing the case. Second-draft cases identified relevant features of the context more fully and successfully; more significant connections were drawn between the context and the problem as the analysis and writing processes proceeded.

• Combining the social and artifactual means for facilitating reflection in this assignment proved powerful in its interactive effect during the writing process. In the actual writing, the teachers created a tangible representation of problematic occurrences in their classrooms. Once involved in writing, the teachers became conscious of what they did and did not remember, and what details (important or less important) they needed to include to make their point and present their cases more fully, accurately, and convincingly. The social exchange that followed the writing could not have occurred in the same form without the written material to stimulate it, the teachers report (Richert, 1989). Similarly, the writing itself would have taken on less meaning, would have been less rich in its description, and less accurate, without the collaborative conversation.

• The solution section of the cases was included so that the teachers would push their thinking to a point of considering possible outcomes and their consequences. The solutions sections of these second drafts included ideas from both the initial presentations *and* the collegial discussion of the case in the initial case conference. In order to underscore the idea that educational problems typically have many possible solutions, the teachers were encouraged to include more than one possible solution in their final write-up. If these particular cases were used in other teacher education settings, the solutions as well as the commentaries could be eliminated. In fact, different parts of the case could be used for different purposes depending on the goals of the teacher educator using the materials.

THE DUMPING GROUND
Mandy McManus

Context

Allentown is an island community of about 75,000, located in a large metropolitan area. Although it is home to a burgeoning industrial park and a large Navy base, Allentown is essentially a small town in operation and feeling. Its schools are largely populated by children whose parents and even grandparents roamed the same halls and had the same teachers. School faculties have sizeable numbers of Allentown alumni. This old guard, mainly white and middle-class, has seen the influx of various immigrant groups (Vietnamese, Korean, Filipino, Chinese, and so forth) and upscale professionals into its older homes and new developments on its own Harbor Isle.

Allentown has two comprehensive high schools, drawing from different ends of the island, as well as Island High, the continuation school (an alternative high school for potential dropouts or students with discipline problems). The boundaries of Allentown High contain the more prestigious locations in the city, while those of Eureka High have always enveloped Navy and public housing projects. To many Allentown residents the relative prestige of the two high schools is a factor of these boundaries.

Like the city itself, the schools in Allentown have historically functioned independently, without much interference from the central administration. For the last 3 or 4 years, there has been a concerted effort on the part of the superintendent and staff to rectify this situation—to bring schools in line. Currently, a single curriculum is being established, and it is being met with considerable outcry and alarm. Allentownians like to remain outside the mainstream.

Problem

Teaching at Allentown High is often like the position of the Red Queen in *Through the Looking Glass*: you must run as fast as you can simply to stay in the same place. Nowhere is this more true than in having to stifle everyone else's urge to fill your classes with kids who are not "making it" somewhere else. By "everyone," I refer to those who apparently have the power to single-handedly lay waste to your classroom—vice-principals, counselors, and special education teachers.

Often these students are added to your roster in the name of enhancing the child's education. When I was recently assigned two learning-disabled students (tenth-graders) in a competency math program designed for seniors, I was assured it was because "they can really learn something with you." My objection to the inclusion of these boys was met by the counselor with the proposal that all I needed to do was to give the students a daily assignment and send them to the special education room for help. The fact that this would summarily negate the voiced purpose of this programming (that they would learn more by being in my class) was lost on the counselor. Unfortunately I was not furnished with any of these students' testing records, which might have aided my assigning them work, nor was I given any books or materials to use with them. In addition, the suggestion to send them for individualized help is untenable because problems beyond basic arithmetic are outside the range of skills of those on hand in the special education room.

Sometimes administrators make selections justified by educational purposes, but actually based on political grounds. In my second year of teaching I was assigned to teach all four remedial math classes in the school. Ostensibly this was due to my counseling background; that is, I could better understand the needs of my students and more effectively teach them. In actuality, as I later learned, the decision was based more on the active dislike of remedial classes by the two other math teachers. Therefore, I was "stuck."

Occasionally, the programming of difficult youngsters is openly acknowledged to be for other than academic reasons. A sophomore was added to the competency math class by a vice-principal at our school. The reason was simply that the student's behavior was so poor that he could not function in an art class (!) and there were no other classes that period to try. This boy's mother, who works in the high school, was also putting pressure on the administration to keep him in school at all costs. Placing him in my class was simply choosing the path of least resistance.

This "dumping" of students is harmful in the short run because of the unfair burden it places on the rightful students in the class. A teacher's time and energy are almost always overbalanced in the direction of those who should not be there in the first place. In the long run, this practice may seriously contribute to the burnout of dedicated personnel. Added to this is the practice of burdening new teachers with all the difficult, deadend classes. If all of your students are those who hate your subject, it is hard to remain optimistic and upbeat. You start to see your students the way the vice squad views transients on skid row: they must be up to no good.

Solutions

This problem is probably best addressed on a whole-school level. Acknowledging that the problem exists might lead to the establishment of a joint teacher-administrator group to tackle the placement of difficult students. Ideas and solutions not clearly evident to a lone counselor or administrator may appear. At the very least the teacher saddled with these students will have a resource and a tribunal.

On the department level, in the high schools, teachers should reach agreement on the fair division of classes and duties. Even the placement of certain individual students might be put on the "agenda." Departments should put pressure on administrators to "give them a fair deal" when hours for classes and prep time are decided so that alternative (and appropriate) options are available for students experiencing difficulty, and so that teachers will have adequate time to deal with the extra problems that arise from working with a remedial student population.

On a personal level, the teacher must resolve to actively protest obviously bad assignments and inappropriate placements. Keeping in touch with the decision maker about the progress of these students in your classes is one method to try to keep from being "hit" again with this type of programming.

Commentaries

Middle School Science Teacher. I can sympathize with your problems of student placement and assignments. Often the teachers with the worst assignments are the ones who are polite. In my first teaching year I was given only the lowest science classes. The students either had behavior problems or they could not speak English. I accepted this because I was new. Now I really act nasty if someone tries to give me an unfair program, and I get what I want because I am nasty. I really do not like to be nasty, but someone who will not be nasty gets the bad assignments. I like your solution better. A committee of teachers and administrators making the selections would be better.

I also get the "you're more understanding" line, and I do not know how to deal with it except my old standby nastiness.

Your writing style is great!

Secondary Resource Specialist. Teaching at the other end of the spectrum, I feel that the problem of dumping students into a classroom where the teacher feels she is overwhelmed with special education students (as I am) should be directed toward the administrators. Most resource specialists realize which teachers are best chosen to mainstream their students. If they resent having any special education students in their classes, the special education instructor should be notified either formally or informally. Nevertheless, teaching lower-level classes—basic skills—seems to be the *right* situation in placing special education students.

She adds later: I can empathize with your feelings in teaching students who belong in your class. But it is a long chain of command. As a resource specialist, I have 15 students in my class, whereas the actual number who should be classified in the program is three. The wide range of skills is also obvious in my special education classroom because most students are evaluated late in their schooling. I'm also "knee deep" in the dumping-ground syndrome. Keep up the good work!

High School Administrator. The problem of finding the correct placement for a student involves funds and teacher ratio. Until the state changes its funding practices, there will be continuing problems in this area. Some possible solutions are

1. A committee of counselors, teachers, and administrators who review the placement of difficult students; the committee meets weekly and puts their collective heads together in dealing with each individual case and often finds creative solutions
2. A study hall that is really a "holding tank" of sorts
3. One-to-one peer tutoring programs that can work with the study hall
4. Reducing class size through negotiations when there are several high-risk students in any given class
5. More communication from the special education office about the high-risk students with records, and so forth

TEAM TEACHING WITH AT&T
Claudia Staniford

Context

The school is a large elementary school in a lower-income neighborhood in a large metropolitan area. There are approximately 25 teachers for 650 students. The transiency rate of the students is high, with many students transferring in or out of the school each semester. The internal climate, or morale of the teachers and staff, is extremely low. I am new to the school, so I have not been able to pinpoint the source of the low morale, but I have seen the principal's lack of teacher support and awareness of teacher needs, and I have seen a high percentage of teachers who have worked 20 years in the district and have become disillusioned or discouraged with the school and district administration. There are a number of outstanding teachers at this school who work together in organizing school assemblies and science fairs and who open their classrooms and teacher resources to new or interested teachers, but they are few and carry the brunt of the burden for the entire school. On the whole, most teachers at this school do not find or create a supportive environment conducive to team teaching.

My class is part of an experimental program in the district to determine if smaller class size will raise student standardized test scores, student skills, and student self-esteem. This experiment is funded through the state superintendent's office, and schools were chosen to participate on the basis of low test scores and their high student transiency rate. I was hired at this school in February to work with an outstanding and devoted 20-year veteran teacher whose fourth-grade classroom was chosen as the one class at this school to participate in this program. I received 10 students from her classroom, 2 students from another fourth-grade classroom, and 3 students from a third classroom. The cooperating teacher kept 15 of her original students, and I was given a classroom for my 15 students. We are viewed as one class of 30 students in two separate classrooms.

The program expectations state that we emphasize test-taking skills and language-based curriculum and that we team teach. The logistics of team teaching can vary. We are currently team teaching a unit on animals. She has chosen an activity of animal research reports, which she teaches to her own class and to my class. I have chosen an activity of writing animal legends, which I teach to both classes. We also, once a week, team teach a math enrichment activity. We team teach on a daily basis, and either we switch classrooms or our students switch classrooms. We discussed the opportunities for ourselves and our students. And we got along immediately, on both a professional and friendly level. However, we were both aware of the tremendous pressure to raise our students' skills, because the success of this experimental program would be determined by the results of the standardized tests that students would take in April.

Problem

The problem we face is that we do not have the physical time to adequately plan and prepare for our team-teaching curriculum and activities. Our two classes share two prep periods per week; one on Monday mornings and one Tuesday afternoons, for an hour each day. We schedule meetings for these prep periods to prepare the following week's curriculum, activities, or team teaching, but we find the prep times slip away in dealing with more prevailing crises or daily responsibilities. On paper, we have 2 hours a week to plan our regular lessons and activities. Individual class planning is delegated for the weekends. In reality, by the time the students are assembled in the morning, walked down to the prep teacher's classroom, and picked up at the end of the hour, our hour is reduced to 40 minutes. By the time necessary business in the classroom or office is completed, we are left with 20 minutes 2 days a week to plan together. When all is said and done, our lunch recess of 40 minutes is similarly reduced to 15 minutes of free time. My team teacher is responsible for an afterschool tutorial program from 2:40 P.M., when school is dismissed, to 3:40 P.M. on Tuesdays, Wednesdays, and Thursdays. I am responsible for another tutorial program from 2:40 P.M. to 3:40 P.M. on Mondays and Fridays. Because we tutor many of the same students, we cannot coordinate our afterschool program to meet the same days. If we schedule meetings to follow our afterschool program at 4:45 P.M., we are so exhausted and bleary-eyed that the creativity and idea exchange, which are the exciting and crucial elements of team teaching, are simply not there for us.

Our problem is complicated by the fact that we are under tremendous pressure to raise our students' skills so their success will be visible on the standardized test. The district needs documentation that smaller class size will, in fact, raise student test scores and student skills. And although I feel that the measure of my students' progress cannot be determined solely by a standardized test, I want the experiment to succeed so that it will be continued on a broader scale next year with more schools and more classrooms. This means that when working with our students, whose math and reading skills range from the first- to the fourth-grade level, we have to develop a curriculum that will emphasize these student skills. Team teaching is an invaluable experience for our students and ourselves as teachers: our students learn cooperation, they have the advantage of two teachers with different strengths, more creativity is brought to the classroom and teaching experience, and we, as teachers, benefit from the collegiality and enriched curriculum. However, the real benefits of team teaching are not in the nature of those skills that will be tested on the standardized test. So although team teaching has far-reaching advantages, these advantages and our progress in team teaching will not be measured or evaluated by the district program at the end of the year.

A further complication is that, although the cooperating teacher and I need more time to prepare for our team-teaching activities, I do not feel another prep hour away from my students is a feasible answer. As it is, the 2 hours a week, the school assemblies, and the vacation days are taking away precious moments we need together as a class. By the time the students take the standardized test, we will have had 10 weeks to prepare them. This is, in itself, an absurdly short time to attempt to mark any real student progress; but this is what we have to deal with. I do not feel I can afford, or have the freedom, to take another hour during class time to prepare with my team teacher.

Solutions

My team teacher and I have been using our weekends to spend the necessary hours over the phone to plan our team-teaching activities and curriculum for the following week. This works, but because we are professionals, participating in an experimental program that has certain specifications, one of which is team teaching, we should be given paid time to plan.

Another suggested solution is that we somehow use my team teacher's aide when our classes are combined and while the students are working on independent assignments to plan together. My team teacher's aide, however, is only with her during the reading hour. One reading hour is already taken away by the prep period on Mondays; 3 days of reading is insufficient, and our schedules are too tight, bound by a minimum of time devoted to each subject, to reschedule an additional reading hour later in the day.

I would like to find a solution that gives us time during the day, when our students are working on an independent activity, to plan together.

Commentaries

High School Math Teacher (**Active Union Member**).   If you can get paid time for prep outside of the schoolday, more power to you. Unless you can be funded from outside the district's general fund, both the board of education and the union will fight you. Maybe you could try to get some kind of school activity to help supplement the program you are working with—be careful of the legalities!

What are the consequences of "lack of success" on the standardized tests in the spring? Are you prepared for negative consequences? Do you have any standards of expectation from the state or from the district regarding your experimental program?

Elementary School Teacher.   This is such a wonderful opportunity to really experiment with educational strategies; it is a shame that the district has set parameters that inhibit the chances to get the most information from the project by setting a standardized test goal, a short timeframe measure, and insufficient prep time. This is such a rich experience for you and the children, it would be much more rewarding and informative to have it viewed and measured accurately.

Paid planning time is a real problem for all elementary school teachers, and it is amplified in your team-teaching efforts/experiment. Teachers responsible for teaching multiple subjects must be given credit for the depth of planning done and the time (not calculated in paychecks) put into planning. This is a major problem in the American education system!

Teacher Educator.   What was the rationale for imposing a team-teaching requirement on this situation in which class size was the chief variable? Who decided on how this teaming could be structured? When you team teach, do you try to teach together or differentiate the tasks so only one actually does the teaching?

The situation has ideal elements, if the pressures to "prove" the benefits were not so immediate, urgent, and arbitrary. These factors do make everything appear crisis-oriented and *outcome-* rather than *process*-focused. Under these circumstances you would probably each use your energies better if you reduced the teaming commitment.

Your solution appears to be planning time with pay on weekends? No other plan is acceptable—no aide for more prep time, no desire for giving away in-class time, too tired after school? I think you do need workday time—1 afternoon each week, perhaps, instead of, or in addition to, both preps. I also think the time together for planning is essential for the experiment—even without teaming. Being partners in the project—but not team teachers—might be enough for this first year.

This is a formula for more teacher burnout: too high expectations with no system for systematically analyzing and addressing the problem.

REFLECTIONS ON THE PROJECT

Creating a culture of teaching that supports teacher learning is vital to the health of our educational system. For anyone who has tried to teach, there is no need to argue the enormity, difficulty, or complexity of the task. In order to do what teachers do—especially in the contexts in which they are asked to do it—they need to know a lot, including knowing how to use their professional knowledge for successful classroom practice. The acquisition of teacher knowledge, or teacher learning, is a lifelong process that begins long before teachers enter programs of teacher education and extends long after.

How teachers learn, and from whom or from what, is a question of central concern in current teacher reform efforts. One important source of teacher learning is experience. But learning from experience is difficult. It is especially difficult in teaching, where the work is action-oriented and the pace unrelenting. Teachers have little time to think about what they do. Yet we know that to learn about what we do—to learn from our experiences—we need to think about them in order to make sense of them.

Writing about their work is one way to foster teacher learning from experience. The teachers in the class indicated that the task of writing cases helped them to learn about the issue they described, including its scope, its complexity, and its consequences. By sharing the cases with colleagues in the form of case conferences in which they actually taught one another, their learning was further enhanced.

In a recent paper on teacher learning, Lee Shulman (1988) suggests we consider at least four dimensions of teacher empowerment related to teacher learning: empowerment of the mind, the spirit, the status, and the role. Writing cases as a process of teacher learning empowers teachers in the way Shulman describes. By analyzing and articulating their work, teachers become creators and definers rather than simply dispensers of knowledge. As the teachers in my class described it, the process of creating cases is stimulating, intellectually challenging, and rewarding both in terms of what they themselves learn and in what they contribute to the learning of others through the model's collaborative process. The spirit of service is enhanced, therefore, as teachers take themselves and their professional knowledge seriously; writing cases to be used by other teachers for professional development awakened a spirit of professional ownership and responsibility. As teachers claim ownership of their professional knowledge, furthermore, and as they see themselves as centrally important in defining the knowledge base of their profession, their role shifts to include professional growth, development, and responsibility in new and challenging ways, thus potentially enhancing the status of the profession as well.

Clearly neither casework nor writing cases is a panacea for teacher empowerment or teacher education reform. Schools where teachers work, and programs where they are trained, need considerable rethinking and restructuring if we are actually to create and maintain a profession of critical and creative practitioners who have the skills, interest, and capability of autonomous work and leadership in their field. Equipping students of the profession with the capability of reflective practice, including the ability to think critically and write about their work, however, orients the profession toward those goals. The teacher education structure described in this chapter is a case, if you will, of teacher education practice conceptualized to prepare reflective teachers who can assume such leadership for our profession.

REFERENCES

Richert, A. E. (1987a). *Reflex to reflection: Facilitating reflection in novice teachers.* Unpublished doctoral dissertation, Stanford University, Stanford, CA.

Richert, A. E. (1987b, April). *The voices within: Knowledge and experience in teacher education.* Paper presented at the annual meeting of the Special Interest Group—Research on Women and Education, American Education Research Association, Portland, OR.

Richert, A. E. (1989, April). *Preparing cases promoting reflection: A case for case methods in teacher education.* Paper presented at the annual meeting of the American Education Research Association, San Francisco.

Shulman, J. H., & Colbert, J. A. (Eds.). (1988). *The intern teacher casebook.* San Francisco: Far West Laboratory for Educational Research and Development.

Shulman, L. S. (1988). Teaching alone, learning together: Needed agendas for the new reform. In T. J. Sergiovanni & J. H. Moore (Eds.), *Schooling for tomorrow: Directing reform to issues that count* (pp. 166–187). Boston: Allyn & Bacon.

CHAPTER 9

Case Investigations

Preservice Teacher Research as an Aid to Reflection

VICKI KUBLER LABOSKEY

Since the summer of 1985, the Stanford Teacher Education Program (STEP) has been using what I have labeled the case investigation method. The procedure calls for student teachers to carry out a modified version of case study research. That is, students identify an educational problem or issue of interest, collect relevant data, analyze the data, and produce a case write-up. The result is different from what Lee Shulman has called a "case report," wherein an individual recounts personal experience. The case investigation involves more than a recording of events. However, it is not assumed that either the process or the product is comparable to the more rigorous case studies of fully trained researchers; thus I have coined a new term, "case investigation." "I Just Want to Teach" is a case investigation written by a STEP student, Jan Mahoney, in the fall of 1987. The focus of this particular assignment, the second in a series of three, was to write about herself as a beginning teacher. Students were encouraged to identify an area of interest for them as novice teachers and explore it as broadly and deeply as possible in a concentrated 3-week period. Jan chose to examine her own learning style and its implications for learning to teach.

One further distinction needs to be made; "I Just Want to Teach" is not a "teaching case." It was not produced to inform or stimulate a reader, though the possibilities for doing so are certainly there. The emphasis in the case investigation method is on the author more than the reader, the process more than the product. The purpose is to have the student researcher learn more about an educational topic and, even more importantly, about the processes and benefits of reflective practices, such as case investigations. In reading "I Just Want to Teach," therefore, one needs to consider the content in terms of what Jan may or may not have gained from the enterprise.

THE DEVELOPMENT OF CASE INVESTIGATIONS

Students enter teacher education programs after a long "apprenticeship of observation" (Lortie, 1975). They bring with them many firmly entrenched ideas about what the teaching/learning process is all about. Because these views have been acquired through experiences as students, not teachers, and because these views are, in the main, personal and nonanalytical, many are inaccurate. Since the new experiences and information presented in teacher education programs can become distorted by such "misconception filters," any wrong notions must be surfaced and changed. Teacher educators have been finding, however, that this is an extremely tough task (Feiman-Nemser & Buchmann, 1985; Zeichner, 1987).

The difficulty of the job is compounded by the fact that the period of time in which students are enrolled in a teacher education program is relatively short. This is particularly true of the Stanford Teacher Education Program. STEP is a fifth-year, 12-month program at the end of which the students obtain both a single subject teaching credential and a master's degree in education. STEP students have obtained their undergraduate degrees in a credentialing content area such as math, biology, or English, and most have had very little instruction in the field of education. In the course of 1 year, therefore, these novices must, on one level, meet all of the formal requirements of both a teaching credential and a master's degree. On another level, they must search out and destroy any faulty preconceptions they brought with them, obtain enough rudimentary knowledge about educational theory and practice to facilitate their survival in early classroom experiences, and acquire the tools and attitudes that will allow them to continue to grow as professionals throughout their teaching careers! The challenge thus posed for those of us entrusted with this awesome responsibility is to select and develop techniques that can simultaneously accomplish as many of these goals as possible, as quickly as possible.

Case investigation, in combination with other reflective experiences, seems to hold promise for being one such technique. Educational scholars as far back as Dewey (1910) have been suggesting that research skills and orientations could be useful for teachers. Lortie (1975), for instance, proposes that courses in teacher education be devised to foster the intellectual skills needed for tough-minded assessment and imaginative inquiry, including accurate observation, conscientious recording, and the ability to write clearly; these are the very skills employed in the case investigation method. He believes that such skills will help novices to challenge the results of the "apprenticeship of observation" (p. 241) and to become more intellectually independent in the future.

More recently, Donald Schön (1983) has claimed that reflective practitioners are engaged in a form of research. Therefore professional training needs to include instruction in research methodology, in particular, the process of problem-setting. Schön maintains that most professional education programs fall short by presenting students with dilemmas they are asked to resolve; in "real life," problems do not present themselves in neatly wrapped packages. The practitioner must first figure out what the problem is before attempting to solve it; similarly, the critical task of the researcher is to determine what the question is that the research will try to answer.

But there are many forms of research methodology. Obviously, we could not and would not want to train beginning teachers in all of the forms. A case study derivation seems most appropriate for use with novice teachers. The case study is grounded in the particular; it examines a contemporary problem within its real-life context (Yin, 1984). By using the here-and-now as a focus for research, the student teacher's concern with the practical is acknowledged. However, through the process of investigation, analysis, and writing, novices are encouraged to place the particular into a larger framework—to develop a structure for the processing, storing, and evaluating of educational experience. Furthermore, the case study is most appropriate for answering the kinds of questions teachers most often puzzle over—the "how" and "why" questions. It is even possible to include in a case assignment, as some of the STEP case investigations have, a requirement for using the research and theory from university coursework in analysis; then the students must grapple overtly with the relationship of theory to practice.

Teaching must be both reasoned and reasonable. Teachers must be taught how to reason using substantially supported ethical, empirical, theoretical, and practical principles. They must learn to engage in, what Dewey (1910) calls "reflective thinking." According to him, the critical factor in "good thinking" is learning not to accept suggestions uncritically:

The most important factor in the training of good mental habits consists in acquiring the attitude of suspended conclusion and in mastering the various methods of searching for new materials to corroborate or to refute the first suggestions that occur; to maintain the state of doubt and to carry on systematic and protracted inquiry—these are the essentials of thinking. (p. 13)

The purpose of case investigations is to help students learn how to think reflectively and to develop a long-term inquiry orientation toward their teaching. This is not to say that the aim is for practicing teachers to continue to carry out thorough case investigations, although the possibility would be available to them. What is hoped is that in the process of doing these assignments, novice teachers will learn some important lessons. They may learn to appreciate the complexity of the teaching task without becoming overwhelmed by it; in carefully analyzing one piece of the puzzle, students often find that other pieces fall into place more easily. In addition, they may learn how to approach future problems more systematically and be reassured by that ability. They may learn the importance of triangulation—the need to gather more data from a variety of sources before drawing any conclusions. They may learn "epistemic humility," a term used by Nisbett and Ross (1980) to describe an understanding that one's interpretations of events are inferences deriving from personally held theory (Buchmann & Schwille, 1983). Teachers will know, therefore, that although they must make decisions and act upon those decisions, they need to remain open to alternative perspectives and continue to investigate the multiple ramifications of their actions. This will require careful record keeping and systematic review.

Quotes from STEP-student participants over the last 3 years will serve to illustrate some of the lessons that can be learned:

The exciting thing about this process is becoming conscious of what I have been doing unconsciously. Although I observed my master teachers for almost a full semester, I had in mind the kinds of things I wanted to do before that, and I didn't change my mind as a result of the observations. I didn't ask myself why I wanted to do it the way I did it; it just seemed the clear and obvious way. When I was forced to examine my choices and actions, I realized that the real models I had had were my own teachers, not the teachers I observed. I was acting on what had worked for me, what had generated my interest in literature and education. I had internalized a model of teaching based on my own model of learning.

Writing in a journal really helped keep my thoughts on target when so much was happening. What's really amazing to me is how much things change from day to day. That means you've got to monitor your work for a long time to get some accurate data. I think I'm getting better or I'm learning how to monitor, to see.

After finishing my first case study on Larry, I realized that I must be more careful in assessing students in the classroom environment. I cannot rely on my hunches about how a student performs or behaves. I concluded that, as a teacher, I must try to push myself beyond the comfort level of just watching a student at various moments and assuming a set behavior. This experience encourages me to be more open-minded and reflective in teaching. I also see the value and, indeed, necessity of observing students in many different settings and endeavoring to reformulate my notions and assumptions whenever possible. When a teacher decides he/she has "figured out" a student and, thus, stops questioning, that teacher will do the student a great disservice.

THE METHOD OF CASE INVESTIGATION

Case investigations can be a single assignment for one teacher education course or be part of a larger research-training package. In the Stanford Teacher Education Program we have tried several variations. One year the students did a single case assignment in one of their courses; another year the students did four investigations, one per quarter, each focusing on a different one of Schwab's four "commonplaces of teaching"—student, teacher, instruction, and context (1978).

Necessary conditions for the implementation of the strategy are first that students be engaged in simultaneous field work and coursework. They must have a practical context, where they are either observing or teaching, in which to carry out their research. They must also have an instructional situation, such as a teacher education course or seminar, where they can learn methodology and discuss progress. Second, there must be several meetings devoted to training in the appropriate research techniques prior to, or during, the first case investigation assignment. Finally, the students must have access to a knowledgeable facilitator, such as an instructor or supervisor, who can assist them in the course of completing the project. This individual must be able to offer guidance in and answer questions about all of the various components of the process—problem-setting, data gathering, data analysis, and write-up.

As an example, I will describe how the case investigation technique was implemented in STEP in 1987–1988, the year "I Just Want to Teach" was written. During the summer quarter, the first in the program, the students were assigned to observe in a Stanford-based Upward Bound class each morning, Monday through Thursday. On Fridays, all of the 65 STEP students met together for a 3-hour seminar session called "practicum." As part of their summer practicum requirements, students were assigned their first case investigation. The focus of this assignment was the high school student; each STEP student was to do a case investigation of one Upward Bound student. After some preliminary observations, the novices were to isolate a question about their observee that they wanted to investigate. Then they were to carry out research in an effort to answer the target question.

The students were introduced to this first case investigation assignment in gradual stages over the course of the summer. Some or all of each Friday morning practicum session was devoted to instruction in the procedures for carrying out a case investigation. First, the students were taught how to engage in systematic observation of their case subject. Particular emphasis was given to the distinction between description and interpretation. They were given handouts with a sample format and comprehensive explanation of the procedures. They engaged in various practice exercises. For instance, in one session a STEP supervisor taught a lesson to a group of STEP students while the others observed. Then the participants were debriefed on the lesson. Finally, all students met in small groups led by supervisors to discuss their reactions and observations. Again, specific emphasis was given to the separation of interpretation from description. Students were given subassignments to carry out specific observations of their case subject, and the progressive results were discussed in several whole- and small-group meetings.

As time went on, the focus of these discussions became question formulation. As students shared their observations in practicum, supervisor meetings, and individual conferences, they were assisted in the identification of a particular issue of interest. They were guided in how to develop from the area of concern a specific research question that would be suitable for a brief case investigation. They were given a very concise overview of the most critical and appropriate points from Yin (1984) on case studies and Miles and Huberman (1984) on data analysis in qualitative research. The point was made that the question may change over time, but that the changes should be well documented and that the final question needs to be clearly stated and thoroughly addressed.

The students were also given instruction in how to carry out a research interview. They were provided with sample questions and given the assignment of interviewing their Upward Bound student, provided the student consented. It was also suggested that they try to interview other individuals, such as their student's teachers, dorm counselors, friends, and parents. The pros and cons of tape recording and note taking were discussed. At this point, other sources of data were also described: cumulative records, course pre- and posttests, and other artifacts from class work.

Finally, the STEP students were taught how to do data analysis and case write-up. The actual paper assignment was distributed at this time, and samples from the previous 2 years were put on reserve in the office. They were, however, encouraged to avoid the examples if at all possible and attempt to have the style and format of their particular case derive from their own questions and data. The samples provided represented a wide variety of approaches to the assignment. Again, individual and group assistance was provided as needed during the course of data analysis and write-up. Once the case investigations were submitted, I read all of them and gave thorough feedback on the content and the form. In many instances, the student's STEP supervisor also read the case and gave additional feedback.

In the fall the students were given their second practicum-associated case investigation assignment. This time the focus was to be on the teacher instead of on a student, and the teachers in question were to be themselves. This assignment was carried out during their first quarter of actual classroom teaching as an intern or student teacher in a public or private school in the Bay Area.[1] Though little attention was given to further instruction in the processes of case study research, one practicum session was devoted to an explanation of the considerable differences between this assignment and the previous summer's case investigation. Less emphasis was given to the development of a specific question; they were instead encouraged to identify an area of interest for them as a beginning teacher and explore it as broadly and deeply as possible in a concentrated 3-week period. The questions posed were: What is it that concerns you most about your own teaching? Which of your beliefs or practices would you like to know more about or just understand better?

INTRODUCTION TO THE CASE

The case I have included in this chapter was written in response to the latter assignment described above. Therefore it was the second case written by this student during her second quarter of the program and her first quarter of teaching. The student author is Jan Mahoney, a credential candidate in science during the 1987–1988 STEP year. As will be clear from reading the case, teaching is a second career for Jan; she left a successful career as a research scientist and administrator to join the program.

In reading the case, it is important to keep in mind the purpose of the assignment. The case investigations were designed with the dual aim of having preservice teachers learn more about a specific issue but also, and more importantly, learn more about how to continue learning and why it is essential to do so. In this case the author focused upon her own learning style and its implications for the process of learning to teach.

The case is followed by three commentaries. The first is by a student who attended STEP during the same year as the author and, thus, carried out the same assignment. The second is by a recent graduate of a different teacher education program who had never done an exercise like this one. The third is by an educational scholar and the former director of STEP. All of the commentators were reading the case for the first time. They were asked to focus upon how the writing of the case was useful to the author and upon their particular perspective on the value of this technique in general. In addition, they could comment upon their reaction to the specific content of the case based upon their own knowledge and experience.

I JUST WANT TO TEACH
Jan Mahoney

Friday afternoon, June 19, 1987, I walked out of my empty office and closed the door on a 10-year career. My desk job at a major pharmaceutical firm had run its course—the thrill was gone and things were quite routine. After many empty days and thoughtful nights, I made a change I knew I needed. Looking back to when I first started that job, I had said to everyone, "I like my job—I'm learning a lot and I seem to catch on to it quickly." The people I worked with were impressed that I picked up the rather complicated organizational structure and intricacies of international clinical research. New material in a new field for me, cardiovascular medicine, was abundant and often overwhelming. At times I was impatient with my lack of knowledge and had to "fake it" in situations that I found myself in. But there always seemed to be a basic level of confidence in my own skills as a researcher and scientist that carried me through some rough times. Continually practicing the new administrative skills I was developing, I found my confidence growing slowly. I avoided making mistakes at almost any cost in order to maintain a shaky sense of self-esteem. However, in spite of my doubts about my own capabilities, a very important job was getting done. Praise and positive feedback were common, and a real sense of accomplishment was experienced with the completion of a major registration package.

But now I just want to teach. Not exactly—I made a decision to learn how to teach. It seems that I had forgotten about the means to the end; forgotten about what learning is like. I knew I liked teaching (my limited experiences told me that). What I was soon to be reminded of is that the learning experience and the teaching experience have been very different for me. Perhaps the very basis of my desire to teach is to help others through what has often been a painful experience for me. Until I began to write this paper, I had never considered this possibility.

As I looked through my journal notes, reflections, and observation critiques, and as I examined my reactions in preparing to write this case study, I experienced a deep sense of how difficult learning to teach has been for me. In considering my learning style and how it affects my development as a teacher, I will reflect on practice, point of view, patience, and, finally, on learning to learn to teach.

Practice

I am learning by doing. It is probably like a "total immersion" language course—you are surrounded by the content that you are attempting to assimilate. Originally, I had planned the immersion process to be gradual. My teaching assignments for the summer had been to present only two lessons during the Upward Bound program, both of which went well and were confidence builders. Small-group work and some limited student contact in developing a case study were my first small steps(!) into classroom teaching. My placement in the fall followed along the "gradual" plan—I had two biology student teaching positions that I felt represented a sufficient challenge for the next stage of my development as a teacher. Limited, gradual exposure to classroom responsibilities began. I was amazed at my difficulties with even such small aspects of teaching as taking roll. My respect for the teaching profession continued to grow as my exposure to the many-faceted role of "teacher" increased.

Five weeks into the first quarter, I was suddenly presented with the opportunity to take on an internship. A general science section was created to ease the overcrowded classes that started this year. With advice from people whom I respect and based on my own considerations, I chose to end my gradual indoctrination into teaching and began to practice—for real. The week I chose for my journal was the third week of my internship. I was now teaching. It was *me*—planning lessons, making up handouts, fixing jammed copiers, and seeing how fast 50 minutes of prep period go by. I juggled preparations for labs with my afternoon Stanford classes and spent early mornings and late nights on a daily basis preparing for this one class. Even with an incredible investment of time and energy, it seemed I was practicing "survival" in the classroom. I felt like a lion tamer in the lion cage—wanting to get the best out of the lions but also wanting to remain in one piece! My class is a semi-low-ability class with a high percentage of minority students. It is a required course. I practiced my entire repertoire of classroom management techniques, oftentimes without success. Classroom control is a big issue, and feeling things are out of control is a big fear. Practice without success causes major concern—it is demoralizing and demeaning. The key seems to be to practice only one thing at a time. In a postobservation discussion I realized this even more. One comment in my journal is, "I think the students are running this class at times." In my desire for things to go well, I give them too many chances to misbehave. I need to practice what I want to achieve—simple behavior expectations. These classroom management challenges would not have existed in my biology classes. I need to learn these skills, and I will learn them through practice. Ego bruises seem to be part of my practice. It has been especially painful for me, and I am aware of how it feels not to do something well.

My practice seems to require some direction. A person could practice golf or tennis, but without coaching from an experienced athlete, the practice may be in vain. Feedback is critically important and direction is essential. I am fortunate to have access to both.

Point of View

Invaluable to my development as a teacher is another's point of view of what happens in my classroom. However, I have approached situations in which I am being observed with some anxiety and the feeling that there is an extra expectation to "perform." It is important to me to be thought well of by colleagues and to have any weaknesses well hidden. I would like the students in my classroom to behave—to make me look like a good teacher and worthy of a favorable evaluation. I realize, however, that this would not contribute much to my learning how to teach. Instead, I need to seek out another's insight into what I do not see, hear, or feel during class. I need to know, in spite of any possible embarrassment.

When Edward observed my class, the students were especially active and full of energy. A lab and lecture situation demanded all my skill in classroom management and resulted in success being measured as "no one was hurt" and "no equipment was broken"—not my idea of objectives in a lesson plan! Edward left saying, "I'm overwhelmed; I'll have to discuss this with you later." I was close to tears (as has been the case more than once). However, his insight during our discussion was positive and very helpful. He congratulated me on being able to do what I did with such a difficult group. He gave me some suggestions, such as slowing the pace, using more demonstrations, and stressing repetition. I knew I was probably overlooking these things. What was most interesting is that he saw things that I had hoped had occurred, when my only memory of the class was my difficulty maintaining control.

This also was the case when I was observed by a STEP colleague. Again close to tears because of the difficulty I had experienced with a class session that was being observed, I was glad that she pointed out things that I had not noticed due to my overall concern with class control. In both these observations, the class had been especially troublesome. People had seen me at my worst and still could find a few positive points and some helpful suggestions. Unfortunately, my own ego may be in the way of my learning from being observed. I do not like to fail, and I want others to see me as a success. Learning implies that we are not a success from the beginning. I have great trouble with this.

I have made it a practice to write "reflections" after each class. I have reviewed these occasionally, noting that I forget to put my own suggestions into practice. I seem to be better able to implement the suggestions of others than my own, although if I were to summarize my own style of learning, it would be "self-criticism." Learning from myself in order to avoid criticism from others, I have developed a strong sense of what I do wrong. Strong, perhaps, but probably not accurate. Really learning requires an accurate, not necessarily "safe," point of view.

Patience

I want to be a good teacher, *now*! I do not like being not good at anything. My life shows a trail of activities in which I have had success, but these activities have been carefully chosen to ensure success. I do not like to fail. In learning how to be a teacher, I have had to face far less than my optimum level of success. I have never chosen to learn from failure, just to avoid it. However, since I know well that my point of view is not likely to be accurate, my own idea of failure just may be only my own. I find myself often feeling like shifting into avoidance gear. I want to be good—but I want to be good now. My lack of patience for my own learning process is significant. To learn, it requires that each step be endured, not skipped in favor of an easier path.

In conclusion, learning how to teach has presented me with major challenges relating to my own style of learning. In looking at how I have dealt in the past with learning the skills associated with a new career, I see that my learning style seems to be well established. Certain aspects of learning embody some difficult challenges. Practice is essential; learning without practice is incomplete, slow, and unlikely to result in success. However, practice means opportunity for failure and success.

Another's point of view is essential. "To see ourselves as others see us" would allow us to have a more accurate basis on which to base the direction of our development. It is difficult to put aside concern about criticism, but it may become easier with practice(!).

It is difficult to learn to be patient while learning. It seems to be easier to have patience with others as they learn. As a teacher, one must be sensitive to the challenges and difficulties involved in learning, which are often those I have outlined in this paper, such as the fear of failure, lack of practice, wrong point of view, and lack of patience. Learning is the reason I chose to go into teaching. The absence of learning appears to be boredom, which is a path I have known in the past. It seems that learning to teach is a path in the other direction, and in spite of difficulties along the way, I have not chosen to leave it. In learning as I teach, I have a sense of what my students experience. Knowing my sensitivities and concerns associated with learning, I can relate to aspects of learning that go beyond pure content and actually form the framework and mechanism that allow the content to be absorbed. Learning to teach is harder than I ever imagined. The content is the easy part. I still "just want to teach."

Commentaries

Pata Suyemoto (New Teacher, Stanford Teacher Education Program). What struck me as I read Jan's case study was how hard it is for those of us who are used to continual success, who are used to getting As in school, who are used to praise—to be suddenly faced with a situation where we cannot be the stars we would like to be. Through her case study, Jan confronts this issue and seems to come to a better understanding of how her own standards and academic fears interfere with her learning to teach.

Jan's high standards for herself make it difficult for her to accept mere "survival" in the classroom. She wants to be great—right away. She acknowledges her impatience and realizes that learning to teach takes time. Although Jan seems aware that the learning she did as a scientist at the pharmaceutical company is different from the learning she did while in STEP, she does not explore why they differed so greatly.

Unlike subject-matter content, which can be learned in solitude, learning to teach requires a complex interaction on many levels simultaneously. Not only does the teacher need to be able to process the content material on a higher level of understanding than her students, she must also be able to transmit effectively this focused information; she must contend with 30 or so discrete personalities as well as the collective personality of the class as a whole; she must manage the mundane but necessary details of the roll, the tardies, the announcements; and she must deal with her colleagues and administrators. I wonder how many different sections of the brain are called into action at once! Coming from a professional situation where, I assume, she had more control over her learning situation, Jan could not be prepared for the circus called the classroom.

Certainly entering the STEP program straight from my undergraduate studies (after a few detours), I was not prepared for the diverse demands that were made on me when I entered the classroom. I often left the class muttering, "But I am only one person." The skills needed to be a good classroom teacher cannot be, as Jan discusses, learned without practice and feedback from others.

However, allowing others to see you "fail" can be difficult for anyone, especially someone who has always succeeded. Jan fears letting others see her weaknesses despite her knowledge that by allowing others to see her blunders she can learn. I found her comment about her self-criticisms insightful. She says, "Learning from myself in order to avoid criticism from others, I have developed a strong sense of what I do wrong. Strong, perhaps, but probably not accurate." From her experiences with observations, Jan has realized that she does not always see the good "stuff" that happens in her classroom; instead, she focuses on the negative. She cannot see the whole picture. She is blinded by her desire to avoid criticism, yet she is also blinded by her own expectations. She has an understanding of what her observer wants to see and what he expects to see. These expectations probably mirror Jan's own concept of what comprises a "good class." I would guess her preconception of others' expectations interferes with her ability to see her classroom clearly.

Through her case study, Jan seems to gain insights into her personality and her learning style. She analyzes her motives and her actions. She identifies her defenses and her fears, hopefully making way for more insightful and productive learning. The case study provides documentation of experience that Jan can review and reflect upon later in her development. Thus she can see how she changed and if her problems are recurring.

This aspect of writing self-case studies is particularly useful for novice teachers. My own case study allowed me to examine and reflect on my inability to discipline students at the very beginning of my teaching career. Now, I do not expect this problem will dissolve; however, I hope over time I will gain greater insight and a broader range of skills for dealing with the problem. By rereading my case study, I can not only see how far I have come, but I can rethink my impressions at that time and build on my previous thoughts. Writing self-reflective cases serves an immediate function of identifying and articulating concerns and a long-range function of documenting ideas and actions.

Mary Fenner (New Teacher, Non-STEP).   In reading "I Just Want to Teach," I felt Jan's frustration and exhilaration as if they were my own. I recently graduated from a teacher education program and have experienced the same fact that "learning how to teach is harder than I ever imagined." Jan very eloquently pinpoints major elements in student teaching that I feel are common in our two programs and experiences. The importance of practice, different points of view, and patience does influence our development as teachers.

I am very interested in this case study approach, for my training did not include anything like this. This case study allows the author to express great personal growth, after much inward reflection, and to share these experiences with others. This would ease the extreme isolation that can be felt as a student teacher. The program I attended never allowed for this sharing of personal feelings on any of the elements of learning how to teach. I was fortunate and could verbally share these feelings, both triumphs and frustrations, with a very good friend in the program. It is always reassuring to know that "you're all in the same boat." I would have welcomed this type of case study assignment in our program, especially if they were shared among the participants.

Nel Noddings (Teacher Educator and Researcher).   Jan obviously learned several important things from her case study: that learning can be difficult, that practicing in public can be frightening, and that coaching can be invaluable. Her comments on the excruciating experience of "failing in public" made me reflect on how we might make trying, feeling, and trying again more respectable. All of us who have studied math and science know that we fill our wastebaskets with failed attempts to solve problems, but, of course, we do this in private. Our teachers and colleagues get to see only the successful products we turn in. We are very rarely asked to think on our feet—to share our bright ideas, forays into blind alleys, inept fumblings, and fortuitous recoveries. We need to make public practice respectable, because it is clearly important pedagogically.

Jan's reflections were directed at herself learning to teach. I was somewhat dismayed that they got stuck there, even though she says at the end, "In learning to teach, I have a sense of what my students experience." That is good, but it may not be accurate. Jan wants very much to learn how to teach, and it is still enormously difficult. Think what it must be like to face learning tasks in which you have no interest at all! Jan thinks she has failed because she cannot accomplish certain intellectual goals with students who are not motivated to learn what she has been told must be taught.

In this area, we teacher educators do not do a very good job. We lead our preservice teachers to believe that experienced teachers (or researchers—some wonderful folks!) know how to get people to learn even when they prefer not to be in class at all. What experienced teachers really know, of course, is how to survive such classes with a minimum of guilt and damage to their egos. We simply do not have trustworthy solutions to this problem. I taught one such class every year for 12 years along with regular college prep and advanced classes, and I never came close to a solution.

All this is not to say that nothing can be accomplished in such classes or that there are no rewards in teaching these groups. I liked the students very much, and some of our discussions and informal exchanges were memorable for me and probably for them as well. But if I made an impression or helped them at all, it had little to do with math. I got better achievement scores out of them than other teachers got with similar groups, but I know I did not teach them how to think mathematically. Until the structure of schools changes so that teachers can work with fewer students over longer periods of time—so that trust can be established and personal aspirations raised—nobody can accomplish the high-sounding academic goals we talk about so glibly and persistently.

When I reflect on the pain that Jan and other novice teachers have suffered in oppressive situations, I suspect that the best thing we could do for large groups of at-risk students is simply to refuse to teach at all until this selfish society provides the conditions that will make real teaching possible.

CONCLUSION

Jan Mahoney learned some important lessons in the process of doing her case investigation, lessons that should serve her well in her development as a teacher. And she is not alone. Many of the STEP students who have been doing these assignments over the last 3 years seem to have learned a variety of lessons, lessons ranging from very specific technique to very general philosophy. These latter statements cannot be supported scientifically as yet, although the preliminary results of a larger study still in progress have been promising (LaBoskey, 1988; LaBoskey & Wilson, 1987; LaBoskey &

Wilson, 1988). Clearly, more research needs to be done on the effectiveness of this and other techniques in teacher education. In the meantime, I believe the case investigation, if carefully controlled, is a worthy addition to our repertoire.

The primary admonition I would give to any who would like to try the technique is that the students must be closely monitored by knowledgeable instructors throughout the process of case development and write-up. In addition, very thorough and insightful feedback and debriefing needs to follow the write-up. As is typical of even our best instructional efforts, not all students learn the lessons we would like for them to learn. Because the lessons learned from this particular technique seem to be so personal and so powerful, it is especially important that continual guidance be provided.

Second, I would suggest that more attention and value be given to the process than to the product. That is, I believe that the exercise can be valuable for students who are not strong writers. Though the case may not be eloquently written, important lessons may still be learned.

Some of the cases, like Jan's, are well written. The topics and styles are enjoyable and informative for the reader. Such cases may be useful to others as well as to the authors, as the commentaries in this chapter have demonstrated. These cases could serve as case reading material for future teachers and professional educators in ways similar to those discussed in other chapters of this book.

Teaching is a very human enterprise and, thus, extraordinarily complex. We cannot ever hope to understand it well enough to control it. Nonetheless, teachers must teach; they must attempt to assist from 20 to 180 young people a day grasp some new fragment of subject matter. In doing so, they must try to take into consideration individual personalities, learning styles, knowledge structures, and current states of mind—and how those may interact with a particular lesson content in a particular instructional context. The bottom line is that novice teachers need to learn how to turn an impossible feat into a manageable task. And, most importantly, they must learn to do so in ways that will be most likely to promote the long-term well-being of the people involved. For such an undertaking, we cannot afford to produce teachers who are either too tentative or too certain. Case investigations require students to use inquiry skills in the exploration of very real educational situations. In the process of arriving at often astounding and always provisional conclusions, novices can learn means for attacking problems within a perspective that acknowledges that there can be no final answers, no ultimate solutions. An impossible feat can become a manageable task—no more and no less.

NOTE

1. During the academic year, all STEP students teach two classes in the mornings in a local public or private school. These assignments begin when the placement school begins in the fall and end when that school is out in the spring. This field work can consist of two student teaching periods, two internship periods, or one of each. The students must be on campus for one additional period for preparation and meetings. The academic-year practicum sessions meet biweekly for 2 hours in the evening.

REFERENCES

Buchmann, M., & Schwille, J. (1983, November). Education: The overcoming of experience. *American Journal of Education*, pp. 30–51.

Dewey, J. (1910). *How we think*. Boston: Heath.

Fieman-Nemser, S., & Buchmann, M. (1985). *The first year of teacher preparation: Transition to pedagogical thinking?* (Research Series, No. 156). East Lansing: Michigan State University, The Institute for Research on Teaching.

LaBoskey, V. K. (1988, April). *Schön into the practice of teaching: Proceed with caution.* Paper presented at the annual meeting of the American Educational Research Association, New Orleans.

LaBoskey, V. K., & Wilson, S. M. (1987, April). *The gift of a case study pickle: Case writing in the education of reflective teachers.* Paper presented at the annual meeting of the American Educational Research Association, Washington, DC.

LaBoskey, V. K., & Wilson, S. M. (1988, April). *A case investigation method in teacher education: Learning lessons about learning lessons.* Paper presented at the annual meeting of the American Educational Research Association, New Orleans.

Lortie, D. C. (1975). *Schoolteacher: A sociological study*. Chicago: University of Chicago Press.

Miles, M. B., & Huberman, A. M. (1984). *Qualitative data analysis: A sourcebook of new methods*. Beverly Hills, CA: Sage.

Nisbett, R., & Ross, L. (1980). *Human inference: Strategies and shortcomings of social judgment*. Englewood Cliffs, NJ: Prentice-Hall.

Schön, D. A. (1983). *The reflective practitioner: How professionals think in action*. New York: Basic Books.

Schwab, J. J. (1978). The practical: Translation into curriculum. In I. West-bury & N. J. Wilkof (Eds.), *Science, curriculum, and liberal education* (pp. 365–383). Chicago: University of Chicago Press.

Yin, R. K. (1984). *Case study research: Design and methods.* Beverly Hills, CA: Sage.

Zeichner, K. M., & Liston, D. (1987). Teaching student teachers to reflect. *Harvard Educational Review, 57*(1), 23–48.

CHAPTER 10

Classroom Management in Elementary School

Using Case Reports to Bridge the Gap between Theory and Practice

JEAN L. EASTERLY

In the winter quarter of 1985 I taught the first classroom management course in the newly revised elementary credential program at California State University, Hayward. During that first quarter, I lectured and the student teachers read their textbooks and supplementary materials. The course included activities that reinforced important concepts, a simulation, and some modeling that I provided. At the same time, student teachers spent more than half of the week in student teaching. My attempt at bridge building was to invite student teachers to share management problems they encountered during student teaching. In actual practice, problems were shared only by the more vocal students as time permitted. Clearly a more systematic bridge was needed. I chose the format of the case report, a self-reporting of classroom events. This format provided the needed link between the classroom management course and the student teaching experience.

I have continued teaching this course in subsequent years, refining the class structure based on experience with each new class. This chapter, which is based on that class as it developed, describes:

- The context in which classroom management experiences are translated into case reports
- The rationale for using the case report
- Teaching with case reports

- The development of the structure for a case report
- An example of one case report with commentary
- Implications for teacher preparation

BACKGROUND INFORMATION

Elementary student teachers at California State University, Hayward complete a bachelor's degree, normally in liberal studies, and then enroll in a fifth-year credential program. Student teachers begin the program as a member of a team of 35 full-time credential candidates who simultaneously take courses and participate in student teaching during all three quarters of the program. During the second quarter students enroll in a classroom management course, a course in social-cultural foundations, and methods courses in science, social studies, and language arts. Three and a half days are reserved for student teaching, and the remainder of the time is spent in courses. Course assignments draw from the student teaching experiences and provide a variety of frameworks for linking theory and practice.

In my course on classroom management, I organize my lectures around six approaches to classroom management: (1) group process, (2) instructional, (3) authoritarian, (4) intimidation, (5) behavior modification, and (6) socioemotional climate. Each of these approaches describes a different role for the teacher with specific strategies. We also discuss eight different models of classroom management described in our primary text, *Building Classroom Discipline* by C. M. Charles (1989). These models included those of Kounin, Redl and Wattenberg, Ginott, Glasser, Dreikurs, Jones, and Canter, as well as a neo-Skinnerian model. The students are familiar with most of these approaches and models of classroom management before they begin writing their case reports.

RATIONALE

The case report provides a structured link between the classroom management class and the student teaching experience. I have found that the procedure of writing about a management problem faced during student teaching has a profound impact on the student teachers. It appears to alter their student teaching experience.

Writing the case reports involves a number of activities. As background for this assignment, student teachers collect information about their schools, classrooms, communities, and students. They must decide whom to interview, which documents to read, and whom and what to observe. This kind of data collection has several implications. Rather than haphazardly learning about their environment, student teachers become involved in a structured data-gathering process that, once learned, may be repeated in future situations. Second, students have opportunities to test their theoretical knowledge of models and approaches to classroom management presented in class against real problems in their respective classrooms. Rather than learning about classroom management from one master teacher, student teachers bring additional alternatives with them. Finally, the structure of the case report provides a framework for reflection and analysis rather than assuming that this process will naturally arise during conferences with master teachers.

TEACHING WITH CASE REPORTS

While the case report shapes the nature of the student teaching experience, it simultaneously enriches the classroom management course for my students and for me as an instructor. We use case reports in a variety of activities throughout my course. Before students begin writing their own case reports, they have opportunities to critique other reports written by student teachers in previous classes. They then write their own reactions to the case using the six questions that are listed in the "Commentary" section of this chapter. Finally, I give them written commentary by other student teachers and master teachers so that they have opportunities to extend their thinking about the particular case.

After critiquing several cases, the students write their own. They then present the cases to their peers within small groups—first describing the problem and soliciting alternative strategies, then presenting their alternatives, solutions, and analyses of the case. They add richness to our class deliberations about theoretical approaches and models of classroom management strategies because these discussions are rooted in practice.

I have compiled the best case reports of the past 4 years to use as supplementary materials for subsequent classes. I have also used these reports in courses and workshops designed to help master teachers to work more effectively with student teachers. By asking these experienced teachers to write commentary, I have been able to compile layers of commentary for each case. These interpretive comments provide a bridge between novices and experienced teachers. Novices are able to benefit from the written analyses of experienced teachers. And veterans are able to understand better the struggles of student teachers who face for the first time the formidable arena of classroom management.

Perhaps most important for me as an instructor is that these case reports provide opportunities for me to learn from my students. Instead of visiting 175 different classrooms in a year, I now have access to specific snapshots that increase my knowledge of the diversity of one metropolitan area, the nature of its discipline problems, and the thinking of my student teachers.

DEVELOPING THE CASE REPORT

I have continued to refine the structure of the case report during the last 4 years, based on the suggestions of student teachers who have completed this assignment and master teachers who wrote commentaries. The original assignment provided few guidelines, because I was uncertain how to structure it. For example, the initial case reports lacked information on the context of the school and classroom, which made it difficult to evaluate how the student teacher handled the particular situation described. As missing elements that would help the analysis of the problem were identified, I added specific questions to the assignment that improved the quality of later case reports.

One outcome of the structure of the current case report was the improved reflection and decision-making skills of my student teachers. In many ways, their discussion of issues of teaching appeared more like those of seasoned teachers than student teachers. Instead of talking about the "best" solution, they talked about alternatives. They had a detailed knowledge of the school, community, and students. They thought about the implications of their present decisions on future decisions rather than being solely concerned with survival tactics. With the addition of specific guidelines, student teachers were assisted in actively learning that which is worth knowing prior to making a thoughtful decision.

Students use four sources for their case report: (1) data collection completed by student teachers about their respective schools, classrooms, communities, and students; (2) the problems in classroom management experienced during student teaching; (3) course lectures in classroom management; and (4) models from the textbook

Typically, four or five student teachers are clustered in one elementary school and are therefore able to share the data-collection task. This includes interviews with the principal and a review of demographic data about the community. Each student teacher is then solely responsible for the information about his or her own classroom and respective students. Student teachers describe a management problem that they had successfully handled and choose alternative solutions from the approaches described in the class lectures and/or the models outlined in their textbook. This kind of data collection is reinforced by a very similar assignment in the course on social-cultural foundations.

INTRODUCTION TO THE CASE

The case that follows is a good example of a case report. The student teacher's description of the context of the school and classroom is thorough, and her candid reflection on the problem illustrates the struggles and personal growth of this novice. She also avoids the pitfalls of drawing conclusions without specific supporting documentation. Of even greater importance is her willingness to accept responsibility for her initial lack of success. She identifies those factors that impede success and makes plans appropriate for a student teacher. She goes beyond merely filling in the blanks by describing the educational background of parents and their vocational aspirations for their children. For example, she raises the issue of geographic mobility and later describes it as an issue for one of the "problem" children.

Originally entitled "Back Row Buddies," the student teacher retitled the case report "Free to Be Me." She indicated that this report reflected her feeling of freedom to try out different approaches and strategies during her student teaching because of the accepting school climate.

FREE TO BE ME
Catherine Bueno de Lorimier

Context

The School and Classroom.   The subject of this case report is Freedom Elementary School, situated in the middle of a quiet suburban neighborhood community. This K–6 school is comprised of 13 teachers who manage many staggered and split classrooms. Students are grouped by ability within their classrooms for most subjects. Additionally, there are two GATE (gifted and talented education) classrooms for the middle and upper grades, which are almost completely managed through learning centers. The development staff of six personnel includes a school psychologist. A physical education teacher and a parent-led FAME program (famous artists and musicians experience) contribute to the supportive, well-cared-for atmosphere of the school, which is further reflected in the newly remodeled library, clean grounds, and carefully gardened lawns and flower beds. The most visible personnel include the personable vice-principal who also teaches in the GATE program, the friendly janitor who calls everyone by name, and the humorous, health-conscious athletic director. The development staff works closely with the parent association in regard to decision making about programs such as a science fair and a young authors' writing competition.

The school's organization and community support are additionally reflected in Mr. Gunther's kindergarten classroom, which was my student teaching assignment for 7 weeks. The class of 29 students is divided into an an early group of 15 students and a late group of 14 students. The early group comes an hour before the late group, which stays an extra hour after the others have gone home. The separate hour thus gained for each group is devoted to the most intensive learning subjects: reading readiness, math, language arts, social studies, or science. For their intensive first hour of class, the 15 early students are divided into three smaller groups of five students each. Grouped by ability, these groups participate in the activities of three different learning centers, assisted by a teacher, an aide, and a parent or student teacher. The same routine is used at the end of the day for the late group, which also works at a more elevated level for their intensive work hour.

The middle of the day, when all students are present, is devoted to calendar and opening exercises, children's educational television programs, music and rhythm activities, storytelling, filmstrips, sharing time, or library trips, depending on the day of the week. A 45-minute block of play activity time is allotted each day, and the children choose their activities and agree to stay at the table or in one area for the entire time.

The Community.   The majority of the surrounding community is Caucasian, with a relatively large concentration of East Indians and some Asians, blacks, and Hispanics. The economic status of most families is middle to upper-middle class, reflected in the smaller single-unit dwellings surrounding the school and the new, larger housing developments within 5 miles of the school's location. Twenty of the 325 students at Freedom Elementary qualify for the reduced-fee lunch program, and 14 have limited English proficiency, making this a fairly homogenous school overall. The age patterns of the families correlate with the housing patterns: younger couples live nearest the school in the smaller dwellings, and older, more established families reside in more affluent neighborhoods nearby. Four children live in a Rubikon (group) home, and four live in foster homes. About one-third of the children are raised by single parents, and the majority live in nuclear families. Crime in the suburban area is minimal.

In regard to the educational background of parents, all have a high school background and most have attended college; many are professionals themselves and wish to continue the tradition for their children. Most expect that their children will attend college and gear them to do so. One community college is located within 2 miles of the school site.

Approximately 40 percent of students remain in the school from kindergarten through sixth grade. About 33 percent of the families are geographically mobile, and Freedom Elementary is used for temporary placement of students until a permanent school is found.

Background on Students.   The students in my kindergarten class range from 5 to 7 years of age, three having repeated the year due to emotional, academic, or social immaturity problems. Generally, the youngest children are the least mature and are placed in the early group. One child cries for her mother about 3 days out of the week, but the rest seem emotionally secure about attending school. This group has quite a few thumbsuckers, and many of them are physically small.

The late group has larger, more physically and verbally mature children. They are also quite a bit more independent in doing their work and relating socially. Six children out of the entire class work with a speech therapist twice a week.

The following are descriptions of the principal students involved in this case report. One 7-year-old, Arnold, has two deaf parents and a slight hearing impairment in one ear; he is for the most part verbally understood by all his classmates and teachers. He has a slight tendency to be impatient and overexcitable.

Benjamin has been medically diagnosed as hyperactive. He takes medication at home to aid this problem. I observed his temperament as fluctuating from very cooperative and sedate to very demanding, stubborn, active, and defiant of directions from any adult, including my master teacher. It is not clear if this is due to the amount of medication he receives or if his moods change randomly.

Kevin has a family in the process of moving to another state. This student is very affectionate and in need of attention. He is clearly distressed about the impending move and the absence of his father, who is setting up new employment. I recognized this through a picture he drew of his family in which he told me each member was crying because they were moving away.

A black boy, Carl, lives with his grandmother and calls her "mother." He apparently never knew his father, and he has little contact with his real mother. Carl has been a discipline problem since the beginning of the school year, often speaking out of turn or using his size and strength to bully others on the playground. Mr. Gunther has been using a neo-Skinnerian system to encourage good behavior by awarding him happy, straight, or sad faces in his special booklet at the end of each day, depending on his behavior. When Carl earns five happy faces in a week, he is given a cracker. This system is well understood and supported by his grandmother at home, and it seems to work on an intermittent basis.

One student, John, arrived at Freedom Elementary in the middle of the school year, the same week I began my student teaching there. His family moved here from Tennessee. According to his mother, this highly verbal child was socially adept with girls but was disliked by boys because he was too aggressive in speech and actions, such as hitting others on the playground.

Description of the Problem

My difficulty with the students did not arise on an individual or small-group basis. In these situations, I was easily able to remind students of the correct behavior standard I had established and keep them on task at their tables. However, in the large-group setting, I found it very difficult to gain and maintain the attention of the entire group, especially during the opening exercises on the rug. Girls would sit next to their friends and chatter, squirm, and play with each other's hair. Boys would sit next to their favorite buddies and poke each other, talk, or cause others to become defensive and speak out because their wiggling invaded another student's space. This often happened on the outer periphery of the large semicircle of children, and the crowded space made access to every spot almost impossible for me. The problem children I mentioned tended to set the tone for the neighboring buddies around them. When I first began the opening exercise routine, I noticed that only some children would pay attention; quite a few could not respond to my direct questions, even when I used their names to address them. I found myself wasting half of the time asking individuals to look up to the front, listen carefully, and do the three things Mr. Gunther had established with them: sit with legs crossed, hands in the lap, and mouth closed.

I had mistakenly expected the children to respond to me just as they did to Mr. Gunther. My initial attitude exposes my naiveté about the situation. In retrospect, I can see that the children were testing me as a new teacher, so I could not automatically expect the same respect and responses that they gave to my master teacher. Also, the opening exercise was very routine, and I did not initially feel assertive enough to try to take ownership of my master teacher's system to make it work for me. Lastly, I needed more experience working with this age group and not letting their misbehavior fluster me and affect the entire lesson. Using positive reinforcement, time-outs, and the ripple effect, as my master teacher did, did not seem to be effective enough for me. What I needed to do was cut down on the amount of time spent disciplining so I could have the children concentrate on the lesson.

Viable Solutions

After some thought about different ways to approach the discipline problem, I came up with the following possibilities:

1. Utilize the group process approach and really focus on maximizing students' accountability, participation, and attention, as Kounin describes.
2. Employ effective movement management, such as vary the tempo and sequence of activities within the instructional approach, also advocated by Kounin.
3. Gain strict control of the students through an authoritarian approach. I could set rules and follow through on limits (Canter); withdraw as an authority figure, and give the students the responsibility of dealing with the problem (Dreikurs); use mild desists, hints, and "I" messages (Canter); or

use proximity control such as eye contact, facial expressions, and body language (Jones).
4. Use harsh reprimands and sarcasm (Ginott) within the intimidation approach.
5. Use a neo-Skinnerian behavior modification approach and utilize "catch 'em being good" techniques, encouragement (Ginott), or tangible reinforcers.

Solution

I used a combination of parts of all of these approaches (except the intimidation approach) with an emphasis on Dreikurs's power-seeking model. I chose to employ movement management, picking up the speed and varying the sequence of my presentation. I also made the children pay closer attention by holding them accountable through the use of more drill questions, which I made into a game. For example, when I asked the name of the month and received an answer, I would circulate to ask the same question of other students. When they were all adept at that question, I would change to ask them the day of the week. Then I would alternate these questions, having them see how quickly they could respond if they paid attention.

I was most pleased with the behavior of my "problem" students after utilizing Dreikurs's power-seeking approach. On the playground one day I "caught" Benjamin and Carl "being good" (behavior modification) and took advantage of the situation to ask them to be the line leaders coming in from recess. I asked them to model the correct behavior for the rest of the class as they came in from recess and sat on the rug and gave them the title "class leaders" for the day. I told the entire class they need to watch these boys because they were going to show everyone the correct way to sit and listen. These boys, whom I situated on different sides of the semicircle, and other students on subsequent days, really took their responsibility to be extra good to heart. They went as far as to ask others around them to be quiet, sit still, and listen during the opening exercises. After doing this only one day with each of the most problematic children in the class, I found that encouragement and "catch 'em being good" techniques had a much quicker and lasting effect. Benjamin and Carl, who used to be the most stubborn of students, were now very cooperative whenever I asked a favor. They were finally being noticed for something besides a mistaken goal!

Throughout my weeks in the classroom, I became more adept at using eye contact, "I" messages such as "I can't hear," and proximity control, even on the rug. All I needed to do was ask the children to spread out their half circle when sitting down so that I could have easier access to them. By concentrating on the most problematic children, I found that the ripple effect naturally took place. The buddy system was more likely saved for recess time.

Analysis of Solution

I chose this solution because I wanted and needed to gain ownership of my master teacher's lesson. Thus, by using a tempo change, encouragement, "catch 'em being good," and giving responsibility to problem students, I found different techniques than my master teacher employed to have the children respond to me and listen to the lesson. I did not see the need to use tangible reinforcers, so I decided to reserve that strategy for a later time when I might really need it.

I took contextual variables into account by primarily concentrating Dreikurs's approach on my problem students. I wanted to give them positive attention in my approach, because all of them seemed to be going through changes or difficulties in their personal lives, and the reality was that they did need attention. Because their behavior could set off the class in one direction or another, I needed to concentrate on them as "classroom leaders" to be assured the rest of the group would "copy cat" and cooperate.

My master teacher influenced my choice in that I wanted to employ a different strategy from the one he used so the children would respond to *me* during the opening exercises. Thus I avoided time-outs, talking about the "three things" to remember, and using the ripple effect too often, because those were *his* strategies. After I tried Dreikurs's model once, he commented positively on its effectiveness.

For this situation, my decision to combine the various approaches was better than utilizing only one approach or simply continuing to work within Mr. Gunther's routine. That is because I was a new teacher trying to assume the lesson established by another, so I really needed to establish my separate expectations and routines. In my own classroom later I may well utilize the ripple effect, time-outs, and maintaining three strict rules.

In the future I will remember the effectiveness of Dreikurs's model with power-seeking students. I found it especially useful because it did not condemn those students who were possibly emotionally upset. Rather, it gave them the chance to gain attention through productive responsibility.

Commentary

The commentary which follows is compiled from written reactions of student teachers enrolled in my classroom management courses as well as master teachers enrolled in supervision classes. I developed the questions (in italics) to provide a structure which guides the reflections of both student teachers and master teachers.

1. *Did the student teacher consider all contextual clues when choosing the solution? If you said no, explain your answer.* The student teacher describes the backgrounds of five students in great detail yet does not appear to connect the specific nature of these backgrounds with her solution. In fairness, she does link her use of positive approaches to the fact that each of the five boys seemed to be experiencing difficulties in his personal life.

Her knowledge of the early and late groups probably contributed to her selection of such techniques as movement management and group focus. However, she does not make a direct connection between the descriptions of the two groups and the selection of these strategies. While this background information probably directed her choice of alternatives, she seems to be unaware of its influence at the conscious level.

In many ways the most important contextual variable appeared to be the master teacher and the approaches he used. Foremost in the student teacher's mind was establishing separate routines so that her students would respond to her as a unique human being rather than a carbon copy of the master teacher. This added dimension is candidly discussed by the student teacher and probably is at work for all student teachers at the subconscious level.

2. *Is there important information that is missing? If you said yes, explain your answer.* While the case report was very thorough, there is some missing information. It is not clear why five of the boys were singled out as setting a negative tone for other students sitting close to them. While the girls were described generally as chattering, squirming, and playing with each other's hair, none were described individually. It could be argued that the reason for choosing to describe two of the five boys in detail was linked to the fact that two of them, Benjamin and Carl, were asked to be line leaders because they were

good on the playground. While we might assume that Arnold, Kevin, and John were also asked to be leaders, this designation is not clearly established.

Based on the student teacher's comments, it appears likely that the master teacher's classroom management strategies worked very well for him, except with Benjamin. If so, this should have been stated.

Given that students were seated in a semicircle, it is not clear why the student teacher had difficulty gaining quick access to each child if it became necessary.

3. *Would you propose additional alternatives?* The semicircle arrangement of the master teacher was never questioned but, rather, simply accepted by the student teacher. This is not surprising in light of the tremendous power that master teachers have to influence novices in their classrooms.

The use of a whole circle would give students more physical space and probably increase their ability to pay attention to the student teacher. Consideration should be given to separating certain students from each other and/or giving assigned places.

4. *Are there any alternatives which are not viable?* Research does not support the use of sarcasm and harsh reprimands that make children "lose face" in front of their peers. The use of sarcasm should not be attributed to Ginott. Instead, Ginott warns against its use because of the negative impact on children.

Under viable solutions, the student teacher talks about withdrawing as an authority figure and giving students the responsibility to deal with the problem. This solution is based on the student teacher's perception that students are seeking power by challenging her authority. The behavior described as power-seeking was a combination of girls chattering, squirming, and playing with each other's hair while the boys would talk and poke at each other. Actually, these behaviors seem quite normal, especially when young children are placed so close together physically and when no attempt is made to separate "buddies." Perhaps it seemed like power-seeking to a student teacher who was struggling to take over the "command" of this portion of the kindergarten morning. Were the children really challenging the authority of the student teacher or is this the way it felt to her? If the latter is true, then Dreikurs's power-seeking approach does not appear to be a viable solution.

5. *Was this the best solution?* While this solution appears to be a very good one, the student teacher may want to think about the reward aspect in the context of fairness to all students. If used on a long-term basis, it will become clear that to be a chosen leader in this class, one must be "bad" first and then do something "good" so that the teacher will reward you. Under this regime, the consistently "good" students will get left out. What would happen if the most attentive students were chosen to be leaders?

Typically, one solution is better than another because it directly addresses the needs of students within the context of the classroom, school, and community. Instead, the solutions chosen revolved more around selecting alternatives that the master teacher did not use than with choosing what was best for the present situation. Perhaps this is an inevitable struggle and balance point in any student teaching experience. Yet should student teachers discard an alternative that works in order to be a unique person?

6. *What could be done to improve this case report?* The student teacher indicates that Carl is black. If being black in this classroom is a problem, then more explanation should be given. Otherwise, it is not helpful to understanding this case report and should be dropped.

When teachers encounter power-seeking students, Dreikurs encourages teachers to redirect students' ambitions to be in charge by giving them positions of authority. In this case report, the student teacher did redirect students' ambitions. However, her main emphasis was on "catch 'em being good." Therefore, Dreikurs's power-seeking approach, as explained in the solution, should be renamed as an approach that combines redirecting students' ambitions and behavior modification.

CONCLUSION

What does all this mean and what lessons can be learned? First, student teaching has always been viewed as the most important learning opportunity in a teacher preparation program, with methods courses as separate from and not having much relationship to student teaching. The synergy between the two needs to be tapped and the case report format provides that vehicle.

Student teachers need to be taught to reflect on practice and to make wise decisions in systematic ways. To leave these two vital skills to the experience of student teaching is to short-change the preparation of future teachers. The case report provides specific guidelines that assist in building these skills.

The skills of reflection and decision making do not take place within a vacuum. During the classroom management course student teachers are required to present their case reports in small groups. I ask that they present the context of their problem as well as the problem, then invite the other student teachers to identify viable alternative solutions and the best solution. Only after that process is completed do they share their alternatives and solution. In the end, student teachers are exposed to a lifelong process of learning from one another in a collegial setting.

While reflective discussion among student teachers is important, it is not enough. Commentary compiled from other student teachers and master teachers needs to be added.

The benefits of the case report do not stop with student teachers. They have the potential to enrich university classes in addition to providing a vehicle by which master teachers and university faculty can better understand the world of the student teacher. It may even be possible to construct an assessment tool for prospective teachers that can evaluate their readiness to assume full responsibility for classrooms.

REFERENCE

Charles, C. M. (1989). *Building classroom discipline*. New York: Longman.

Part III

PROSPECTS
AND
LIMITATIONS

CHAPTER 11

Using Cases to Develop Teacher Knowledge

A Cautionary Tale

GRACE E. GRANT

I had thought that the path between using case studies to under-stand experienced teachers' teaching of critical thinking and using that same information to build prospective teachers' understanding of how to teach critical thinking was short and direct. I was wrong. The short, direct path, instead of leading to an analysis of the content-based pedagogical understandings I had intended, led to a more superficial analysis of generic skills. As a result, this is a cautionary report on the potential for cases to misrepresent what we know about teaching, even for those who have constructed them. My purpose is not to argue against the use of cases in teacher education, for I am enthusiastic about their potential; rather, my purpose is to speak of the difficulty in incorporating them effec-tively.

I choose to introduce cases of teaching critical thinking into the courses I teach for two reasons. First, they highlight the complexities of teaching and call teacher knowledge to the forefront in under-standing teacher performance. Teaching students to use higher-order thinking processes—those processes that require the manipulation of information rather than the reproduction of knowledge—requires more than the refinement of discrete, teaching skills. Students must think *about* something. Teaching critical thinking, therefore, is based upon a teacher's broad and deep understanding of subject matter (see L. Shulman, 1987) and requires a presentation of that under-standing in multiple forms as work activities for students. Thus critical thinking is context-bound. Its effective strategies vary by subject matter, by an individual teacher's conception of that subject matter, by the way that conception is represented in work tasks for students, and by a teacher's ability to engage and sustain student attention in those tasks. Moreover, by combining information about academic work that students and teachers are trying to accomplish and their organizational demands, these cases highlight the fundamental tension between organizational and instructional processes in classrooms. They call attention to the significance of this tension for both order and achievement. Cases of critical thinking deserve attention for a second reason, the centrality of schooling. The secondary school is currently the only social institution specifically designed to develop these cognitive skills in adolescents. If higher-order thinking is not promoted in the course of learning to read, compose, and calculate, a student may never have an opportunity to move beyond the literal interpretation of information. No other social organization—not the peer group, the family, religion, or the work site—requires analytical thought in any sort of systematic matter. Thus, if reasoning is not expected as a part of secondary classroom activities, it may never be developed. I wanted prospective teachers to understand both the complexity of teaching critical thinking and its critical importance.

BACKGROUND INFORMATION

My interest in using cases in teacher education arose primarily from a line of research I began in 1984 while a MacArthur Research Professor at Occidental College. That spring I spent 8 weeks in the classrooms of seven secondary teachers who had been identified as able teachers of critical thinking. My purpose was to identify pedagogical skills for teaching reasoning that could be developed in prospective teachers. I observed in these classrooms, read the texts, listened during discussions, watched demonstrations, and read course descriptions, classroom handouts, assignments, and information recorded on chalkboards and bulletin boards. I also interviewed the teachers about their goals for students, their understanding of subject matter, their principal activities directed toward accomplishing these goals, their concerns in working with this group of students, and their recent professional development activities.

The following summer, as I was analyzing the data, I read *Habits of the Heart* (Bellah, Madsen, Sullivan, Swidler, & Tipton, 1985). Influenced by the structural organization of that text, I began to think about the seven teachers as case studies of critical thinking. I developed a preliminary narrative account on each teacher. These accounts took the form of an educational criticism (Eisner, 1985); that is, a description and analysis of one classroom experience, a session occurring toward the end of the observation period that is representative of the major conventions of that classroom. Events that preceded or followed each experience were included to illustrate recurring and unique features. These original accounts advanced notions about the structure of curriculum content and the ways that structure is translated into work tasks for students; they also offered interpretations of classroom management in relation to these goals. An analysis of the work of four of these teachers is reported in *Teaching Critical Thinking* (Grant, 1988). The case of Bob Post is the descriptive portion of one of these case studies.

A second influence on this work has been J. Shulman and Colbert's (1988) work with intern teachers. Following participation in the Workshop on Case Methods in Teacher Education at the Far West Laboratory in November 1987, I revised the four case studies into cases by reducing their length and withdrawing any analysis. I also added questions about each that would serve as the basis for discussion about the role of subject matter and pedagogy in teaching critical thinking.

I then began to use one case as the basis of discussion with preservice teachers in a general secondary methods course. This course considered the key concepts and skills needed in curriculum development and instruction for secondary students: curriculum concepts, methodologies, planning skills, and teaching skills. It identified organizing principles for curricula and developed a repertoire of teaching strategies. In addition, the course provided an opportunity to synthesize and apply these principles and cognitive skills in reflective teaching sessions, in a curriculum design project, and in a short teaching experience in a secondary school. The course enrolled equal numbers of undergraduate and graduate students from all teaching fields.

Prior to discussion of this case, students had identified key concepts in their teaching field drawn from their own subject-matter background, from a discussion with one of their major professors, and from their reading of a methods text and the California state curriculum framework for their teaching field. They had read *Teaching for Thinking* (Raths, Wasserman, Jonas, & Rothstein, 1986). They had demonstrated teaching skills in one reflective teaching session and served as a peer coach in critiquing two additional sessions. And they had participated in one classroom of a neighboring public high school for 3 hours a week for at least 3 weeks.

Prior to reading the case of Bob Post, we had discussed one review of research on cognition (Sykes, 1985) and Doyle's (1983) concept of academic tasks. Sykes's summary identifies five characteristics of learning drawn from advances in cognitive psychology and information-processing research in the past twenty-five years.

1. The image of academic tasks is one of incredible complexity.
2. The well-structured problems of academic study bear little relation to the ill-structured problems of real life.
3. Cognitive activity is differentiated into metacognitive, performance, and knowledge acquisition components.
4. Prior knowledge plays a critical role in problem solving.
5. Both the concreteness/abstractness of a situation and its social relations serve as cues for intelligent behavior.

Thus the basic unit of education is the task, which draws attention to the products students must produce, the operations that are to be used while working. From this view, the best approach to teaching critical thinking and problem solving is within the traditional areas of the curriculum.

Doyle's conception of academic tasks is also useful in understanding the difficulties in teaching reasoning. Two structural features of student work tasks exacerbate a teacher's difficulty in managing critical thinking tasks: ambiguity and risk. Some tasks, such as objective tests, because they call upon the retrieval of information from memory or routine and have highly certain evaluation criteria, are low in ambiguity. Higher-order thinking tasks, such as essays, are much more ambiguous. The task does not prescribe particular ideas to use, an appropriate organizing structure, a sense of adequate development, or the logical relation of ideas; and the criteria for effectiveness are less predictable. The wider the gap is between the known and the unknown, the greater the students' risk of failure. It is the ambiguous and risky nature of critical thinking tasks that makes them more difficult for teachers to manage in classrooms (Doyle, 1986). Thus structural features of the academic task place specialized demands upon the interactive skills of teachers.

To promote these understandings, three questions directed my students' reactions to the case of Bob Post:

1. How does Bob teach his students to think about the concept of "economic self-interest"?
2. How does this method influence his students' skills in thinking critically?
3. What did Bob's students learn about the concept?

Armed with these questions, my students read and studied the case at home and prepared a written commentary, using these questions to guide their comments. Together, we discussed the case and their reaction to it.

THE CASE: BOB POST[1]

Bob Post is an energetic, slightly balding, slightly disorganized, unassuming, and thoughtful historian at Castile High School. In its demographics and program, this school has little to distinguish it from other public suburban high schools. It is a school of 1,561 students, one of seven comprehensive and continuation high schools in a high school district in the West. Because of its attractive programs and reputation for good teaching, its recent decrease in student population has not been as dramatic as at other district schools. A more significant change, however, the result of a district transfer policy, is an increasing ethnic population. In 1984, Castile's minority population was slightly smaller than the district's, 23.9 percent compared to 26.0 percent. Here, minority students are Asian American (13.1 percent), Hispanic (8.4 percent), African American (2.1 percent), and American Indian (0.3 percent).

Moreover, in order to meet the needs of a more varied student population, Castile has diversified its strong academic program for college-bound students. A 1982 accreditation self-study report described its present comprehensiveness:

> Castile still draws a rather large portion of very able students. The school finds it must offer two to three sections of advanced placement work for all four years in English and three years in the social sciences. This year advanced placement sections are also offered in chemistry and mathematics. In addition, the school finds an increasing number of minority students enrolled and also increased numbers qualified as educationally handicapped. . . . For the first time, this school year Castile qualifies as a Title I school and has been assigned a team of experts to aid in the new programs.

Castile's faculty members have accepted responsibility for these curricular changes; they assume that the task of improving teaching is a collective responsibility. As a group, they accept the obligation to serve student learning needs and to see curriculum development projects through. As a result, there is frequent talk about the practice of teaching and an opportunity to design and evaluate materials. One catalyst for this dialogue on important curricular issues is the weekly schedule. Meetings for faculty and students have a regular place on Wednesday mornings; then, in the first hour of the day, staffs, departments, clubs, or individuals meet to set policy, design activities, or discuss assignments.

Other than a supportive weekly schedule, which also includes an hour of released time daily for department heads, Castile teachers have typical material support for their work. They have generally large classes (ranging from 22 to 39 students), grade their own student papers, perform their own clerical tasks, and teach a traditional five-class schedule. It is in this environment that Bob Post works to develop critical thinking.

An experienced teacher, Mr. Post exudes the confidence and openness conveyed by his customary dress: an open-necked, button-down shirt, a brown corduroy jacket, and tan pants. One Wednesday morning in April he was leaning on his podium, a transformed audiovisual cart on wheels that held his notes and materials and followed his wanderings, at the front of Room F5 as his first-period honors history class entered. Stepping into the classroom, students automatically checked the roster on the back wall, where scores from last Monday's quiz had been posted. A bright, eager group of 38, they entered with energy, found their seats, and chattered easily with friends, their voices ricocheting off bare classroom surfaces. They filled nearly all of the 40 desks crowded into this small room.

Mr. Post took roll silently this morning, noted Beth's absence on the appropriate slip, and returned papers to Amy and Carin. He closed the door, circled the left side of the room, and rolled his podium to a more central location.

"Okay," he began. "Can I have your attention now, please?" Thirty-eight students hurried to finish their conversations. Mr. Post picked up a dittoed page containing the essay questions for the current unit on "America Secedes from the Empire" and held it up for reference. "Today, I'm going to proceed a little differently than I have for a while." This was today's experimental approach to discussion, the reason for Mr. Post's unusual hesitancy. Charles leaned forward to talk with Brian, in the seat in front of him. Mr. Post frowned toward their corner of the room and the conversation ceased. He leaned on his elbows over the rolling podium, glanced for a moment out the window.

"Today," he continued, "I want you to forget about me as a teacher, although I will retain certain things. Like I'll look at somebody who's working on geometry, Christopher." Mr. Post straightened and peered at Christopher in the last seat of the second row; Christopher closed his book. "Now, today I'm going to play the role of a substitute teacher. So I want you to think about me as Mr.—— anybody want to give me a name?"

"Jones," came one reply.

"Yeah, Jones."

"That's good. Jones."

"What about Jellyblob?" Joseph suggested from the back.

Mr. Post wrote "Jellyblob" on the board, then began pacing at the front of the room. His students giggled at his chosen pseudonym. "But," he emphasized by a direct stare at Joseph, "I will still retain my prerogatives. Essentially, today I am a substitute. And let me tell you my problem." Mr. Post-Jellyblob began pacing again, stopping at the left corner to glance at the view from the window. "My problem was I came to school early but Mr. Post was late; and when I finally got my instructions, they said to go over two essay questions that students are going to write on Friday. Before class, as I was coming in, I pulled out my copy of the questions and read it over." Tom shifted in his desk and it scraped the floor. "It said something about the boys telling me what it is all about. But I frankly don't understand——Mr. Post said that probably the girls will do a lot better job than the boys at explaining their essays."

"No way!" Joseph burst out.

"I don't know. Mr. Post may have been wrong. But the question is——and let's focus on that," Mr. Post-Jellyblob read from the dittoed page that was still in his hand, "'man is basically motivated by his economic self-interest.' John, would you help get us started here? I frankly don't understand what that quote means."

John's answer was mumbled and drowned in his classmates comments.

"Okay, I had the wrong impression." Mr. Post-Jellyblob moved half-way down the first aisle on the left before continuing. "It's the young ladies who are going to help me." He repeated the question again, then called on Vicki.

Hands in his pockets and staring at the floor as he listened thoughtfully, Mr. Post-Jellyblob walked back to his podium as Vicki also struggled to explain economic self-interest. "Well, economics is what——started with the colonies. They all tried for a little economic respect, and when they couldn't do it, they set up these restrictions and took them through the society to all levels."

"You know," Mr. Post-Jellyblob looked up from his listening and, bending forward, commented, "I thought the question was gobbledy-gook. But I'm not sure that that's not gobbledy-gook, too." He wrote "economic self-interest" in large block letters on the chalkboard. "I imagine Mr. Post doesn't print as well as that, does he?" There was a chorus of responses to this personal aside. The quality of Mr. Post's chalkboard writing and artwork was a subject of much discussion. Nonetheless, his graphic representations of concepts and their relationships are a salient feature of this classroom experience.

"Is this simply saying," he pointed to the words, "that people, that all of us—you and me and everybody else—are basically after the big bucks? Elizabeth?"

"Yes. I think that when it comes down to people doing anything it's because they're angry because they're losing money or because they're being stopped from making more money. People are motivated by that and just want more money."

Mr. Post-Jellyblob continued to direct the discussion from an exploration of the motivations for political conflict toward an application of these principles to the events in American colonial history from 1600 to 1770. He asked Ruth to speak louder so David could hear her comment about the Stamp Act.

"I *said* that England was taking money from the colonies without the colonies' consent. Okay? Thus the colonies felt that it was wrong, and so instead of paying England, they boycotted and started the Revolution."

Okay," Mr. Post-Jellyblob continued. "So the change—if I understand what Ruth was saying—the change, the movement in history, comes from the boycott. The boycott was really what was happening and if one wants to understand that boycott, what one does is look to the fact that the colonies are getting pinched economically. They're concerned about having to dish out the money for stamps. Susan?"

"It wasn't really against the colonies that the Stamp Act was looking. The Stamp Act came about because England had got itself into——was worried about being able to take care of its debts. So I think it was more the English that were causing the conflict because the colonists were just protecting what was rightfully theirs. It was a matter of principle."

Greg, however, was not as convinced as the others that the Stamp Act was motivated purely by economic considerations. He asked for clarification on the political changes. In replying to this request, Mr. Post-Jellyblob called his students' attention to an earlier reading in the unit. "Jensen," he began, referring to the author of their reading, "Jensen seemed to be saying that there was quite a movement of people to gain political power in the colonies. I thought he said something about the Stamp Act being used to gain political power. Susan?"

"Yes, the colonists were using the fact that they were being taxed without representation as——the principle was wrong then so they were using it as a basis to rebel. It wasn't really economic, but it was more the principle of the matter that they were being taxed without representation. And it meant that they were trying to gain more than lower taxes; it was their means of rebellion so they could gain more advantage and political power."

"Okay, so you feel, then, if you were writing your paper, at least one part of your paper would argue that the colonists were concerned with political issues. That was really what was motivating them, and that they were sort of covering up, maybe, some economic questions."

Susan continued, "They were economically motivated, but we were motivated by principles."

"Interesting thesis," Mr. Post-Jellyblob noted. "Do you understand what Susan is saying? She's suggesting that maybe change comes from economic motivation in England coming into conflict with political motivation in the colonies." He wrote these terms and their sources on the board. "Now, Mr. Post says that I'm supposed to divide the time equally between these two questions——do I still have half an hour left there?"

"You have 4 minutes," several reminded him.

"Four minutes!" His students giggled at Mr. Post-Jellyblob's consternation. "Okay, let's see how helpful the men can be, very quickly." He read the second essay question, a comparison of readings by Jensen and Rossiter on the Declaration of Independence. "Tell me, Anthony, how did Rossiter look at the Declaration?"

"Umm, I guess he was against it," Tony mumbled.

"He was against the Declaration of Independence? He was not, my good man. John?"

"Well, it was an agreement between all the people, he would have said, that made the Declaration of Independence. So everybody had consensus. Some people went half-way and other people went half-way, and they agreed on the middle road."

"So the Declaration, you feel, in Rossiter's view, represents the consensus viewpoint of all the colonies? Good. Mr. Post left some kind of note saying that the Declaration of Independence represented a consensus of American opinion and was a document that symbolized, then, some Americans coming together. Denis, tell me, how does Jensen view that Declaration?"

Denis sat lost in thought.

"Mr. Post was right. The boys must have slept last night." Just then the bell rang, indicating the end of the first period. Mr. Post, back in his own role, interrupted its buzzing. "Rossiter and Jensen seem a little weak in this discussion. Now, the Declaration of Independence represents something very clear to Jensen. You ought to be able to recognize that. Please take a look at that issue and check your understanding of it. If you don't understand more than we discussed today, you will not be able to write your essay on Friday. Okay, have a good day."

Mr. Post's students picked up their books and spilled into the corridor outside.

Four Student Commentaries

Tina Cabriales, Prospective English Teacher. Based on the given transcript, Bob teaches his students to think about the concept of economic self-interest mainly by providing a scenario in which students feel less conscientious about the "teacher-student" role and more concerned about becoming involved in the discussion. By creating an environment that invites students to offer responses without the "worry" of answering to the "real" teacher, Bob is essentially teaching his students to not be afraid to think. It seems to me that the concept of economic self-interest almost becomes secondary to Bob's primary goal: to encourage critical thinking and to have students venture and risk trusting themselves.

This method influences his students' skills in thinking critically by creating a framework within which students may draw their own conclusions based on knowledge and imagination. Bob does not "give away" the lesson; he makes his students learn it.

About economic self-interest, Bob's students learned that there really aren't any "right" or "wrong" answers, but rather, answers that can only make sense or not make sense based on intelligent collecting of data and evidence. Mostly, Bob's students learned that finding correct answers is a process, instead of a product.

Todd Stoney, Prospective Physical Education Teacher. I like how Mr. Post taught his class for a number of reasons. (1) He presented a situation where the students feel in power by turning himself into a substitute, which makes students both ask and answer questions. The students set up the class. (2) He makes assumptions that the girls will do better and sets up a competition. The boys tended to lose interest, but the girls put them in a pressure situation and they responded. (3) He maintained power yet allowed the students to have fun by giving (or taking) the name "Mr. Jellyblob." (4) During a period when the students have trouble speaking about economic self-interest, he turns attention to the writing on the chalkboard and once again everyone gets involved. (5) He made them think they learned a lot by essentially going "Wow, we used the whole period" on economic self-interest.

Jaimez Belmudez, Prospective Spanish Teacher. Bob teaches his students to think about the concept "economic self-interest" by having the students engage in teacher-student interaction. He listens to the students; therefore, more original thinking takes place. Bob lets the students do most of the thinking. He only directs questions and interprets whatever the students have said.

Bob uses five kinds of strategies described by Raths and colleagues (1986): (1) "Listening to students" creates original thinking on the part of students. (2) "Appreciating individuality and openness" involves students in a "thinking act," instead of initiating a search for the correct answer. (3) "Encouraging open discussion" gives the students an opportunity to discuss, analyze, and think critically with the teacher. (4) "Promoting active learning" lets the students participate in the thinking process. (5) "Accepting students' ideas" encourages them to think more carefully and not to give up if they say something that does not sound correct. Other strategies that Bob uses are "nurturing confidence," "giving facilitative feedback," and "appreciating students' ideas."

The students learned to associate the concept "economic self-interest" with the American Revolution. It is not really important what they learned, but how they learned it. That is, the thinking that took place during the discussion is more important than the details they might have learned.

Tom Lind, Prospective English Teacher. Bob starts by setting the stage for his lesson: he informs his students he will be taking on a different role. By assuming the role of the substitute, Bob puts students in the position of having to help him, rather than the other way around. He then challenges the students by setting up factions—boys versus girls—to stimulate the search for answers. All this before even stating the question. He prepares his learners to learn. He states the question, then claims he does not understand it at all—a way of forcing the students to concentrate, it seems. When the boys fail, he further challenges the girls by telling them that they are going to help him. He asks a question, gets a response, clarifies the response, then calls on a student to agree or disagree. He continues to clarify and simplify student responses, leading them in an almost step-by-step fashion toward the concept. At one point he brings up previously studied information, but he approaches it in a way that tells the students he is not sure of himself—this might motivate them to go back to the work and *be* sure. His pattern of clarification, pointed questioning, and simplifying eventually gets the students to the objective.

The questions Bob asks come right after clarifying an issue that a previous student brought up, so the students have a well-organized concept to go from. He basically takes one concept and asks for an opinion, gets another concept from that opinion, and then asks another student for his or her response to the most recent concept. He puts pressure on the students by playing the role of a substitute who is unsure of his detailed knowledge of the material, saying "maybe" or "I thought," trying to elicit a correcting response from a student. He also starts with a very general concept and leads the students, by steps, toward the ideas he is looking for. I think the role-playing idea is a good one, and the basis for why this lesson seems to work.

ANALYSIS

These four student commentaries on Bob Post reveal a clear understanding of generic pedagogical skills for teaching critical thinking. Most students comment on the importance of the classroom atmosphere to intellectual risk taking, Bob's willingness to listen and clarify student thinking, and empowering students to think for themselves. The commentaries also recognize, to varying degrees, the sexism inherent in the boy-girl competition. But none fully recognizes the important role of subject matter in shaping his discussion. As Tina states, "It seems to me that the concept of economic self-interest almost becomes secondary to Bob's primary goal: to encourage critical thinking and to have students venture and risk trusting themselves." Jaime adds, "It is not really important what they learned, but how they learned it."

Despite my own understanding of the importance of pedagogical content knowledge, my students did not learn it in analyzing this case. I had written the case to discover principles Bob used in teaching critical thinking. In discussing it with prospective teachers, I was not seeking further discovery of that meaning, as J. Shulman & Colbert (1988) did in asking intern teachers to write cases of their own world and their work. Instead, I sought a focus on the variety of possibilities in the relationship between content and pedagogy in teaching. This difference in purpose requires an entirely different set of instructional strategies and thoughtful handling of the case in order not to misrepresent the complexity of teaching. Like the distinction between the history teacher and the historian (Wilson & Wineburg, 1989), the goals of the instructor of cases differ from those of the writer of cases. As a case writer, I sought to broaden our understanding of teaching critical thinking through the creation of new case studies. As a teacher educator, my aim was not to create new knowledge, but to use cases to create new understanding in the minds of my students. Like Bob's teaching of economic self-interest, I had to both deeply understand the content of teaching critical thinking and never forget that the goal of this understanding is to foster it in others. My students' misunderstandings of Bob's knowledge base, in my view, stem from my failure to adequately support their learning.

First, neither the background knowledge discussed prior to the case nor the structuring of the commentaries focused sufficiently on the important role of subject matter. I had unfairly assumed that my students understood the concept of pedagogical content knowledge and that the presentation of Sykes's (1985) and Doyle's (1983) work would complement that concept. Instead, since neither Sykes's summary of information-processing research nor Doyle's concept of academic tasks is content-specific, my students followed the model presented to them immediately prior to the discussion of the case. The fact that none were specialists in history might also explain why they could not comment with specificity about the appropriateness of this method for the concept of economic self-interest. But their disciplinary background is not sufficient to explain the failure to recognize the relationship between content and method. Had they understood the concept of pedagogical content knowledge, even though unable to explain whether or not this strategy was appropriate for teaching economic self-interest, they could have raised questions about appropriateness. Like the experienced high school social studies teachers in Peterson and Comeaux's study (1985), these prospective teachers could articulate with elaboration and detail which activities Bob chose to teach or why he chose to intervene in managing student behavior, but they had difficulty in explaining the rich understanding Bob used when anticipating students' misconceptions of a concept or when selecting one concept instead of another. My students' statements reveal a meager vocabulary for discussing this knowledge: their conceptions of pedagogical knowledge, knowledge of self, and knowledge of students are blurred and fuzzy. As a result, teacher knowledge is missing from the language they use in communicating the reasoning of their professional decisions and actions. A more appropriate introduction to this case would be to introduce this language through a review of L. Shulman's (1987) conception of the knowledge base for teaching. As teacher educators, one way we can strengthen the conception of teaching as cognitive work is by introducing the components of teacher knowledge into professional language.

Second, I failed to structure the commentaries to focus on pedagogical content knowledge. My discussion questions failed to indicate one important focus for their commentary. In fact, they overlooked altogether the importance of Bob's background understanding. Although I asked students to respond to how Bob taught the concept of economic self-interest, I did not ask about his understanding of that concept. I had unfairly assumed that my students understood their role as commentators and could structure their reactions coherently. Instead they responded to my questions in sequential isolation. Because writing a commentary is a complex task, it must be assigned with careful attention to the manner in which ideas are generated. Like all well-designed writing assignments, it must specify the focus or purpose. A more fruitful strategy might have been to ask students to focus on pedagogical knowledge, to generate their own questions about the case related to this concept, and then to respond to one of them. A second kind of structuring organizes the layers of commentaries on a case and presents interpretation from a variety of points of view. Responses from experienced teachers, teacher educators, or educational researchers could have shown the variety of possible deliberations about Bob Post as well as identifying key principles of teaching. Especially when discussed following the student responses, these additional commentaries could have modeled important understandings that prospective teachers are only beginning to develop.

Third, as a means for understanding the complexities of teaching critical thinking, one case is insufficient and, in fact, misrepresents the very complexity that I hoped to teach. By using only one case, I failed to provide sufficient opportunity for my students to learn how to teach reasoning. In order to convey a comprehensive view of teaching and to promote reflection, case methods must permeate the entire professional education of prospective teachers rather than represent a single assignment. One case cannot convey the variety or the consistency in Bob's conception of history. The persona of Mr. Jellyblob, for example, is only one of a number of content-specific strategies Bob uses in teaching history. All are related to his conception of power as central to historical events, but not all are as personally dramatic as Mr. Jellyblob. A series of three or four cases of Bob Post could communicate that complexity more accurately. What is needed is a library of cases to learn about teaching critical thinking, about teaching reproductive thinking, both from Bob and from others. As teacher educators, we know that it is incorrect to assume that simply giving teachers this information and time in classrooms will automatically strengthen their domain-specific knowledge and transform them into reflective teachers. Such an assumption oversimplifies the complex process teachers undergo in developing their knowledge base.

Rather than leaving beginning teachers to learn through trial and error, teacher education must be redesigned with greater emphasis on what L. Shulman (1987) calls the "wisdom of practice"— the knowledge, skill, beliefs, and values that wise practitioners have acquired through years of experience and reflection. I believe case methods have the potential to make a major contribution to this redesign. But their contribution, as my experience has suggested, is not easily achieved. It requires our dedication to documenting the varied work of wise practitioners. It requires our deep understanding of the relation between case writing and case methods. It requires our best understanding of the complexities of learning to teach. In short, it requires our best thinking, our utmost care, and our constant vigilance.

NOTE

1. This case was adapted from a more extensive case study originally published in *Teaching Critical Thinking* (Praeger Publishers, an imprint of Greenwood Publishing Group, Inc., New York, 1988), pp. 11–15. Copyright

REFERENCES

Bellah, R., Madsen, R., Sullivan, W., Swidler, A., & Tipton, S. (1985). *Habits of the heart: Individualism and commitment in American life.* Berkeley: University of California Press.

Doyle, W. (1983). Academic work. *Review of Educational Research, 53,* 159–199.

Doyle, W. (1986). Classroom organization and management. In M. Wittrock (Ed.), *Handbook of research on teaching* (3rd ed.). (pp. 392–431). New York: Macmillan.

Eisner, E. (1985). *The educational imagination: On design and evaluation of school programs* (2nd ed.). New York: Macmillan.

Grant, G. (1988). *Teaching critical thinking.* New York: Praeger.

Peterson, P., & Comeaux, M. (1985, April). *Teachers' schemata for classroom events: The mental scaffolding of teachers' thinking during classroom instruction.* Paper presented at the meeting of the American Educational Research Association, Chicago.

Raths, L., Wasserman, S., Jonas, A., & Rothstein, A. (1986). *Teaching for thinking* (2nd ed.). New York: Teachers College Press.

Shulman, J. H., & Colbert, J. A. (Eds.). (1988). *Intern teacher casebook.* San Francisco: Far West Laboratory for Educational Research and Development.

Shulman, L. (1987). Knowledge and teaching: Foundations of the new reform. *Harvard Educational Review, 57,* 1–22.

Sykes, G. (1985, March). *Teaching higher order cognitive skills in today's classrooms: An exploration of some problems.* Testimony presented to the California Commission on the Teaching Profession; Claremont, CA.

Wilson, S., & Wineburg, S. (1989). Subject matter knowledge in the teaching of history. In J. Brophy (Ed.), *Advances in research on teaching.* Greenwich, CT: JAI Press.

CHAPTER 12

Teaching and Learning with Cases
Unanswered Questions

PAMELA L. GROSSMAN

While arguments for adopting case-based methods in teacher education are both plentiful and powerful, there are also many unanswered questions about the nature of teaching and learning with cases. Our enthusiasm for a new method that promises to link theory and practice in a way that engages students cannot overshadow the need to understand more about what students are actually learning when we teach with cases or to examine the potential pedagogical pitfalls in using case methods. The purpose of this chapter is to raise questions regarding what it means to teach and learn with cases.

THE NATURE OF CASES

The first question that arises concerns the very definition of "case." What counts as a case when we talk about case methods in teacher education? What are the parameters of a definition for a case that could include the variety of cases represented in this volume? All of these cases share some common characteristics: all are realistic, all provide contextualized accounts of teaching, and all have been used for pedagogical purposes. Yet beyond these broad similarities, the cases differ in origin, in structure, and in the amount of detail included. As we look toward the creation of a case literature for teacher education, how will we begin to construct a "canon" of cases, if we even want to engage in such an endeavor? What criteria will we use? What are the possible genres of cases we might want to consider for a case literature in teacher education?

To a certain extent, we seem to have borrowed our definitions and criteria for cases from the kinds of cases used in other forms of professional education, particularly cases used in law and business (Carter & Unklesbay, 1989; L. Shulman, Chapter 1, this volume). While it may be useful to build upon these models of cases, we must not feel limited by available prototypes but must assess their suitability for the specific world of teaching.

Our implicit definition of a case seems to consist of narrative texts. While most of the cases represented in this volume consist of written texts, teaching cases, at least theoretically, could also consist of videotapes of teaching episodes, primary documents such as teachers' journals, lesson plans, or examples of student work, and fictional or philosophical texts. How might these different versions of cases affect what teachers learn? Do texts and videotapes provide different opportunities for learning? Do prospective teachers approach primary documents differently than they might read narrative accounts of teaching episodes? It seems likely that the nature of the medium for the case will affect both what and how teachers learn from cases.

Many of the current cases are represented in narrative form. Does the narrative structure itself impose a linear quality to a case that may misrepresent the "buzzing confusion" of classroom life? Videotapes of the classroom may capture this quality of teaching with greater accuracy, but they may be more difficult for novices to comprehend (Carter, Sabers, Cushing, Pinnegar, & Berliner, 1987). As we consider the use of narrative in cases for teacher education, perhaps we can learn from the field of literature, in which contemporary authors struggle against the difficulties of representing life within traditional narrative forms. For example, in his novel *Hopscotch*, Julio Cortazar (1966) provides two alternate versions of the novel; the reader can either read the novel straight through or can follow the author's designations at the end of each chapter and literally "hopscotch" through the book in a different order. We need to consider what kinds of narratives best serve our pedagogical purposes in using case methods.

Even cases written as narratives differ in their structure. For example, some cases may be open-ended (see Chapter 3) leaving the resolution of the case open for discussion. Other cases may include the final resolution of the case, as does "Malaise of the Spirit" (Chatper 2). Does the lack of a conclusion in decision-making cases actually promote deeper analysis? Does the inclusion of the resolution to "Malaise of the Spirit" narrow the range of other possible solutions proposed by readers? Our selection of cases should be informed by a greater understanding of how the structure and medium of a case affect teacher learning, rather than simply by our use of precedents from other professions.

The origin of a case may also be an important criterion. In other professions that use case methods, such as law or business, the case must originate from an actual legal ruling or a real business dealing. Some advocates of case methods for teacher education have argued that cases in teaching must also be rooted in reality, representing true accounts of teaching practice (See Chapter 3). What is gained, however, by insisting that cases be "true"? Can cases be realistic without necessarily being real? To illustrate particular dilemmas of teaching, case writers may need to construct cases, elaborating on or altering true events for pedagogical purposes. Would these constructions necessarily disqualify them from inclusion in a case literature? The important point may be the *authenticity* of the case, rather than its depiction of true events. Until we know more about how the criteria of verisimilitude affects what people learn from cases, we will be hard put to argue one way or another.

Cases can also originate from research, as is true of a number of the cases used in this volume (See Chapters 4, 5, and 6). Case study research typically contains "thick descriptions" of teachers and teaching that portray the complexity of teaching; these research reports may represent attractive and available case material, but their very density can make them difficult to use for teaching purposes. In addition, case studies of teaching arose from particular research questions before being adapted for pedagogical purposes. Does their origin in research affect their pedagogical potential? To what extent must readers understand the analytic frameworks that guided the research in order to make sense of the cases? For example the case of George (Chapter 4) incorporates a discussion of the analytic framework of pedagogical content knowledge that informed the original research, a framework Wilson helped develop. Could another teacher educator without the theoretical knowledge possessed by Wilson use this case effectively? How do we develop teaching cases from in-depth case studies that preserve the richness of the original case in versions that are sufficiently accessible and abbreviated for pedagogical purposes?

The question of abbreviation also raises the issue of the amount of detail necessary in cases used for teaching purposes. As the argument for cases includes the importance of contextual information in teaching, cases should include enough detail to provide information about the particular context of the case. Yet the cases in this volume vary widely in the amount of detail provided for readers. How much detail is sufficient to enable the reader to "criss-cross the landscape" of the case (Spiro, Vispoel, Schmitz, Samarapungavan, & Boerger, 1987)? Without sufficient detail, readers may not be able to return to the particulars of a case in their discussions, limiting the usefulness of the original case. Overly simplified cases may also limit the reader's ability to construct multiple perspectives on a case, an important feature of learning in ill-structured domains (Spiro et al., 1987; Spiro, Coulson, Feltovich, & Anderson, 1988). The trade-off, of course, is time. Lengthy, detailed cases consume more outside time for reading and more class time for discussion.

The variety of cases included in this volume might lead to a consideration of different genres of cases. Not all cases necessarily need to look the same nor follow a standard format. Yet different genres are likely to serve different purposes, as is true within literary genres as well. The lengthy, fully elaborated case, such as "Malaise of the Spirit," (Chapter 2) might enable students to explore more fully the complexities of teaching and the interrelationships of many different aspects of teaching. Briefer cases, such as decision-making cases, may focus readers' attention more narrowly and serve to develop particular analytic skills. Cases written by teachers may serve yet another purpose, as teachers learn about their practice in the process of writing (Richert, 1991). Lee Shulman (Chapter 1) provides one version of a typology of cases. J. Kleinfeld (personal communication, August 21, 1990) proposes four genres of cases in her work: dilemma cases, appraisal cases, mixed dilemma and appraisal cases, and research case studies. In Kleinfeld's typology, dilemma cases portray dilemmas of teaching practice that provide students with vicarious experiences; discussion of these cases helps them develop ways of thinking about the dilemmas. In contrast, appraisal cases present examples of teachers teaching specific topics or concepts; their purpose is to help students develop ways of evaluating teaching. Mixed dilemma and appraisal cases represent how a particular teacher responded to a particular dilemma. Finally, Kleinfeld distinguishes research case studies from true teaching cases, a distinction also made by Lee Shulman (Chapter 1).

As we pursue the issues related to case-based methods in teacher education, we need to develop a typology of different kinds of cases and their uses, rather than trying to fit all cases to a particular model. As we begin to develop a research agenda on the effects of case-based methods, we can explore the strengths and limitations inherent in each genre of case, which can in turn inform our use of these cases in teaching.

Finally, we must confront the question of whether or not there are "paradigmatic" cases of teaching (Chapter 1). Is there a virtue in developing a set of cases with which most prospective teachers would become familiar? Broudy (1990), for example, argues that "the key to the improvement of teacher education lies in the identification of a set of problems that *legitimately* can claim to be so generic and so important that all who teach will be familiar with them" (p. 453). While part of the purpose of case methods is to help prospective teachers understand the contingent and contextualized nature of teaching, a common experience with important and widespread issues and concepts through cases might help to develop a common theoretical basis for teacher decision making. Yet even if there were virtue in such a proposal, do we understand teaching well enough to develop these cases? Broudy also bemoans the lack of a "consensus of the learned" regarding teaching, a consensus that is unlikely to develop in the near future. As we look toward the development of casebooks in teaching, we will need to struggle with this issue.

What makes a case effective pedagogically depends to a large extent upon what we mean by learning from a case. As we advocate the use of case methods, we must come to understand the nature of learning from cases and how this learning is distinguished from what teachers learn from other forms of teacher education.

THE NATURE OF LEARNING FROM CASES

Many have argued that case methods are best suited for learning in areas that qualify as "ill-structured domains," domains that are characterized by a great deal of ambiguity and in which "relevant prior knowledge is not already organized to fit a situation" (Spiro et al., 1987, p. 2). Teaching as a field of study would seem to fulfill the criteria of an ill-structured domain. While we can analyze teaching into its component parts for analytical purposes, teachers, of necessity, must orchestrate the whole in classrooms. The classroom is an uncertain domain in which events rarely unfold in the same way twice. As Spiro and colleagues (1988) comment:

> In ill-structured domains, general principles will not capture enough of the structured dynamics of cases; increased flexibility in responding to highly diverse new cases comes increasingly from

reliance on reasoning from precedent cases. Thus, examples/cases cannot be assigned the ancillary status of merely illustrating abstract principles (and then being discardable); the cases are key—examples are necessary, and not just nice. (p. 379)

Spiro and his colleagues also argue that knowledge of ill-structured domains is stored in cases. This may help us understand why teachers talk in terms of stories, as these stories may both help organize their knowledge of teaching and serve as precedent cases from which they reason about current dilemmas.

We need to define more clearly what we mean by learning from cases in the field of teaching. We seem to be arguing that we learn something different from a case than we might if we simply studied a set of general principles or concepts from a textbook. When we talk about learning from cases, are we talking about learning particular content differently or learning a different way of thinking about teaching? The chapters in this volume seem to be arguing for both. The emphasis on using cases to develop reflection among teachers suggests the latter, while the use of cases on classroom management and pedagogical content knowledge suggest the former. These purposes are not mutually exclusive, however, as case methods can hope to develop simultaneously both habits of thought and knowledge of particular content.

The issue of learning from cases is closely tied to our purposes for using cases in the first place. At times, the purpose of a case may be to illustrate a particular concept; a concrete case may help contextualize an abstract principle and illuminate its relationship to classroom practice (see Chapters 4 and 6). At other times, the purpose of a case may be to develop a vicarious understanding of the dilemmas of teaching and to develop ways of analyzing and reflecting upon teaching (see Chapters 2 and 3). In still other instances, teachers are asked to write cases from their own experiences to stimulate a reflective stance towards practice (see Chapters 8 and 9). Each of these purposes suggests that we want prospective teachers to learn different things from their use of cases. Yet how much do we know about what and how people actually learn from cases? We must first distinguish what students might learn from reading and discussing cases and from writing cases. While there may be some overlaps in what is learned, reacting to previously written texts and writing one's own case are likely to lead to different outcomes.

One prominent feature of the cases contained in this volume is the fact that cases tell stories. Stories are powerful; they remain in memory in a way that decontextualized information may not (Bruner, 1986; Coles, 1989). Yet what do people remember most about cases? Do memories of the specific details of a case overwhelm the memory of the general principle or concept abstracted from the concrete case? Will Wilson's students (Chapter 4) remember George's frustrations in teaching theme long after they have forgotten the concept of pedagogical content knowledge, or will students be able to work back to the concept from the fragments of George's story caught in memory? Work in the psychology of decision making suggests that people rely upon the "availability" heuristic (Tversky & Kahneman, 1974) in making decisions, using information that is readily available in memory even if it inaccurately portrays the reality of a situation. A story of a relative's misfortune with an Edsel, for example, may unduly inflate the listener's estimate of the problems with this particular model. The more vivid or emotionally laden stories embedded in cases may be more available to student teachers; how might this affect how they remember and use these cases in their own careers? In turn, how will the characteristics of salience and vividness affect the selection of cases by teacher educators (Nisbett & Ross, 1980)?

Because texts are necessarily underdetermined, it may be difficult to specify exactly what readers will learn from a particular case. If reading is seen as the interaction between the text and the reader within a particular context, different readers will inevitably construct different meanings from a common text. Teachers who use cases must respect the ambiguity of learning from cases and the multiplicity of meanings that may emerge in case discussions. Yet we must also reconcile this feature of learning from cases with the purpose of developing knowledge of teaching from case discussions.

Another issue related to learning from cases concerns the effect of conflicting interpretations of a case on teacher beliefs. Work in cognitive psychology suggests that when presented with contradictory evidence on an issue about which they hold strong prior beliefs, people use the evidence that supports their prior beliefs. In fact, mixed evidence can result in the polarization of initial beliefs (Lord, Ross, & Lepper, 1979). If part of the purpose in using cases is to confront difficult ethical issues in teaching, issues about which teachers are likely to have strong beliefs already, how should we attend to the possible "belief polarization" that might result from a case discussion?

If our purpose in teaching cases is to help students develop a theoretical understanding of some aspect of teaching, we need to understand more about how students construct knowledge from cases. Does theoretical knowledge derive from a familiarity with a variety of specific cases over time, or do we need some theoretical knowledge in order to interpret the cases initially? How much scaffolding should teacher educators provide to help students make sense of cases? Understanding more about how people construct knowledge from their encounters with cases will help us grapple with instructional and curricular issues related to case methods.

Learning from writing a case may differ in important ways from responding to previously written cases. In composing a case, the writer must first distill experience into prose and define the boundaries of the case. This search for the parameters of a case differs from encounters with written texts in which the case has been predefined. Writing a case then can help writers reflect upon what makes particular events puzzling or worthy of analysis—writing a case can serve to frame the nature of the problem (Richert, 1991; Schön, 1983). In both writing and discussing cases, the nature of the issues involved is not necessarily predetermined in the text, nor is the nature of problem resolution. However, writers of cases may propose resolutions to the problems of a case that may close off other potential explanations. The purpose of reflection and self-examination may be served, but for this reason cases written for pedagogical purposes may not translate well into teaching cases for others. Commentaries on teacher-written cases (see Chapter 7) may help offset this particular problem, as the writer's resolution to the case can be examined and made problematic by layers of commentary (for examples, see Shulman & Colbert, 1988). Again, different types of cases may serve distinct pedagogical purposes.

Finally, we must also clarify what our students are *not* likely to learn from cases. As others have stated, cases methods are not an all-encompassing panacea for the preparation of teachers. Teachers must still acquire classroom techniques as well as habits of thought. We need to consider the kinds of learning cases are and are not good for and to understand how cases fit within the larger curriculum of teacher education, which includes field experiences.

THE NATURE OF TEACHING WITH CASES

Finally, what students learn from cases will undoubtedly depend upon how the cases are taught. When we refer to case "methods" in teacher education, we refer implicitly not only to the nature of the materials used—cases—but to the instructional methods that accompany them. However, one could easily imagine an instructional use of cases that thwarted the kind of critical reflection and analysis that we too easily assume results from the study of cases. We need to clarify the kinds of instruction that exploit the potential for learning inherent in cases, as well as considering the curricular issues of sequencing related to the use of cases.

Advocates of case methods assume that something special is called for in the teaching of cases. In their series for preservice teachers, which include cases for disputes, Soltis and colleagues include the following five suggestions for instructors who have not taught with the case method:

1. Establish a good climate for discussion in which individuals may express their own views honestly as well as challenge the views of others

2. Require students to read cases and consider their own responses prior to class discussion

3. Use the same cases from more than one perspective to help students understand the "multi-dimensionality of real-life situations in which different issues come to light when different interests are operative and different questions are asked"

4. Summarize key issues, bring in relevant theoretical knowledge, and bring the discussion to a resolution

5. "Remember, students can learn worthwhile things even when their instructor is not talking" (Fenstermacher & Soltis, 1986, p. xii)

Welty (1989) includes a similar set of suggestions in an article on "Discussion Method Teaching."

In its most common format, the case-based method is a subset of teaching a text through discussion. The criteria Soltis and his co-authors recommend are the necessary ingredients of any good discussion and have long been recommended by seasoned educators (see Schwab, 1954/1978). Many of the recommendations related to the discussion method concern the nature of the social system within the classroom and the related concept of a learning community. In genuine discussions, there is a shared responsibility for the conversation, just as in learning communities there exists a shared responsibility for learning. Part of what we may want to promote through the use of case-based methods, in addition to reflection and decision making, is a learning community of teachers, in which preservice teachers construct meaning together, with the help of teacher educators as facilitators. Another benefit of focusing on the nature of the learning community in case-based methods may be modeling for prospective teachers a classroom environment they can then create in their own teaching.

If we think about case methods as a subset of teaching text, we can learn something from the research on the teaching of literature. All too often, teachers retreat from the goal of "grand conversations" about literature and settle instead for "gentle inquisitions" (Eeds & Wells, 1989), in which the teacher holds a predetermined answer that the students try to ferret out. If our reason for using case methods is to portray the ambiguities and complexities of teaching, we must be wary of leading discussions that turn into inquisitions aimed at revealing the one correct interpretation.

Focusing solely on the development of reflection and problem solving through the use of cases also poses potential problems. In their concern for process and encouragement of divergent thought, discussion leaders can communicate the belief that "anything goes" in case discussions and that all proposed solutions to teaching dilemmas are equally worthy. How do we balance an awareness of the multiple meanings inherent in textual interpretation, while keeping a discussion of the text sufficiently focused? How do we incorporate theoretical material on teaching into discussions that may naturally lend themselves to revelations of personal experience? How do we prevent students' use of conflicting interpretations of cases to confirm their preexisting misconceptions of teaching?

If the potential of learning from cases is to be fully exploited, the nature of the accompanying case discussions is critical. Restricted discussion of a case can lead to overly simplistic conceptions of teaching and its analysis. Spiro and colleagues (1988) argue that

> The complexity of cases requires that they be represented from multiple theoretical/conceptual perspectives—if cases are treated narrowly by characterizing them using a too limited subset of their relevant perspectives, the ability to process future cases will be limited. (p. 378)

For teachers to see relationships between the events of a case and subsequent classroom experiences will require a broad understanding of the initial case, as the specific details of the two are likely to differ significantly. Students' ability to make these connections across cases and from cases to classroom experience will require an understanding of teaching that goes beyond its superficial features. The development of this theoretical understanding may require instruction that allows for multiple readings of a single case over time, in which subsequent readings offer increasingly elaborated understandings and multiple perspectives on the case. Such instruction will also depend upon the curriculum we build with cases.

How *do* we build a curriculum of cases? What should guide our selection and sequencing of cases as we move from the use of the occasional case for illustrative purposes to a professional curriculum centered around cases? The implicit purpose of such a curriculum would be to provide opportunities for students not only to discuss individual cases in some depth, but to make connections across cases. The ways in which cases are sequenced, however, will inevitably help determine the nature of the connections that can be made. What will guide our sequencing of cases? Do we start with simpler cases first, building to more complex cases over time? Do we use several complex cases over the course of a class or program, returning to these cases again and again from different perspectives? At what point do we introduce the theoretical material that will help students make sense of the cases? If the community of teacher educators can agree on a common set of cases, will it also reach agreement on the conceptual material that will accompany the cases? As more teacher educators introduce case methods into teacher education, we have the opportunity to explore possible answers to these curricular questions.

CONCLUSION

The value of cases for teacher education lies in their potential to represent the messy world of practice, to stimulate problem solving in a realm in which neither the problem nor the solution is clear. Before this potential can be met, however, we must grapple with the questions raised in this chapter, among others. The development of case methods for teacher education must be accompanied by a research agenda that seeks to illuminate what prospective teachers actually learn, and do not learn, from different genres of cases and the instructional methods that best support this learning. Such research could profitably draw upon disciplines as diverse as cognitive psychology, cognitive anthropology, literary studies, and Biblical hermeneutics, as all of these address questions related to the nature of learning from text. Our optimism for the power of case methods in teacher education must be bolstered by our understanding of the underlying questions related to teaching and learning with cases, as well as to issues concerned with learning to teach.

REFERENCES

Broudy, H. S. (1990). Case studies—Why and how. *Teachers College Record, 91,* 449–459.

Bruner, J. (1986). *Actual minds, possible worlds.* Cambridge, MA: Harvard University Press.

Carter, K., Sabers, D., Cushing, K., Pinnegar, S., & Berliner, D. C. (1987). Processing and using information about students: A study of expert, novice, and postulant teachers. *Teaching and Teacher Education, 3,* 147–157.

Carter, K., & Unklesbay, R. (1989). Cases in teaching and law. *Journal of Curriculum Studies, 21,* 527–536.

Coles, R. (1989). *The call of stories: Teaching and the moral imagination.* Boston: Houghton Mifflin.

Cortazar, J. (1966). *Hopscotch.* New York: Pantheon.

Eeds, M., & Wells, D. (1989). Grand conversations: An exploration of meaning construction in literature study groups. *Research in the Teaching of English, 23,* 4–29.

Fenstermacher, G. D., & Soltis, J. F. (1986). *Approaches to teaching.* New York: Teachers College Press.

Lord, C. G., Ross, L., & Lepper, M. R. (1979). Biased assimilation and attitude polarization: The effects of prior theories on subsequently considered evidence. *Journal of Personality and Social Psychology, 37,* 2098–2109.

Nisbett, R. E., & Ross, L. (1980). *Human inference: Strategies and shortcomings in human inference.* Englewood Cliffs, NJ: Prentice-Hall.

Richert, A. E. (1991). Case methods and teacher education: Using cases to teach teacher reflection: In R. Tabachnick & K. M. Zeichner (Eds.), *Issues and practices in inquiry oriented teacher education* (pp. 130–150). London: Falmer.

Schön, D. A. (1983). *The reflective practitioner.* New York: Basic Books.

Schwab, J. J. (1978). Eros and education: A discussion of one aspect of discussion. In I. Westbury & N. J. Wilkof (Eds.), *Science, curriculum, and liberal education* (pp. 105–132). Chicago: University of Chicago Press. (Original work published 1954)

Shulman, J. H., & Colbert, J. A. (Eds.). (1988). *The intern teacher casebook.* San Francisco: Far West Laboratory for Educational Research and Development.

Spiro, R. J., Coulson, R. L., Feltovich, P. J., & Anderson, D. K. (1988). Cognitive flexibility theory: Advanced knowledge acquisition in ill-structured domains. In *Tenth Annual Conference of the Cognitive Science Society* (pp. 375–383). Hillsdale, NJ: Erlbaum.

Spiro, R. J., Vispoel, W., Schmitz, J. G., Samarapungavan, A., & Boerger, A. E. (1987). *Knowledge acquisition for application: Cognitive flexibility and transfer in complex content domains* (Technical Report #409). Urbana-Champaign: University of Illinois, Center for the Study of Reading.

Tversky, A., & Kahneman, D. (1974). Judgment under uncertainty: Heuristics and biases. *Science, 185,* 1124–1131.

Welty, W. M. (1989, July/August). Discussion method teaching: How to make it work. *Change,* pp. 41–49.

About the Editor and the Contributors

Judith H. Shulman is the Director of the Institute for Case Development at the Far West Laboratory for Educational Research and Development. Her research interests focus on both the development of teacher-written casebooks and later impact of these materials in teacher education and staff development seminars. Her publications include *The Mentor Teacher Casebook* and *The Intern Teacher Casebook* (both edited with Colbert), *Teaching Diverse Students: Cases and Commentaries* (edited with Mesa-Bains), and numerous articles in professional journals. Before joining the Laboratory, she spent nearly 20 years in Michigan, where she taught in elementary school and community college, supervised student teachers, and taught children's literature at Michigan State University.

Kathy Carter is Associate Professor in Teaching and Teacher Education at the University of Arizona. She is Advisory Editor of the *Elementary School Journal* and the *American Educational Research Journal*. She currently serves as Vice-President of Division K of the American Educational Research Association. Her articles have appeared in numerous professional journals. Her current work is focused on studies of teachers' knowledge and learning to teach and on the development of a case literature for teacher education.

Jean L. Easterly is Professor of Teacher Education at California State University, Hayward, where she teaches courses in classroom management, models of instruction, and social studies methods. She also serves as Director of the East Bay International Studies Center, a consortium of colleges and school districts that assists K–12 teachers in implementing international teaching content into their classrooms. Author of numerous monographs, chapters, articles, and simulation games, she also serves as a member of the Board of Examiners for the National Council for Accreditation of Teacher Education and as an editorial consultant for *Action in Teacher Education*, the journal of the Association of Teacher Educators.

Grace E. Grant is Director of the Stanford Teacher Education Program at Stanford University. Her research interests center on teaching thinking, particularly subject-specific pedagogy, and teacher development. She is the author of *Teaching Critical Thinking* (Praeger, 1988). Her 15 years as a teacher educator include faculty appointments at the Claremont Graduate School (Claremont, California) and at Occidental College (Los Angeles, California) as well as at Stanford. She received her B. A. and M. A. from Stanford University and a Ph. D. in Education with an emphasis on curriculum and teaching from the Claremont Graduate School.

Pamela L. Grossman is Assistant Professor of Curriculum and Instruction at the University of Washington. Her research interests lie in the areas of teacher cognition and teacher education coursework. Her research on the development of pedagogical content knowledge in subject-specific methods courses has appeared in a number of journals and in her recent book, *The Making of a Teacher: Teacher Knowledge and Teacher Education* (Teachers College Press, 1990). She has used a variety of case methods in her work as a teacher educator.

Judith Kleinfeld is Professor of Psychology at the University of Alaska, Fairbanks. After getting her doctorate from the Harvard Graduate School of Education, she set off for Alaska, which offered virgin territory for researchers in virtually any field of education. Her interest in cases developed from a research project which showed that the stories village teachers told about their teaching experiences were far more valuable to prospective teachers than the generalizations of the research. She collected stories of teaching dilemmas in the form of cases. These cases became the basis for an experiment in teacher education—the creation of a problem-centered, case-based teacher education program analogous to the problem-centered approach to medical education developed at McMaster University and at the New Pathways Project of the Harvard Medical School. This program, Teachers for Alaska, is pioneering ways of organizing teacher education around the complex real-world problems of teaching.

Vicki Kubler LaBoskey is Assistant Professor in the Department of Education and Coordinator of the Multiple Subjects Credential Program at Mills College in Oakland, California. She received her doctorate in curriculum and teacher education from Stanford University. Her dissertation, entitled *An Exploration of the Nature and Stability in Preservice Teachers*, received two awards, including the American Educational Research Association's Division K Outstanding

Doctoral Dissertation Award for 1990. Previously she was an elementary classroom teacher for 8 years in schools in East Los Angeles and San Jose, California. She has also served as the associate director of the Stanford Teacher Education Program and Upward Bound. Her professional interests include the development of reflectivity in preservice and inservice teachers, case methods in teacher education, the development of the field-work component of preservice education, and cooperative learning.

Katherine K. Merseth is the Director of the Comprehensive Teacher Education Institute and an Adjunct Assistant Professor of Education at the University of California, Riverside. She also holds a Research Associate Appointment at the Harvard Graduate School of Education. Her research interests are in teacher education, beginning teacher support, and the case method of instruction. She is the former Director of Teacher Education at Harvard University and an experienced secondary mathematics teacher and public school administrator. She holds a doctorate degree and a master of teaching degree from Harvard University, a master's degree in mathematics from Boston College, and an undergraduate degree in mathematics from Cornell University.

Anna E. Richert is an Assistant Professor of Education at Mills College in Oakland, California. In both her teaching and her research she is examining notions of teacher learning and reflective practice. She locates her case methods research into nested frames of teacher learning at one level, and into the moral and ethical imperatives of teacher decision making and knowledge construction at the next level. In 1989 she received a research award from the Association of Colleges and Schools of Education in State Universities and Land Grant Colleges for her research on the use of case methods to enhance teacher reflection. She is the author of numerous publications on both teacher reflection and the use of cases for teacher learning.

Lee S. Shulman is the Charles E. Ducommun Professor of Education at Stanford University. From 1963 to 1982 he taught at Michigan State University, where he was Professor of Educational Psychology and Medical Education and founding Co-Director of the Institute for Research on Teaching. He has previously written about case knowledge and teaching in articles in *Educational Researcher, Harvard Educational Review,* and *The Handbook of Research on Teaching.* A former president of the American Educational Research Association, he currently serves as President of the National Academy of Education.

Suzanne E. Wade is an Associate Professor in the Department of Educational Studies at the University of Utah, where she teaches courses on reading methods and the diagnosis and remediation of reading disabilities. She received her Ed. D. from Harvard University Graduate School of Education. She spent the 1989–1990 academic year at the Center for the Study of Reading at the University of Illinois working with Bonnie Armbruster on a book entitled *Learning from Text* (in progress). Her research interests have focused on the strategies that expert readers use to learn from text. More recently, she has been investigating how interest affects selective attention and recall, a project funded by the Spencer Fellowship Program.

Suzanne M. Wilson is Associate Professor in the Department of Teacher Education at Michigan State University. She is also senior researcher in the Center for the Learning and Teaching of Elementary Subjects and the Center for Policy Research in Education. Her interests include the subject-matter knowledge required for teaching, which she examines through her research on elementary mathematics and language arts instruction and secondary school history teaching. She teaches a range of students, from third- and fourth-graders at a local elementary school, to prospective and practicing teachers, to doctoral students at Michigan State. She has written a number of pieces about her own experiences teaching as well as her observations concerning the relationships between teacher subject-matter knowledge and teacher thinking and action; she is currently working on a book about her experiences exploring these issues.

Index